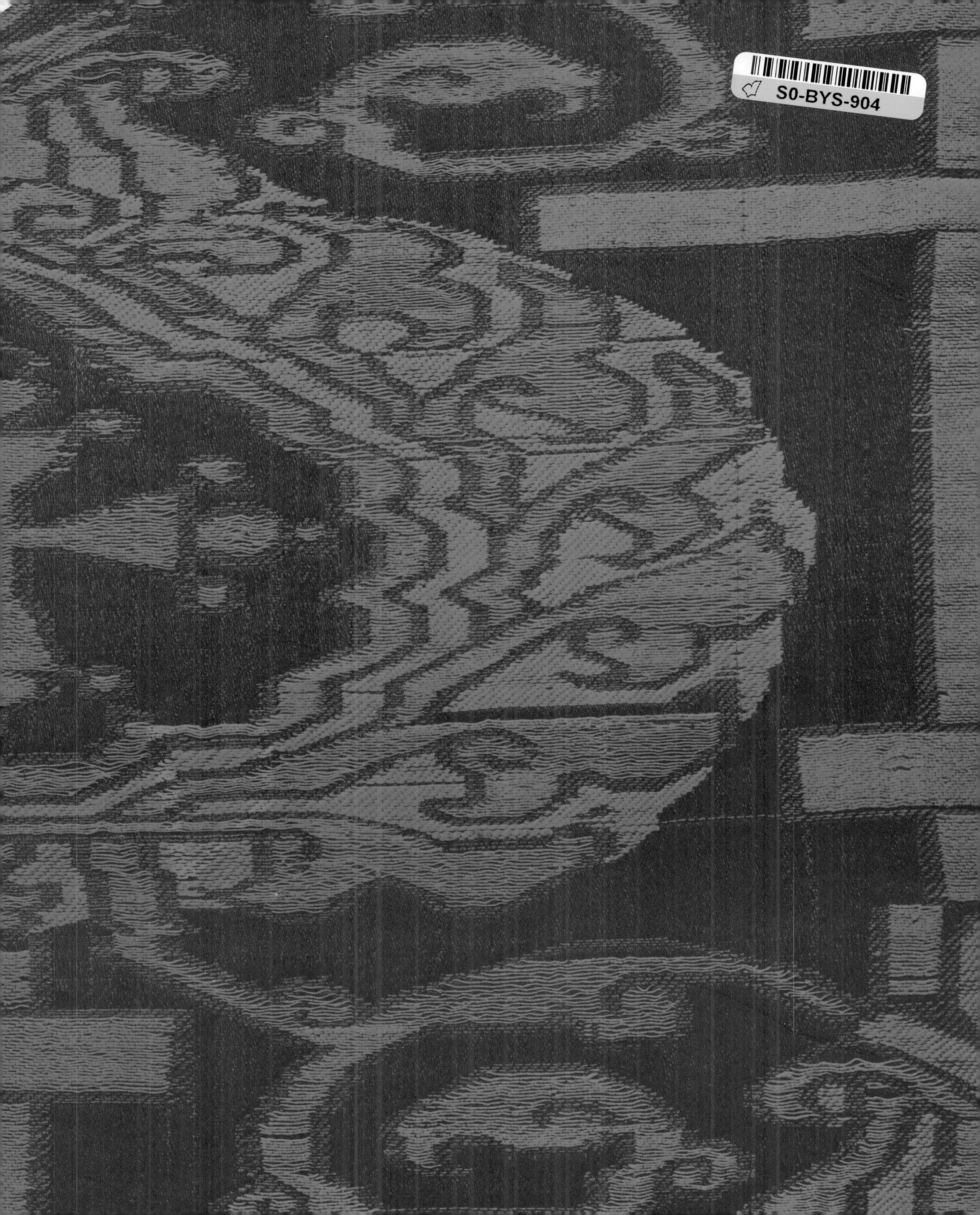

BYZANTINE ART

in the Collections of Soviet Museums

BYZANTINE ART

in the Collections of Soviet Museums

Introduction and Notes on the Plates by Alice Bank

HARRY N. ABRAMS, INC., PUBLISHERS, NEW YORK

AURORA ART PUBLISHERS, LENINGRAD

Designed by Yury Kirillin

Translated from the Russian by Inna Sorokina

Photographs by Lydia Tarasova

Library of Congress Cataloging in Publication Data
Bank, Alisa Vladimirovna.
Byzantine art in the collections of Soviet museums.

Bibliography: p. 337
1. Art, Byzantine—Catalogs. 2. Art museums—
Russia. I. Title.
N6250.B27 709′.02 77-25751

Library of Congress Catalogue Card Number: 77-25751
International Standard Book Number: 0-8109-0726-7

Published in 1978 by Harry N. Abrams, Incorporated, New York
Printed and bound in Hungary

Byzantine art is an outstanding, and in many respects unique, phenomenon in the history of world culture. Emerging on the brink of the medieval period, at a point where the antique society was giving way to the nascent feudal system, the art of Byzantium absorbed the traditions of classical antiquity, and preserved them throughout the thousand years of its existence. This, however, was but one of the several aspects which made of Byzantine art a factor of paramount importance in the cultural evolution of a number of countries in Europe and Asia. A blend of artistic traditions of the various peoples inhabiting the vast Byzantine Empire, this art came to express, with the utmost force and clarity, the aesthetic ideals of its time. Though here, as elsewhere in Europe, art was subservient to religious doctrine, and the necessity to follow the canons set by the Christian church curbed the individual freedom of the artist, yet Byzantine masters achieved unprecedented heights of artistic perfection. Their work possessed a powerful emotional appeal, and addressed itself to much wider circles of society than the art of antiquity had ever done.

Constantinople, the capital of the Empire, was unquestionably the leading centre of medieval culture; its place in the art evolution of the time could be compared to that of Paris during the past four or five centuries. Karl Marx once called Constantinople "a golden bridge joining the East and the West", and this refers to art no less than to any other sphere of human activity.

Up to the seventh century, the Byzantine Empire incorporated many different countries situated on the continents of Europe, Asia and Africa. Many peoples enriched the culture of this powerful state with their ancient artistic traditions. At a later time they, in their turn, were to be influenced by Byzantine cultural traditions. Ancient Russia, Georgia and to a lesser degree Armenia are also numbered among the legatees of Byzantine culture.

Soviet museums own extensive collections of art objects from Byzantium. Viewed in their entirety, they give a more comprehensive idea of the evolution of the various branches of Byzantine art than do the collections of any other single country. Among the works housed in Soviet museums are specimens of the art of painting, of sculpture, and of the minor arts: silver- and bronzework, goldwork, jewellery and glyptics, wood and ivory-carving, *cloisonné* enamels, textiles, embroidery and ceramics.

The wealth of Byzantine collections in Soviet museums is explained by historical reasons.

For a long period of time the Byzantine Empire included the southern coast of the Crimea, with the town of Chersonese (near the modern Sevastopol) which was the bulwark of Byzantine domination in this area. As far back as 1827, excavations were started here, which have been carried out up to the present day with the participation of the Hermitage, Leningrad, and the History Museum, Moscow. They yielded large numbers of jewellery objects, bronze and stone icons, and various articles of pottery.

Byzantine gold and silver wares are found in Central Russia and in the Ukraine, where they occur at different spots once visited by nomad peoples in the course of their migrations. Most of the silver objects from the sixth and seventh centuries, produced in Constantinople, come from the Urals area which had long maintained commercial relations with Sassanian Persia and Byzantium by direct trade routes.

Ancient Russia had close economic, political and cultural relations with Byzantium. Objects of Byzantine provenance reached Kiev and Novgorod, Vladimir and Moscow. Fragments of Byzantine silks have been discovered in the Northern Caucasus and in Transcaucasian regions. Specimens of Byzantine artistic glass have been unearthed during the 1960s at Dvin, the ancient capital of Armenia (now the township of Artashat), and at Novogrudok in Western Byelorussia. A beautiful ivory comb was found during the excavations of the old Russian town of Belaya Vezha, which occupied the site of an earlier Khazar fortress called Sarkel.

Old Russian chronicles and other literary records mention several cases of importation of Byzantine icons into Russia. Byzantine silks adorned with rich embroidery were sewn into robes of state worn by Russian tsars and dignitaries of the Orthodox church. Patriarchs of Constantinople are known to have presented precious gifts to Russian statesmen; these were preserved in the treasuries of the Kremlin cathedrals and in the Kremlin Armoury.

The Arts Museum of the Georgian SSR, Tbilisi, owns a splendid collection of Georgian and Byzantine enamels, second only to the Tesoro di San Marco in Venice. It includes objects from the churches of Georgia proper and of Svanetia, where these treasures accumulated during the Middle Ages together with other art works of Byzantine provenance.

In Russia, the first collections of Byzantine antiquities were started in the second half of the eighteenth century, a period when the emperors and members of the higher aristocracy began to emulate Western European rulers in collecting art objects. The rich collection of gems formed by Catherine II comprised several veritable masterpieces of Byzantine art, such as the cameos of the celebrated collection of the Duke of Orleans, or the chalcedony bust of Julian the Apostate.

Among the antique marbles brought to Russia from the islands of the Aegean Sea by Admiral Spiridov after the campaign of 1768—74 was an early Byzantine marble relief with circus scenes. Originally placed at the Academy of Arts, St Petersburg, it was transferred to the Hermitage after the October Revolution of 1917.

In 1770, a hoard of silver vessels of Sassanian and Byzantine origin was discovered at the village of Sludka (Perm Province). It came into the possession of the Urals industrial magnates, the Stroganovs, and later found its way into the Hermitage.

In 1852, when the Hermitage, hitherto a palace museum practically closed to the public, received a new status of the "Public Museum", its collections already comprised a number of Byzantine antiquities, among them some silver vessels, probably finds from the Urals region. The year 1862 was marked by the inauguration, in Moscow, of the Rumiantsev Public Museum with a department of Christian antiquities. At the same time, a Museum of Early Christian Art was founded in St Petersburg under the auspices of the Academy of Arts. These two museums became important centres of collecting works of art of Byzantine origin.

In the middle of the nineteenth century, a collection of remarkable icons was brought from Mount Sinai by Archimandrite (later Bishop) Porphyry Uspensky. Some of these beautiful specimens of encaustic painting, now the pride of the Museum of Western and Eastern Art, Kiev, are widely known. The examples of later Byzantine painting, once preserved in the Kievan Cave Monastery Museum Zone (Kievo-Pecherskaya Lavra), to all appearances, perished, or were destroyed, during the War of 1941—45. Porphyry Uspensky was not merely an enthusiastic art collector, he was also a self-taught art scholar. Among other things, he gave much of his attention to antiquities from Mount Athos. Another collector of note who contributed greatly to the study of this material was Sevastyanov. He organized an important expedition to Mount Athos in the 1850s. Some of the most remarkable icons in the collection of the Pushkin Museum of Fine Arts, Moscow, and supposedly a few specimens of the Hermitage collection, were acquired in the course of this expedition, a tremendous undertaking for its time. On their arrival in Russia, these icons, accompanied by a vast body of photographic material, copies of frescoes, and fragments of authentic sixteenth and seventeenth century murals, were divided between the Museum of Early Christian Art, St Petersburg, and the Rumiantsev Museum, Moscow.

Further progress in collecting and research was achieved in the middle of the last century, with the formation of the Archaeological Commission and a number of local archaeological societies which organized excavation work in the southern regions of Russia. It was at this period, too, that the first Russian journals of archaeology and art history, such as *Christian Antiquities* (in Russian), edited by Prokhorov, Keeper of the Museum of Early Christian Art, began to publish selected specimens of Byzantine antiquities.

The 1860s and 1870s are associated in Russian art history with the activities of Buslayev, an eminent scholar who laid the foundations of studies in ancient Russian art. One of his students at the Moscow University, Kondakov, was to gain world recognition as a leading specialist in the field of Byzantine art. His extensive travels in countries of the Byzantine world resulted in the publication of a series of monographs on Mount Sinai, Mount Athos, Syria and Palestine, Macedonia and Georgia (his work on Georgian art was written in collaboration with Bakhradze), which greatly enlarged the stock of information available to Byzantine scholars. His *History of Byzantine Art and Iconography Based on the Study of Greek Manuscript Illumination* (in Russian, published in Odessa in 1876) was the first comprehensive survey of the subject; its French version appeared ten years later.

Kondakov worked at the Hermitage as Head Keeper of the Department of Medieval and Renaissance Art. During his years of office he prepared and published such important works as *Histoire et monuments des émaux Byzantins*, Francfort, 1892 (also Russian and German versions), and *Russian Hoards* (in Russian, 1896).

The close of the year 1884 witnessed the acquisition, in Paris, of a most extensive collection of medieval art objects, formed by the Russian art collector Basilewsky. This collection, which reached Russia in 1885, included valuable specimens of carved ivory, bronzework, mosaic icons and enamels, many of them quite unique for their artistic perfection. It formed the core of the Byzantine collection of the Hermitage.

Towards the close of the century, in 1888—89 and in 1897—98, Keeper of the Department of Medieval Art at the Hermitage, W. von Bock, travelled in Egypt. He was one of the first art scholars to develop an interest in Coptic antiquities. Von Bock brought to the Hermitage a great number of objects, some obtained by purchase, others unearthed during the excavations conducted under his guidance. Among his acquisitions were many outstanding specimens of Coptic textiles. Von Bock was the author of interesting works on Coptic art. He explored the connections between Christian art and pagan culture, and pointed out those features peculiar to Coptic antiquities which distinguished them from Byzantine art productions. The Coptic collection of the Moscow Public Museum, which was to become part of the Museum of Fine Arts (later the Pushkin Museum of Fine Arts) with its formation in 1912, was built up at the beginning of the twentieth century on the basis of the collection of Golenishchev, a noted Russian Egyptologist.

In the late nineteenth century, the Hermitage collection of Byzantine coins was greatly enlarged. The newly acquired collections of Photiadis Pasha and Lobanov-Rostovsky took a place of honour among its treasures.

The 1890s were marked by the beginnings of research in Byzantine sphragistics. Here the foundations were laid by Likhachov, who was to become a leading specialist in this field. His studies were closely linked with his activities as collector. Likhachov's excellent collection of Russian icons was partly published in his *Materials for the History of Russian Icon-painting*, an atlas issued in 1896 (in Russian). The collection was acquired in 1913 for the Russian Museum, St Petersburg, but some samples of Byzantine painting later found their way to the Hermitage.

His comparative studies of Russian icon-painting and Byzantine lead seals provided Likhachov with materials for the fundamental work, *Role of the Italo-Greek School of Painting in the History of Art* (in Russian, 1911). Though some of the author's views have not stood the test of time, such as his exaggerated opinion of the role of the Italo-Greek school in general, and its influence on Russian icon-painting in particular; and though his conclusions, unsupported by sufficient proof, have since been justly criticized by Lazarev, yet Likhachov's analysis of iconographic types, based on the study of seals, fully retains its significance up to the present day.

In the last years of the nineteenth century, Ya. Smirnov, an outstanding authority on the art of the Orient and of Byzantium, joined the staff of the Hermitage. During the twenty years of his work at the Museum, Smirnov did much to enlarge the Hermitage collections. He also conducted extensive research in art history, recording the results in numerous publications. Smirnov's works, which display an exceptional erudition and depth of thought, still have a stimulating influence on researchers. He was the first to discuss a number of problems essential to the study of Byzantine art, among them the role of stamps in dating Byzantine silverware.

At the end of the nineteenth century, Russia had a large body of Byzantine scholars. Their works were published in the *Bulletin of Byzantine Studies* (in Russian), a journal founded in 1894, and in other periodicals. The year 1894 saw the foundation of the Russian Archaeological Institute in Constantinople, with the well-known historian Uspensky as director. The staff conducted excavations in areas once forming part of the Byzantine Empire. Several art objects of importance now in the Hermitage collection, such as the sculpture of the Good Shepherd, discovered near the village of Panderma in Bithynia, were acquired for the Museum with the assistance of the Institute's administration.

The late nineteenth and early twentieth centuries were marked by the publication of Ainalov's *The Hellenistic Origins of Byzantine Art* (in Russian; English version published in the USA in 1961). The idea of the influence of the Hellenistic Orient on the formation of Byzantine art, advanced by the author in this research, was a highly progressive one for its time and has since lost none of its importance.

For many years Ainalov filled the office of Professor of Art History at the Petersburg (later Leningrad) University. He also lectured at the Bestuzhev Classes for Women Students and taught at the Institute of Art History. From 1922 to 1929 he worked at the Hermitage.

A pupil of Kondakov, Ainalov may be regarded as the founder of the Russian school of art research in general, and of that of old Russian and Byzantine art history in particular. He trained such prominent Byzantine scholars as Matsulevich and A. Grabar (Paris), such specialists in the history of old Russian art as Sychov and Miasoyedov, and such well-known historians of art as Okunev of Prague and Belgrade, who worked mainly in the field of Serbian art. Ainalov's influence on his formation as a scholar was repeatedly acknowledged by the leading Soviet art historian, Lazarev, in many of his publications.

The list of Russian scholars who worked in Byzantine art history may be further extended. There was Pokrovsky, who did much in the study of iconography during the 1890s; Pavlovsky, the author of a monograph on the Capella Palatina at Palermo (with an album prepared by Chagin and Pomerantsev), which was published in 1890 and long remained the only fundamental work on the subject; Redin, who wrote one of the first really thorough researches on the mosaics of Ravenna, and Panchenko, a specialist in Byzantine history, who started the publication of a catalogue of Byzantine lead seals in the collection of the museum of the Russian Archaeological Institute in Constantinople, and published the reliefs of the Monastery of St John of Studius, which were found during the excavations conducted by the Institute.

Another scholar whose work was connected with the Russian Archaeological Institute was Wulff. He started his career in Constantinople, but later went to Germany. A noted historian of Byzantine art, he was Head of the Department of Byzantine and Early Christian Antiquities at the Kaiser Friedrich Museum. Schmidt, the author of an important work on the mosaics of Karyai Jami, which laid the foundations of all further research in this field, was also a member of the Institute's staff.

On the eve of World War I, Ivan Tolstoy published nine issues of his fundamental work *Byzantine Coins* (in Russian).

To sum up, during the pre-Revolutionary period Russian scholars achieved a steady progress both in collecting and studying Byzantine monuments. There were, however, some circumstances which stood in the way of any signal advance. Highly valuable works of art, such as the icon of *Our Lady of Vladimir*, were regarded primarily as objects of cult. Distorted by later overpaintings, with large areas of the surface invisible beneath extensive metalwork mounts, often stored away in church treasuries, such icons were not available either for artistic appreciation or for scholarly research. Many of the Byzantine monuments, the property of private collectors (Botkin, G. and P. Stroganov, Shuvalov, B. and V. Khanenko and others), were known to a limited circle of art lovers, but for the most part remained unpublished. Authentic masterpieces were preserved side by side with fakes; almost invariably they were lost amidst a congeries of objects of different kind and date. Dispersed among a variety of private collections throughout the country, and even at the Hermitage scattered among different departments, this material could not be viewed as a whole, or studied in its proper context.

The iconographic method of research long persisted in Byzantine studies. Though some eminent scholars held advanced views on problems of their science, most were slow to depart from established tradition. Works with a markedly clerical approach to the subject were common; many were devoid of a true sense of history. Highly characteristic of the period was Kondakov's *The Iconography of the Mother of God* (in Russian, 2 vols., 1914—15). It is based on a great wealth of material which has since been studied by many Byzantine and Old Russian art scholars. But, like many of his contemporaries, Kondakov was unable to define, with sufficient clarity, the national features which mark the art of different peoples: in his day the term Byzantine was understood to cover all art phenomena connected with the Christian East, and it did not occur to the scholars —past masters of the iconographic method—to view Byzantine antiquities as works of art, and to subject them to aesthetic analysis. Only two works, Ainalov's *Byzantine Painting of the Fourteenth Century* (in Russian, 1917)—though containing controversial, and even erroneous conclusions—and Schmidt's book on Nicaean mosaics (original version, in Russian, 1913, unpublished; German version, 1927) placed Byzantine monuments in the general context of art history.

The October Revolution of 1917 marked a turning point in Byzantine studies, as it did in all spheres of social life. Important steps were undertaken towards the safeguarding and preservation of national artistic heritage. Collections whose owners had emigrated were declared the property of the state. Objects of historical and artistic value were assembled in state-owned museums. In the first post-Revolutionary years, the Central Restoration Workshops began to function in Moscow. Their chief concern was the care of ancient paintings. Many Byzantine icons went through the process of cleaning, *Our Lady of Vladimir* being one of the first among them.

The 1920s were a time when such scholars as Lazarev, Brunov, and Matsulevich, who were to become leading authorities on Byzantine art, were starting on their careers. Prominent among the older generation were Alpatov, whose interests at the time lay mainly in the field of Byzantine studies, Protasov, Malitsky and Jurgenson.

During the 1920s and 1930s museum work was undergoing complete transformation. The rapid growth of attendance, and the appearance of a new type of visitor who, with little previous aesthetic experience of the museum kind, sought for knowledge and understanding of art, demanded radical changes in the principles of exposition. To present the viewer the clearest and most comprehensive picture of a given period in the history of culture and art, it was necessary to achieve the greatest possible concentration of relevant materials in the museum exhibitions. To this end, a redistribution of the collections in accordance with the specific aims of different museums was effected, and in great repositories of art treasures, such as the Hermitage, new departments were created. This general policy in the field of museum work led to important developments in Byzantine studies.

The Kremlin Armoury, Moscow, received large numbers of magnificent church vestments, enamels, steatite icons and cameos which had been preserved in the Treasury of the patriarchs of Moscow, in Kremlin cathedrals and in some of the provincial monasteries. The collection of the Tretyakov Gallery, Moscow, was enriched by several remarkable specimens of ancient painting which came from the church of the Vysotsky monastery, St Sergius's Monastery of the Trinity (Troitse-Sergiyevskaya Lavra) and other churches and monasteries. The History Museum greatly enlarged its collections with the accession of new Byzantine manuscripts, icons and archaeological materials. In 1924, the Byzantine Room was opened there. Later some of its icons and a number of specimens of the minor arts were transferred to the Pushkin Museum of Fine Arts.

The Hermitage, however, retained its position as the leading centre for collecting Byzantine monuments. Its acquisition policy in this field was highly consistent. The 1920s witnessed the formation of a Byzantine Section headed by Matsulevich who remained in office for a long period of time. In 1927, the exhibition *Byzantium and the Migration Period* was organized. On display, alongside with specimens of Byzantine art proper, which had been preserved in the various departments of the Museum, were Coptic antiquities and archaeological finds from the northern Black Sea coast area, as well as silver vessels, carved ivories and other Byzantine art objects from private collections, and individual specimens transferred from several museums which seized to exist, such as the Museum of the Stieglitz School of Art and Design, the Museum of the Society for the Advancement of the Arts (both in Leningrad) and some provincial museums of art and culture.

Somewhat later, in 1930 and 1934, the Hermitage collection absorbed a number of Byzantine, Greek and Italo-Greek icons. These icons came from the Department of Old Russian Art in the Russian Museum, Leningrad, where they had been preserved and studied by two prominent scholars, Malitsky and A. Smirnov. Now the collections of the Tretyakov Gallery and the Russian Museum retain just as many specimens of Byzantine icon-painting as are necessary to demonstrate its connection with the art of ancient Russia.

In 1931 the Hermitage received a part of the collection of the former Russian Archaeological Institute in Constantinople. Of interest among Byzantine materials were some of the sculptures and funerary stelae. Highly significant was the collection of lead seals which numbered over 5,000 items. Another important addition to the Byzantine Section was the splendid collection of lead seals formed by Likhachov. It was transferred to the Museum in 1938 from the Institute of History, USSR Academy of Sciences. The extremely rare mosaic icon of the *Four Saints*, once the property of Likhachov, entered the Hermitage at about the same time.

The Byzantine collection of the Hermitage and that of the History Museum continue growing. New accessions come mainly from the excavations at Chersonese. Some, as, for instance, Byzantine silver vessels, come from the Urals area.

Collections of Byzantine antiquities in Soviet museums vary in composition and character.

The collection of the Kremlin Armoury, originally a treasury which grew into what may be called Russia's first museum, was gradually built up in the course of several centuries. The bulk of the collection consists of gifts to Russian tsars from foreign courts, and precious objects belonging to the patriarchs of Moscow. Among them are beautiful cameos of Byzantine work (often in mounts of Russian origin), richly embroidered church vestments, *cloisonné* enamels, articles of gold and silver. These objects are exhibited side by side with specimens of ancient Russian art, as the general character of the museum suggests.

In the History Museum Byzantine antiquities figure mainly as part of the archaeological complexes with which they were originally associated. The collections of the Museum include finds from Chersonese, silverware from the Transcaucasian and the Urals regions, and individual examples of Byzantine art which have had a long history on Russian soil.

The small but choice collection of the Pushkin Museum of Fine Arts comprises icons of high artistic merit, several remarkable ivories, and a splendid cross decorated with *cloisonné* enamels.

The Tretyakov Gallery owns the icon of *Our Lady of Vladimir* and a number of Byzantine paintings which have been preserved in Russia for centuries.

The Novgorod Museum Zone and the Zagorsk Museum also have in their possession some outstanding specimens of Byzantine art.

Examples of Byzantine glyptics are to be seen in many Russian museums. They often have mounts of Russian work, and their large numbers testify that these objects, so easy to carry from one place to another, were rather widespread in Russia.

The collection of B. and V. Khanenko, which forms the nucleus of the Museum of Western and Eastern Art, Kiev, consists of objects selected with excellent judgement. One of the gems of this collection is the rare mosaic icon of St Nicholas. After the October Revolution, the collection of encaustic paintings brought from Mount Sinai by Porphyry Uspensky was placed at the Museum.

The Museum of Ukrainian Art, Kiev, recently obtained by transfer from the town of Mariupol a unique carved wooden icon of St George.

The Chersonese Museum has a permanent source of additions to its stock of Byzantine antiquities in the excavation works conducted in this area. It possesses one of the richest and most varied collections of archaeological finds, highly valuable to the science of history.

The collections of the Hermitage are the richest and the most representative. The materials, viewed in their entirety, give an excellent picture of the evolution of Byzantine art. They include icons, beautiful marbles and bronzes, exquisite silver vessels and carved ivories, goldwork, jewellery, cameos, pottery and glass, *cloisonné* enamels and mosaic icons, executed with the utmost delicacy and refinement. Incorporated in the Byzantine collection are also objects of Coptic and barbarian manufacture, adequately illustrating the role of the cultures they represent in the art of the Empire as a whole. It should be mentioned that both in the Hermitage and in the Pushkin Museum of Fine Arts the bulk of the Coptic collections is associated with the exhibitions of Egyptian art of the ancient and the Graeco-Roman periods. The materials from the area of the northern Black Sea coast, which characterize a phase of social development preceding that of the Byzantine Empire, are displayed at the exhibitions of the Department of Prehistoric Cultures.

Most of the works illustrated in the present Album belong to the Hermitage collection. Also included are the best specimens of Byzantine art owned by other museums than the Hermitage. Among them are some magnificent *cloisonné* enamels now in the Arts Museum of the Georgian SSR, Tbilisi; their Byzantine origin is beyond doubt.

The present publication does not claim to cover the entire field of Byzantine antiquities preserved throughout the country. Such elements of the decorative art as the miniatures, headpieces, colophons and initials which embellish the numerous Byzantine manuscripts in the possession of libraries and of the History Museum, Moscow, have been thought deserving of a special publication, and so have not been included. Monuments of Byzantine architecture in the territory of the Soviet Union, as well as samples of Byzantine decorative sculpture, wall painting and mosaic panels, are not represented either. Of the archaeological finds unearthed in the area of the northern Black Sea coast, only a few unique specimens of Byzantine art and some examples of glazed pottery have been introduced. The lead seals are represented by a small number of specimens selected for their high artistic quality. It has not been judged expedient to reproduce specimens of Byzantine coins, which possess but little artistic merit.

The materials are arranged on the chronological principle. The traditional periodization has been adopted. The Album opens with objects illustrating the art of the period of the fourth to the seventh centuries. Then follow works dating from the tenth to the twelfth centuries, the period of Iconoclasm (the eighth and the first half of the ninth century) being represented by a very few individual objects. The materials illustrating the last period in the history of Byzantine art, the period of the artistic revival under the Palaeologi, have been classified into two groups, those datable to the thirteenth and fourteenth centuries, and those datable to the fifteenth century. Within each of the chronological groups the works are arranged by material.

The Notes on the Plates contain brief information concerning each of the objects, followed by a reference on the principal parallels and relevant publications. The descriptions and references are not intended to achieve the completeness of a *catalogue raisonné*, which is not required in a type of publication we hereby offer to the reader.

The problem of dating the beginnings of Byzantine art has not been solved to this day. What some scholars regard as the art of the Roman Empire in the period of its decline, others see as Early Medieval art. It is difficult to draw a clear line of demarcation between these two epochs of cultural history, for in Byzantium, as elsewhere, the transitional period was characterized by a co-existence of new features with traditional concepts and forms, and the art of the fourth to the seventh centuries presents a picture of opposing tendencies.

Sculpture, a leading branch of art in the antique world, was gradually losing its former importance. Reliefs were gaining predominance over statuary. Sometimes representations were executed in engraving; to set them off, the background was filled with coloured paste.

The museums of the Soviet Union (all except the Chersonese Museum) own comparatively few specimens of Byzantine sculpture.

The marble sarcophagus dating from the fourth century is carved with scenes from the Old and 12
the New Testament. The figures are conventionally arranged in two rows, one behind the other. Their heads are all of the same size (a phenomenon known as *isocephaly*), but the features are individualized.

The marble panel from *c.* 500 A.D. has a cross in low relief on one side, and circus scenes on 13, 14
the other. The background gives no indication of the scene of action. The figures, some of which seem to be floating in the air, are full of movement. Characteristic of the period is the use of a sacred monogram on an object otherwise decorated with purely secular representations. The panel may have served as a chancel-screen in a church.

The sculpture of the Good Shepherd shown as a youth has numerous analogies among the 10, 11
materials of different collections. This symbolic image, extremely widespread in Early Christian art, went out of use in the fifth century. The flat treatment, and the unworked surface at the back, give to this piece of statuary a certain resemblance to relief sculpture.

The portrait bust of Julian the Apostate, carved in chalcedony, is a unique specimen of minor 6, 7
sculpture from the fourth century. The head is worked in the round, the body flat, one forearm almost merging with it. Originally, the wide-open eyes possibly had inlays for the pupils; the hair and beard are treated ornamentally.

Soviet museums are relatively rich in specimens of toreutics, especially objects dating from the fourth to the seventh centuries. Most of them come from the Urals area, some from the southern regions of our country.

The silver dish found at the end of the last century in a burial vault in the area of the modern 1
Kerch, which had once belonged to the Bosporan Kingdom, shows a royal rider identified by Matsulevich as the Emperor Constantius II (337—361). The type of composition, traditional in the art of antique Rome—the victor on horseback, crowned by Nike with a palm branch, and accompanied by a shield-bearer—has been somewhat modified. The steed tramples, not on the body of a vanquished foe, but on his shield, which in this case symbolizes the owner; the shield of

the Emperor, carried by the attendant, bears a Chi-Rho monogram. The costume of the Emperor and the shape of his diadem, as well as the weapons he carries, display features of both Oriental and barbaric influences, and refer the dish to the period of transition from the antique to the medieval world. The techniques of execution and the very method of approach, typical of the time, seem to introduce the viewer to the world of medieval art: the loss of the plastic sense, the use of niello and gilding, and the rendering of the figure, with the rider's legs presented from the side, in accordance with the movement of his horse, while his face and body are shown from the front. The dish is supposed to have been made in one of the workshops of the northern Black Sea coast where, as in other peripheral areas, some features of the new style emerged at an earlier date than in the large cities of the Hellenistic culture.

8, 9 There is also a gold medallion with the portrait of Constantius II. He is shown in profile; the face retains certain elements of plastic modelling, and the dress accentuates the forms of the body.

2–5 A silver ewer from the close of the fourth century was found near Kursk, in the burial of a barbarian chief, together with a frontlet of a horse and some gold costume plaques. The ewer is embossed with figures of the Muses, each accompanied by her name in Greek writing. The design in the lower band shows running animals, with bodies emerging from acanthus scrolls; and the broad band above is decorated with a vine with clusters of grapes. A certain degree of generalization in the treatment of the figures, and absence of strong modelling, distinguish this work from specimens of pure antique art. The reverse of the bottom is marked with a control stamp representing Tyche of Constantinople. This shows that the object was made in the new capital.

Silverwares from the sixth and the seventh centuries are especially well represented. Most of the objects bear on the reverse as many as five control stamps, proof of the high quality of the silver. The stamps, done in a variety of shapes (circles, hexagons, or ovals), bear monograms, inscriptions, and portraits of emperors. By comparing the portraits with those on coins or on lead seals, it is possible to identify the ruler and thus establish the date of the vessel; for the objects were stamped while in the process of manufacture, before the work was completed.

Of the greatest interest are the specimens of Byzantine silverwork discovered in a very rich burial at the Malaya Pereshchepina village near Poltava. The burial also contained numerous gold coins of the first half and the middle of the seventh century (the coins had holes struck in them, for use as ornaments), and objects of Sassanian, Turki, Sogdian, and even local provenance.
66–68 The most remarkable of the finds is the celebrated paten which used to belong to the bishop of the town of Tomi (now Constanţa) in Rumania. The Chi-Rho monogram is encircled with a band which bears an inscription telling that the paten was "ex antiquis renovatum" by Bishop Paternus. The ornament on the border is typical of the Byzantine art of the fifth and sixth centuries. Soldered on over the border design—probably in the process of "renovation", and quite in keeping with the practices common in barbaric art—are metal settings for precious stones. The burial
62, 63 also contained a patera and a ewer which served, as stated in the inscription on the reverse of the handle of the patera, for the ablutions of the officiating priest during the service. The handle of the ewer is topped by the figure of a fantastic animal, which had an apothropaic function — to protect
70 the liquid in the vessel from evil influence. There was also a large amphora, silver gilt, with three ornamental bands, the one in the middle composed of plant ornament with the head of an old man personifying Ocean. This design has a close analogy in one of the motifs of the mosaic floor in the Great Palace in Constantinople.

We have seen that even vessels used in the ritual of the Christian church often show an influence of ancient Greek and Roman art. This influence is still more strongly expressed in objects
of secular character. Typical of the sixth and seventh centuries were such dishes as those decorated with scenes showing Silenus and a maenad (connected with the cult of Bacchus), Meleager 84, 83
and Atalanta, Athena deciding the quarrel of Ajax and Odysseus, Venus in the tent of Anchises, 60, 61, 72
or the feeding of the sacred serpent. *Trulla* handles usually bore the figure of Poseidon (Neptune), 53, 54, 87
the god of the sea. In treatment, however, these scenes in a greater or lesser degree differed from
their antique prototypes. While in the dish with Meleager and Atalanta landscape is still given 83
a great importance, and an attempt is made to create a sense of depth by applying the technique
of chasing in rendering the foreground, and that of engraving in representing the background; yet
no such tendencies can be observed in most other works of this kind, where the place of action is
indicated, if at all, by a few purely conventional details. A comparison of the Byzantine seventh
century ewer representing Nereids with the Roman second century dish illustrating the same sub- 88–90
ject, will reveal a difference in treatment: the Byzantine master did not try to present water but
indicated the place of action by a symbolic use of fishes, shells, etc. A similar approach is seen in the 85–87
decoration of the *trulla* with fishing scenes, which has on the handle the traditional image of Neptune with a trident.

Conventional features are obvious in the rendering of architectural motifs in the dish with
Venus in the tent of Anchises, a work which seems to anticipate the flat backgrounds used in icons 72
of later date. Curiously enough, this comparatively early dish (*c.* 550) is in many respects farther removed from the antique prototypes than some of the specimens of toreutics dating from the middle of the seventh century. This suggests the existence, at the same time, of several workshops, some of them showing a more conservative attitude towards the artistic traditions inherited from the past, others with a tendency towards innovation.

The *trulla* with fishing scenes, and the ewer with the Nereids, display motifs of Alexandrine 85–87
scenery. Another instance of this is the *trulla* with the scene of two Erotes measuring the height 53, 54
to which the Nile has risen, within a border ornamented with Nilotic plants and animals. It should be noted that the figure which one of the Erotes marks on the Nilometer is ten ells below the watermark reached by the Nile during the high flood: an error unthinkable to an Egyptian meant little to a native of Constantinople.

A few specimens of silverware are decorated with genre scenes: a shepherd and goats, with 55, 56
a dog in the foreground (close to the Roman prototypes), and a horse under a tree (with a com- 73, 74
position resembling Sassanian plates).

Some articles are decorated on both sides. The reverse might be engraved with plant ornament;
figure subjects are of rare occurrence. There are many dishes having no other decoration but
ornamental rosettes, among them the dish discovered in the Perm District several years ago (now 79
in the Hermitage).

Outside the large group of dishes of different size showing a cross, usually nielloed, within
a wreath, silver objects with Christian symbols and motifs are rare. We have a reliquary in the 75–77
shape of a sarcophagus and a censer excavated at Chersonese, with busts of Christ, the apostles, 81
the Virgin and angels, and youthful saints, in medallions, some encircled with beading. While the Virgin has as yet no features of the canon, and is rather close to the type of a Roman matron, other representations show, in their ethnic type, a Syrian influence. Undoubtedly Syrian in origin

78 is the well-known paten with a cross guarded by two angels, and the rivers of Paradise. In some points of style and technique (type of faces, rendering of draperies) it differs from purely Byzantine work, showing an influence of Sassanian art.

Christian motifs are also used in the decoration of early Byzantine glassware. Here, too, dif-
24 ferent methods of treatment may be recorded. The bust of St Peter engraved on a piece of gold foil placed between two layers of glass, resembles a Roman portrait sculpture; the subject of
25 Abraham's Sacrifice, executed in the same technique, is treated as a genre scene. We know vessels decorated in the same way, and probably coming from the same workshops; some of them show secular subjects, others portraits, or even motifs connected with other religions than Christianity.

A different treatment of Bible subjects is seen in the glass patera of the fourth century, found
26–29 near the village of Podgorica (now Titograd, Yugoslavia). The design is executed in engraving. The figures are no longer anatomically correct; the drapery folds are rendered by a rhythmically repeated pattern; but both men and animals are presented with great freshness, even naiveté, of vision, and an extraordinary power of expression. Inscriptions in Latin show that the patera was produced at a western centre of glass manufacture. The style reveals an unquestionable influence of the art of barbaric peoples.

15 As unique of its kind as the patera from Podgorica is the bronze polycandelon. Found in the 1850s in a fifth century burial near Orléansville in Algiers, the polycandelon reproduces, with remarkable accuracy, the form of a basilica very widely spread in the fifth and sixth centuries.

During the fourth and the fifth centuries, the bronze lamps retained their traditional form; often, however, they were decorated with the Chi-Rho monogram.

Ivories hold an important place among the collections of Byzantine art objects in Soviet museums.

The first period in the development of Byzantine art is represented by such forms as diptychs commissioned by newly elected consuls, and pyxides. The date and provenance of each consular diptych can be established with perfect accuracy from the evidence of written records which give
32–34 the precise date of the consul's inauguration. On these grounds, the consular diptych of Areobindus
36 is dated to 506, and the fragment from one of the wings of Anastasius's diptych, to 517. Only the
30, 31 diptych with circus scenes, executed with exquisite craftsmanship and preserved whole, offers no evidence for exact dating. It may be, however, assigned to the second half of the fifth century, by comparison with other related works. The choice of subject matter—circus and theatrical scenes—was connected with the custom which prescribed that the consul should give seven performances for the benefit of the public, and distribute coins, by way of celebrating his election. This was one of the usages inherited by Byzantium from ancient Rome.

The Latin (and not Greek) inscriptions on the diptychs, the figures of genii, the use of allegory, etc., are also elements which continue the Roman tradition. But at the same time, there are in evidence a number of features characteristic of a new ideology, then in the process of its formation. Thus, personages of high rank are made larger in size than people of less consequence; the figures of consuls are static and treated according to the canon, while those of the actors, though arranged to form conventional compositions, and differing in size to indicate the relative importance of the characters they impersonate, are rendered with vividness and expressive force.

The date and origin of the pyxides with scenes from the Old and the New Testament are far more difficult to define. These objects differ in two respects: firstly as regards style, and secondly

in the ethnic characteristics of the persons represented. Such pyxides as those with the scenes of the
life of Jonah or of Joseph are close to the antique; the figures, carved in high relief, have natural 41,42,39,40
dynamic poses; the structure of the human body is shown carefully. Other works, as, for instance,
those with scenes of the life of Moses, or the three youths of Babylon, are executed in lower re- 47, 48, 49
lief; here the figures are of a more massive build and the faces, of an Oriental type. Oriental
features are still more pronounced in fragments of ivories with Gospel scenes, found in the Caucasus, 51, 52
and also in the part of a diptych carved with the Annunciation and Proof of the Virgin; they may 50
well have been made in Syria or the Transcaucasian regions. These carvings, as well as the pyxis
with Gospel scenes, are invested with deep and strong emotion.

Thus, the two opposing tendencies which operated in the art of toreutics—the continuation of the old artistic tradition, on the one hand, and the search for novel means of expression, on the other—are also recorded in the ivory-carving of the period. The same duality in the choice of subjects, with secular and mythological motifs used side by side with Biblical or Gospel scenes, is also reflected in glyptics, jewellery, and even coin and seal-making.

This co-existence of motifs is exemplified by the sixth century gold chain of stamped plaques, 95
with a large medallion suspended from it. The plaques bear the busts of two emperors flanking
a cross, and the medallion shows the Emperor Constantine the Great being crowned by two figures,
one personifying the sun and the other the moon, with birds drinking from the fountain of life
underneath, and a border of plant scrolls within an outer band of animals chasing each other.

The goldwork of the fifth and sixth centuries is characterized by the predominance of the technique of openwork creating a strong play of light and shade (also highly favoured by contemporary stone-carvers). This can be seen on belt plates, earrings and necklace plaques. Some of the specimens show an influence of barbaric art, either in shape, as belt buckles, or in the technique of decoration, as objects with stone or paste inlays. It should be noted that Byzantine goldwork in its turn often provided models for barbaric metalworkers who imitated objects of their choice in bronze or copper.

The lead seals mainly bear the figure of a goddess with the cornucopia, or Nike, the goddess 115
of victory. With time, Christian motifs also penetrated into sphragistics, as well as into coinage.

Early Byzantine icons known at present are few in number, though the findings from the monastery on Mount Sinai, including the icons brought to Russia by Porphyry Uspensky, formed important additions to our stock of specimens of Byzantine painting. Four of the icons belong to the Kiev Museum of Western and Eastern Art.

The earliest icons were executed in the very same technique of encaustic which had been
used in antique painting (e.g. the Faiyum portraits). They exemplify different stylistic tendencies.
The two main trends formed in Late Hellenistic portrait-painting, the naturalistic and the spiritual,
are also represented in Byzantine icon-painting. Indeed, the distinction between such examples
as *The Virgin and Child* and *St John the Baptist*, on the one hand, and *Sts Sergius and Bacchus* 109–113
on the other, does not rest solely on extraneous circumstances, such as the different measure of
ability in their authors, or their association with different artistic centres. The choice between freedom of attitude and a strictly frontal position of the figures, or the pictorial and linear treatment,
was a matter of principle, and probably reflected the conflict between the sensual rendering of a religious image, and its abstract interpretation, which reached its height during the Iconoclast movement of the eighth and the early ninth centuries.

The minor arts were doubtlessly well developed during the period, but our information on the subject is practically confined to the descriptions of individual specimens of particularly high artistic quality, which occur in written sources. As for the works themselves, only a few surviving fragments of silk textiles can be with confidence assigned to this period, in addition to coins and seals. The silks come from the excavations in the Northern Caucasus, and thus serve as evidence of the fact that the Great Silk Route traversed this region. This gives them great historical value.

The formation of a new ideology, a process marked by a long struggle of conflicting tendencies, resulted towards the middle of the ninth century in a final triumph of the medieval outlook. During the tenth and eleventh centuries the characteristic features of Byzantine art, already fully formed, found their strongest expression in wall and icon-painting, in manuscript illumination, and in the minor arts. Works of Byzantine art became widely spread not only within the Empire, but all through the contemporary world. Their influence is felt in the productions of local masters.

This period is represented in Soviet museums by a variety of materials. One of the most remarkable art forms is illustrated by a rich collection of *cloisonné* enamels in the Arts Museum of the Georgian SSR, Tbilisi. Many specimens were preserved for centuries in Georgian and Svanetian monasteries: a memory of the close links which had once bound Georgia with Byzantium.

Among the early specimens dating from the tenth century is the icon from Shemokmedi
184, 185 with the scenes of the Annunciation and the Descent into Limbo, archaic in their composition.
Busts of Christ and the apostles, and of the healers Pantaleon, Cosmas and Damian, complete the decoration of the icon. The silver mount of later date is chased on the reverse with a leaved cross within a border of floral ornament. This composition has numerous analogies among eleventh century works of art; it is seen on a silver reliquary in the Hermitage collection, once richly decorated with enamels.

Many Byzantine and Georgian enamels of different periods were incorporated in the famous
190,191, triptych of *Our Lady of Khakhuli*, a relic preserved in the Ghelati Monastery.
186–188 *Cloisonné* enamels, with their bright, pure colours on a gold ground beautifully harmonized
with the spiritualistic outlook of medieval society. The art of *cloisonné* enamelling developed within a short period of time in a number of countries, Georgia and Ancient Russia among the others. It is interesting to note that Byzantine enamels of the tenth and eleventh centuries were mounted
180, 181 in the cover of the Gospels of Mstislav, which was altered in the mid-sixteenth century, side by
side with enamels of Russian work. The combination of local and ancient Byzantine elements in the decoration of a single object shows that old models were highly venerated.

Among other representations, the Khakhuli triptych numbers a rare specimen of the art of
187 the portrait, showing the Emperor Michael VII Ducas (1071—1078) and his wife Maria, daughter
of the Georgian King Bagrat IV. Similar figures can be seen on the famous *Pala d'oro* made in
190, 191 Venice at about the same time. The figures of the apostles in the Khakhuli triptych are close in
treatment to those on the well-known Limbourg staurothèque of the tenth century.

Crosses discovered in Georgia, some of them with cast reliefs or embossed decorations in combination with *cloisonné* enamels, have close parallels among Byzantine art objects. Among them are specimens made by Constantinopolitan masters, like the reliquary cross (acquired in
176 Kiev) with the busts of the Four Evangelists and exquisite geometric designs.

A small Byzantine icon with the Crucifixion was found at Staraya Riazan with a rich treasure
178 of objects of Russian work; icons of this kind occur in the territory of Ancient Russia.

Alongside with *cloisonné* enamels, which testify to the contacts of Russia and Georgia with the Byzantine Empire, Soviet museums own specimens which reached our country in more recent 197–201 times. Thus, the staurothèque with the Deesis, recorded at the beginning of the present century in the Saidnaya Monastery near Damascus, came to the Hermitage from a country residence of the Emperor Nicholas II where it had probably been brought in connection with the celebration of the tricentenary of the Romanovs' rule in 1913. At some period in its previous history, a missing enamel plaque with the figure of the Virgin was replaced by another executed in crude chasing.

The composite icon and reliquary of the eleventh century, with the Crucifixion, saints, and 192–195 Gospel scenes, had a long and complicated history. The subjects are mainly executed in the technique of *cloisonné* enamel, with the exception of *Christ in the Sepulchre*, a plaque somewhat later in date, which displays certain traits of the *champlevé* technique. The central plaque is distinguished by the utmost delicacy of workmanship which is quite astonishing in such details as the centurion's shield, about 1 cm in length, decorated with the figure of a bird and a border of precious stones.

The embossed representations of saints are of different date. This is clear from their style. The busts in medallions, flat in treatment, with the hair and beard rendered by an ornamental pattern, were made in the tenth or eleventh century, and widely differ from the half-length figures in the margins, facing the centre, with the forms rendered three-dimensionally, which are datable to a time not before the end of the thirteenth century.

A comparison of earlier enamels, such as the figures of the apostles on the cover of the Gospels of Mstislav or those on the Khakhuli triptych, with works of later periods, will show a gradual development in the pattern of the partitions which finally came to form a dense network of lines filling the entire space of the draperies. No technical reasons can be assigned for this process, whose results are well exemplified by the icon of *St Peter* which is dated by Amiranashvili to the 183 thirteenth century—too late a time, in our opinion.

The evolution in artistic enamels is beautifully illustrated by two versions of the *Descent into* 182 *Limbo*, of which the earlier comes from Shemokmedi, and the later is now in the Kremlin Armoury, Moscow. The enamel in the Armoury shows a far more complicated composition resembling a painted icon of the same subject in the collection of the Hermitage. The arrangement of the figures is less conventional; most of them, however, are shown frontally. Exaggerated attention to detail, and a certain crudeness of execution, seem to point to a provincial provenance.

The icon of *St Theodore Spearing the Dragon* was made at the turn of the twelfth and the 196 thirteenth centuries: here the main contours are executed in *champlevé* enamel, a technique widespread in European countries, and the details, such as the hair, in the *cloisonné* technique. St Theodore, a character derived from folklore tradition, is shown here as an epic hero. This deviation from the Byzantine canon, usually so strictly enforced, was only possible in an object of lesser intrinsic value: the icon is made of copper, not of gold.

The ivories of the period are as well represented in Soviet museums as enamels. They include a unique plaque with the Emperor Constantine VII being crowned by Christ. A comparison with 122 the coins of this ruler shows that the face of Constantine VII is a portrait. The execution is characterized by plastic modelling, particularly in the face and the hands; the draperies, in both figures, repeat the body contours.

Ivory-carving of the tenth century was influenced by a neo-classicist tendency, which characterized the court-painting of the period. This influence is clearly expressed in the triptych with

123–127 the Forty Martyrs of Sebaste and Warrior Saints. The martyrs standing naked on the frozen surface of Lake Sebaste, are presented in a variety of postures: their faces express suffering, each in its own individual way. The bodies are rendered with marked attention to muscular structure. Only a somewhat constrained execution, and the repetition of certain details, betray a lack of freedom in the master who was evidently copying an older original. Curiously enough, this work, in which the classicizing tendency is so strongly pronounced, also reveals an Oriental influence: the shields of two of the saints in the side wings, and the scabbard of the third's sword, are decorated with inscriptions in ornamental lettering imitating Arabic characters. The classicizing tendency is also felt in the figures of the saints, modelled on the type of philosophers of antiquity. They are carved in such very high relief as to stand almost free of the background, like round sculpture.

136–139, 140, Other works of the same period are close in style to contemporary icon-painting: the diptychs
143, 144 and parts of triptychs presenting the Feasts of the Church, sometimes forming a whole series.

If works of religious art display a strong influence of antiquity in the field of form, those of a secular nature reproduce subjects and characters of classical mythology. Wooden caskets were
130–135 decorated with carved ivory plaques showing mythological scenes and figures of dancers, actors and musicians. Mythological subjects were not always familiar to the ivory-carvers; unable to grasp the content of the scene, they let it fall into pieces; there was no unity of action, the characters were presented as the master's imagination prompted, the nude figures provided with clothing, and the treatment as a whole was far from the aristocratic classicism of the religious representations described above. It is not improbable that the plaques were produced for sale and stocked against future demand, not executed on commission for an individual patron.

All the caskets, irrespective of the subjects they illustrated, whether classic or Biblical, had the same ornamentation consisting of rosettes or a star motif, characteristic of other art works of the period as well. Fragments of ivory plaques decorated with rosettes have been excavated on a variety of sites, some of them in the territory of the Soviet Union (Western Byelorussia, Smolensk area and other places). This shows that ivories were widely exported from Byzantium.

141, 142 An ivory comb was discovered during the excavations of the ancient town of Belaya Vezha, which stood on the site of the Khazar fortress of Sarkel. It is decorated on one side with the scene of Heracles (or Samson) and the Lion, and on the other, with the figure of a peacock, and a hound chasing a hare. The carving is rather crude, the proportions of the figures are somewhat squattish, the compositions overcrowded. The comb was probably made in one of the provinces—not in Constantinople—but it is unquestionably of Byzantine work.

Some of the carved stone icons of steatite or schist, produced in the eleventh and twelfth centuries, were imitations of ivory-carvings, executed in a cheaper material. Among them are works
145, 146 of excellent craftsmanship, as for instance the icon of *St Demetrius Mounted.* This specimen shows an influence of classic art. Most of the icons, however, are nearer in treatment to spiritualized images, probably borrowed from miniatures. The stone icons frequently show warrior saints; this suggests that they may have been particularly popular among soldiers.

The art of working hard stones, inherited from antiquity, also flourished. One of the best
153 specimens of this art is the small vase of agate; its bowl is decorated with a network pattern of thin gold lines, with rosettes, and Greek characters forming an inscription round the rim (hitherto undeciphered, probably a cryptogram). Vessels of this kind served as models to Russian stone-carvers, who produced similar objects.

Most Byzantine cameos preserved in the museums of the Soviet Union found their way to Russia many centuries ago. Some of them have mounts of Russian fourteenth to seventeenth century work, with the names of the owners inscribed on them.

A few of the cameos reflect the classicizing tendency. This group is exemplified by specimens in translucent semi-precious stones, carved in high relief with images showing an influence of antique
art: for instance, the chalcedony cameos with St Basil, or Sts George and Demetrius. Another 162, 163
group is closer to the tendency of the Comnene period; it includes cameos showing Christ Enthroned, or the bust or half-length figure of Christ. Heliotrope was commonly used in cameo- 161, 164
carving; such gems as those of lapis-lazuli owned by the Kremlin Armoury are extremely rare. 155, 159

Lead seals became particularly widespread in the tenth and eleventh centuries; many are of 168–175
exceptional interest as documents throwing light on the political life of the epoch. They are often executed with a mastery which makes of them true works of art. Objects of this kind mainly show the figure of the Virgin or the saints; less common are figure compositions and portraits of emperors. The inscriptions on the reverse, containing the name, title and rank of the owner, are not infrequently executed with a high degree of artistic perfection.

During the tenth, eleventh and twelfth centuries, the art of metalwork retained the high level reached during the preceding periods. True, we have few specimens of goldwork, but there is enough silverware at our disposal to help us form an idea of this branch of art as well. In contrast to the pre-Iconoclastic period, most of the objects surviving from the tenth to twelfth century
are connected with religious practices, as e.g. staurothèques (containers for the cross) usually 207, 208
decorated with the scene of the Crucifixion, the figures of saints (mostly busts in roundels), and representations of the Emperor Constantine and St Helen. The ornamental motifs were akin to those used in manuscript illumination.

A rare octagonal reliquary shows, alongside with the customary details of decoration, chased
portraits of the Emperor Constantine Ducas and his wife Eudocia. In form it is a replica of the 205, 206
baldachin over the tomb of St Demetrius at Thessalonica. The warrior saints represented on the reliquary are reminiscent of the figures carved on ivory and steatite icons.

Of great interest is the image of the Virgin and Child in gilt bronze, incorporated in a large 188
seventeenth century Georgian icon. It was repeatedly reproduced by Georgian masters; one of
the copies, made of gold, shows a local modification of the Byzantine prototype. It is not improbable 179
that Byzantine icons were commissioned as models for reproduction by local masters.

Works made in precious materials were often repeated in bronze or copper. Several such 209, 210
copies, probably once mounted on a wooden panel, have been excavated at Chersonese. They may have been imported, or produced locally.

Evidently Byzantine in origin, though probably manufactured in provincial workshops, are the silver vessels, most of them intended for secular use, with chased decoration, sometimes
heightened with engraving or nielloed. Notable among this group of objects is a bowl (one of its 212–214
handle missing), with St Theodore in a roundel on the bottom, and a Greek inscription running around the rim, with the name of Theodore Tourkelus, the owner of the bowl. The walls are decorated on the outside with real and fantastic creatures, birds and animals, devouring each other; there are also a few human figures. These images have parallels in the art of the Balkan countries, and are probably connected with the idea of the Last Judgement; in form, however, they are reminiscent of Near Eastern art.

Other vessels, generally also having a central roundel on the inside of the bottom, are adorned
with figures of hunters, epic heroes, musicians, acrobats, girl dancers, etc. One of the bowls, of a
215–217 shape resembling the Russian *bratina* of later years and scratched on the reverse with an inscription in Old Cyrillic, is decorated with small embossed scale-like shapes, each of those in the upper
row bearing an element of a feast scene; below are real and fantastic animals, birds, and plants.
On the bottom is an image of St George, with his name in Greek characters. Along the rim are
figures of running animals.

218, 219 Animals of the same type, executed in the same technique, decorate another bowl embossed
with figures of men under arches. To judge by one of the subjects identified as the Ascent of
Alexander the Great, the figures must represent characters of fiction.

Objects of this kind may be regarded as associated with a third, orientalizing trend in the development of Byzantine art, which existed side by side with the classicizing and the spiritualizing tendencies. This trend, which has certain features in common with the art of the Near East, seems to have been popular among the townspeople in the provinces of the Empire. Its existence is attested by numerous finds, mostly coming from excavations: articles of silver and bronze, such as bracelets and rings, and bone plaques carved with bird and animal motifs and ornamental designs.

227–232 Examples of this orientalizing style are numerous among glazed pottery, objects widely used
in everyday life. The specimens preserved in Soviet museums are mainly derived from excavations on the site of the ancient Chersonese.

In the ninth and tenth centuries, glazed pottery was decorated with impressed figures of birds
and animals, often confronted or placed back to back. During the later ages the technique of in-
cising through slip, with subsequent coating with transparent glaze, became predominant. Pottery
252 designs included such motifs as the fantastic bird called the *Sirin*, the griffon, animals in combat,
and other subjects widespread in the art of the Near East as well. There are also human figures,
among them Dighenes Akrites, the hero of the Byzantine epic. Representations of Christian saints
are less common. Specimens of painted ceramics form a group apart.

Icons hold a central place among objects of Byzantine art.

During the eleventh and twelfth centuries, the importance of icon-painting grew considerably as compared with the preceding period. The technique of encaustic was replaced by a new method, that of painting in egg tempera.

235, 236 One of the most remarkable specimens of the period is the icon of *Our Lady of Vladimir*.
It was highly venerated in Russia, often copied, and repeatedly "renovated", so that the faces
alone have survived from the Byzantine original. The image, at once highly spiritual and permeated
with deep human feeling, has a powerful appeal. The expression is one of mixed sadness and
severity; the mother's anxiety for her child's fate and the strength of the love which binds them
are rendered with exceptional force. The composition, the colouring, the plastic modelling of the
faces, all serve to convey the main idea. This lyrical image of the type known as the Eleousa
(Tenderness), came to be one of the most popular in Russian iconography.

Another outstanding work, evidently made in Constantinople, as was *Our Lady of Vladimir*, is
237, 238 the icon of *St Gregory the Thaumaturgus*. This painting displays a close connection with murals,
mosaics and frescoes produced in the eleventh and twelfth centuries. The flat treatment and the
severe simplicity of style are excellently suited to the stern dignity of the saint's face and figure,
and help to create an image far removed from the world of men. The colouring serves the same

purpose. It is based on a harmony of golden-yellow and brownish tones; the dark blue band round the collar of the chiton alone sounds a contrasting note. In spite of the predominantly linear treatment of the draperies, the forms of the body are felt beneath the clothing. There are elements of modelling in the rendering of the features; the hair is painted ornamentally. This icon is one of the best samples of the spiritualizing trend in the art of the period.

The fragments from a *templon* (a row of icons surmounting the chancel-screen) show two 243, 244
subjects, the Descent into Limbo and the Pentecost. The scenes are arranged under arches resting
on columns, a characteristic feature of the time, reflecting the position of the paintings in the
interior of the church. The laconic composition, the conventional treatment of both landscape
and architectural backgrounds, the frontal poses of the figures, and the severe simplicity of the
colour scheme are typical of the twelfth century mosaics and murals.

Another fragment from a *templon* presents the Apostle Philip and two warrior saints, Theo- 239–241
dore and Demetrius. The figures are disposed under arches supported by columns of elaborate
shape. The faces expressing strong religious feeling, preserve, nevertheless, faint traces of the por-
traiture of the Late Hellenistic period, more exactly of the Faiyum portraits. Another icon of the
three warrior saints, with the proportions of the figures somewhat shortened and the colours rich
and bright, probably comes from a provincial workshop. The icon of *St Pantaleon*, also displaying 234
certain features of Late Hellenistic art, is at present variously dated by the scholars.

The *Transfiguration* (and its companion piece, the *Raising of Lazarus*, in a private collection in Athens) has a red background rare in Byzantine painting, probably a distant echo of the art of Late Classic where it was widely used, as for instance in Pompeian murals.

The monumental style, and the close connection with architecture, two features distinctive
of the painting of the period, also characterize the art of sculpture where relief is the dominating
form. The figures of Sts Peter and Paul under arches, carved on two slabs discovered among the 247, 248
ruins of a church in Bulgaria, may be regarded as typical specimens. They are flat, yet the draperies
follow the body contours. The decorated arches and the knotted columns on which they rest, are
common in works of the minor arts from the eleventh and twelfth centuries; they occur in decorative
sculpture as well. There is no way of establishing whether the reliefs are the works of a Greek or
a Bulgarian, but their close association with Byzantine sculpture is beyond doubt.

A most remarkable art object which had long interested Russian scholars recently became
available for study. It is an icon of *St George* in carved wood, with the full-length figure of the 266–268
saint surrounded by scenes of his life. A rare specimen illustrating a combined use of carving and
painting, this icon is probably the earliest known work executed in this technique. Its iconography,
style, and the ornaments which fill the spaces between the scenes in the margins suggest that the
St George was produced on the brink of the thirteenth century. The scenes of the saint's life may well
be reproductions of miniatures in manuscripts, while the main figure has certain features in common with steatite icons. The place where the work was produced has not so far been identified;
but such is the case with most specimens of Byzantine wooden sculpture. The icon of *St George* was
found in a church at Mariupol, a town where the Greeks living in the Crimea had been forced to
move in the eighteenth century. It has some points of resemblance with the sculpture and metalwork from Georgia; this seems to justify the supposition that the icon may have been made at
Trebizond, a centre which had close political ties with Georgia, and which played a most important
role during the period of the Crusades.

The natural process of evolution in Byzantine art was interrupted in 1204 when Constantinople was seized by the Crusaders. This event was, however, beneficial to the development of local art centres, no longer dependent on the capital. Here the artists, compelled to leave Constantinople, found refuge. The splendid revival of art after the restoration of the Empire in 1261 is an enigma to the historians. Byzantium, economically weakened, deprived of a large part of her former possessions, no longer able to play a leading role in world politics, nevertheless retained, throughout the last centuries of her existence, a place of importance in the development of medieval culture. Byzantine art reached a new height at the end of the thirteenth and in the first half of the fourteenth century. This is clearly illustrated by the monumental painting and icons of the period, and also by examples of contemporary artistic embroidery.

Soviet museums own numerous works of Byzantine art dating from the fourteenth and fifteenth centuries; some of them reached Russia at that distant epoch.

Among them are specimens of miniature mosaics, datable to the end of the thirteenth century.

The exquisite art of miniature mosaics was practised in court workshops of Constantinople
262 after 1261. Notable among the specimens at our disposal are two early icons, *Christ Emmanuel*
261 (badly damaged, from the P. Sevastyanov Collection), and *The Prophet Samuel.* These works are
characterized by a sparse use of smalts, the irregular shapes of the tesserae, and a rather dark colouring. The elongated proportions of the figures, the flowing draperies, and the use of highlighting and rose carnation tints in modelling the faces are features of the new style. They are to
269 be seen in *The Prophet Samuel*, and in the painted icon of *Christ Pantocrator* shown full length.

265 The marble relief with St Luke was in all probability carved in the late years of the thirteenth
century. It shows certain elements of plastic modelling (cf., e.g., reliefs of Bulgarian provenance) and a free arrangement of drapery folds which follow the forms of the body; the figure has much free background space. Comparison with other related materials helps to define the relief as a work of the Italo-Byzantine school.

Also datable to the beginning of the Palaeologue period are some specimens of the minor arts.
259, 260 One of them is the gold icon of the *Virgin and Child*, with the Virgin seated on a throne which is
placed at an angle, so as to achieve a greater sense of space, and the Child clinging to her in a transport of tenderness, his cheek pressed against hers. Another remarkable work is the silver mount for an icon of the *Virgin and Child*, made in the late thirteenth and early fourteenth centuries. Its most outstanding feature is the portraits of Constantine Acropolites and his wife, with individualized features and the details of clothing and headdresses carefully rendered. Most half-figures of saints shown in the margin face the central image, differing in this respect from analogous representations in the works from the eleventh and twelfth centuries when the strictly frontal arrangement was obligatory. While the floral designs filling the background of the icon have a certain affinity with the embossed ornamentation of the previous epoch, other elements of decoration, resembling filigree work, are quite typical of the Palaeologue period, as, for instance, the distinctive openwork bosses which were to become a favourite feature not only in chasing but also in stone and wood-carving.

Specimens of the art of glyptics are difficult to date; but some of the gems clearly show the characteristic traits of the so-called Palaeologue style: the mild expression in the face of Christ, in the jade cameo with Christ Pantocrator, or the affected elegance of pose in the figures of Sts Gurias and Abibus in another cameo.

The development of mosaics during the first half of the fourteenth century can be traced by
comparing the icons of *St Nicholas*, *St Theodore*, and the *Four Saints*. The tesserae, which tend 246, 264, 263
to decrease in size, and to assume a more regular geometric form, are arranged with greater regularity. As regards style, the later specimens show a stronger modelling both in the faces, which have smaller features and a less severe, more mild and benevolent expression, and in the hands (for example, the hand of one of the four saints).

The icon of *St Nicholas*, which has been found during the recent restoration to be of the same date as its silver mount, is more traditional in execution than the other works. Yet the mount includes elements of decoration unknown prior to the end of the thirteenth century, and typical of the closing phase in the evolution of Byzantine silverwork. We mean not so much the filigree design, which adorns the edging of the icon and fills the margins and the lozenges in them as the above-mentioned openwork bosses of interlace pattern. Consequently, the icon itself could not have been made before the end of the thirteenth century.

Of the icons painted in egg tempera in the first half of the fourteenth century, two are of superior merit. One of them shows the Twelve Apostles, the other, the Annunciation.

The icon of the *Twelve Apostles* reflects the changes which are also observed in the mural 270
paintings of the period. The figures are no longer static: the apostles are represented in the attitudes of persons in conversation with each other. The faces have a plastic quality, enhanced by the use of high lights; their features are individualized. The draperies are rendered in detail, with a multitude of folds revealing the forms of the bodies. The work is distinguished by a rich colour scheme and a pictorial manner of execution.

In the *Annunciation* there is no impetuous movement. The figures are full of dignity. Unity 272, 273
of action is achieved by gestures rather than movement. The background of buildings with a velum thrown over the tops, a typical feature of the architectural backgrounds of the period, is organized so as to create a sense of deep space. In the middle ground is the figure of a servant girl standing behind a column, with her arm round the shaft. The faces are modelled by the use of high lights
and rose carnation tints. The colouring is restrained, much more so than in the *Dormition of the* 274, 275
Virgin, of about the same date. The latter work, though also marked by a complex of features characteristic of the epoch, displays a much more elaborate iconography, and includes a large number of figures arranged in several superimposed rows.

The small icon (perhaps originally part of a diptych) with Six of the Twelve Feasts of the 278
Church reflects the tendency towards the diminution of forms which is felt even in the murals of the period. Most of the scenes exhibit features of the early Palaeologue style: violent movement, as in the figure of Christ in a flowing cloak in the *Descent into Limbo*; strongly dynamic attitudes, as of Christ in the *Crucifixion*, with the Virgin and St John in a transport of grief; the sense of depth in the architectural background, as in the *Dormition* and the *Entry into Jerusalem*; elements of landscape background, as the cliffs in the last mentioned scene, etc. The icon shows a close affinity with a part of a mosaic diptych now in Florence. The diptych, in its turn, is very closely related to the celebrated mosaics of the early fourteenth century in the church of the Chora Monastery (Karyai Jami) in Constantinople.

Characteristic of the fourteenth century is the icon of the *Virgin of the Eleusa* (Tenderness), 276
highly popular during the closing period of Byzantine art. Also characteristic of the time is the
Prophet Elijah in the Wilderness, a powerful image reminiscent of the type of antique philosopher, 271

amidst a rocky landscape, to which it is differently related as to size than are the human figures in works of the eleventh and twelfth century art.

281–284 The icon of *Christ Pantocrator* holds a central place among the later Byzantine icons in the Hermitage collection. Two portraits of donors with accompanying inscriptions, from one of which only traces remain in the lower portion of the left margin, the other opposite in the right margin, help to establish the exact date of the work. The donors, the Grand Stratopedarch Alexius, and the Grand Primicerion John, founded a monastery of Christ Pantocrator on Mount Athos in 1363. This is the year when the icon was painted, and it is important in dating other works stylistically related to *Christ Pantocrator*.

The face and hands of Christ are modelled by vivid touches of white, arranged with greater regularity than in works of earlier periods. The *clavus* has gold hatching typical of later icon-painting. The deep blue tone of the *himation*, characteristic of Byzantine painting produced in the capital, was originally heightened by similar touches of white.

The large panel with St John the Baptist, executed in a somewhat unusual colour scheme, refers to approximately the same time as *Christ Pantocrator*. Probably once part of a Deesis, it is distinguished by an original treatment of the face which seems to be divided into parts, each enclosed by a separate outline, as in certain works of Serbian and Macedonian provenance.

According to Lazarev, this phase in the evolution of Byzantine painting is also exemplified
288 by the icon known as *Our Lady of Pimen* (from the name of Metropolitan Pimen who is believed
to have brought it from Constantinople in the 1380s). This scholar regards it, however, as linked with the earlier artistic tradition.

Very few works of applied art from this period have come down to us. The political and economic situation was not propitious to the flourishing of most minor arts. The ivories and enamels are represented by only a small number of specimens. By contrast, artistic embroidery is best known for this period; and it is precisely by embroideries, more than by works of any other of the minor arts, that we can judge of contemporary painting.

Outstanding among the works of this class are two *sakkoi* and an *epitrachelion*, once owned by the Moscow Metropolitan Photius.

The stole is embroidered with eighty-eight roundels enclosing miniature busts of saints, joined so as to form a single uninterrupted pattern: this reflects a general tendency observed in the art of the time, towards breaking up the surface into a multitude of small units. The shoulder parts are embroidered with figures of the Virgin and St John. The elongated proportions and graceful attitudes of the figures are also typical of the period. A half-length figure of Christ facing slightly left is wrought in a roundel at the top; the mild expression in the face of Christ is the same as in contemporary painted icons. The embroidery is executed in silks of pale, light colours.

In the two *sakkoi*, the features of the style predominant during the Palaeologue period are
305–307 still more strongly pronounced. The so-called Minor *Sakkos* is generally regarded as the earlier of
the two, and this view is borne out by the manner of its execution. The scenes and individual figures filling the surface of the Minor *Sakkos* are better suited to the shape of the vestment, and form
300–304 a clearer compositional design than in the Major *Sakkos* where no structural connection can be felt
between the elements of decoration and the object itself. In its overcharged composition and the obvious fear of vacancy the Major *Sakkos* is remindful of the Byzantine murals of the later period, which show a complete loss of unity with the structure they decorate.

Features of the new style are also observed in the execution of individual compositions (on both of the *sakkoi*). The strong curve given to the body of the suffering Christ in the *Crucifixion*, the refined proportions of the figures flanking the cross in the same scene, the strong dynamism of the *Descent into Limbo*, the increased importance of the narrative in most subjects, all these have direct parallels in specimens of late Byzantine painting. Another characteristic trait is the use of portrait representations: conspicuous among the decorations of the Major *Sakkos* are the groups of Basil, Grand Prince of Moscow, with his wife, and John Palaeologue, Emperor of Byzantium, with his wife. It is interesting to note that the portraits of the Russian rulers are accompanied by inscriptions in Old Cyrillic while all the other texts, including the one which refers to the embroidered portrait of the Metropolitan Photius, are in Greek writing.

Deserving of interest are also the textiles of which the vestments are made, magnificent satins
of Byzantine work. The *sakkos* of the Metropolitan Simon is of particularly great beauty. It was 308, 309
manufactured at the end of the fifteenth or the beginning of the sixteenth century.

The name of Photius is also connected with the splendid gold mount of the icon of *Our Lady* 310–314
of Vladimir. The question of its provenance has not so far been decided. Certain technological features distinguish it from specimens of contemporary Russian goldwork: this has been conclusively shown by M. Postnikova-Loseva. One of these features is the use in the designs of thin metal strips soldered on edgewise, like the partitions in *cloisonné* enamel, a technique widespread in Byzantine metalwork. The decoration also includes some ornamental motifs, which have numerous analogies among Byzantine objects of art dating from the period since the end of the thirteenth century. The inscriptions in Greek—not only the names, but also a long text on the unrolled scroll in the *Presentation in the Temple*—confirm the Byzantine origin of the mount.

The somewhat crude manner in which the Gospel scenes are chased is in striking contrast to the exquisite delicacy of the ornamental background. These scenes, however, reflect the iconography and style of the Palaeologue period. The question arises, which of the art centres of the period could have produced this gold mount, an object so rare for its time? The answer to this question requires special research.

Though the fifteenth century was marked by the appearance of a few works of high artistic quality, the late Byzantine art as a whole showed gradually developing symptoms of decline.

One of the best among the paintings of the period was the icon with the Abraham Etertaining 392, 393
the Three Angels. It embodies some elements newly included into the canon, such, for example, as the still life in the foreground, of tableware, with decanters, vases, a cup, etc., probably reproducing actual types of objects used in daily life. The icon is characterized by the use of gradations of colour, and by the beginnings of the graphic manner, anticipating the dry linear treatment of later periods, in the rendering of the faces.

The linear principle assumed a more developed form in the icon of the *Descent into Limbo*, 315, 316
distinguished by exceptional delicacy and beauty of colour. A comparison of this work with the icon of the same subject painted in the twelfth century will reveal important changes in iconography and style. The later specimen has a more complicated composition and a greatly increased number of figures placed in an altogether different relation to the rocky landscape. The refined proportions of the figures linked with each other by attitude, look and gesture, the use of tonal gradations in the modelling of the faces, and a number of other details clearly illustrate the evolution of icon-painting from the twelfth to the fifteenth centuries.

280 The icon of *The Raising of Lazarus* has several points in common with the murals decorating some late Byzantine church buildings at Mistra. Among the features characteristic of fifteenth century painting, the most important is the elaborate architectural motif in the background and the significant place given to the rocky landscape. Also, such figures as those of the youths in the right-hand corner, who are carrying away the coffin lid—one is shown from the side, the other with his back to the viewer—would be quite unthinkable in earlier Byzantine painting.

317–319 *The Nativity of St John the Baptist* and the icon of *St Gregorius Palamas* probably belong to the late period of Byzantine painting. The former work is remarkable for its bright, joyous colouring, and for the lively genre groups included in the composition. The latter is a rare example of an image presenting a historical personage, and created soon after his death. The dry graphic manner used in rendering the faces, and the complete predominance of the linear over the pictorial principle are indicative of the direction to be taken by post-Byzantine icon-painting in its further development. It is certainly not such uninspired, standardized work that embodies the artistic heritage left to the world by Byzantine culture.

Some works of later Byzantine art show an influence of the mystic doctrine of Hesychasm which taught the necessity to leave the world, to shut out all external impressions, and to concentrate on prayer as a means of achieving communion with God by divine revelation. This trend, opposed to the first shoots of the humanist thought, gained many adherents at a time when the impending fall of the Empire cast its shadow on the minds of men.

During the fifteenth century, the circle round Constantinople tightened; the Ottomans came close to its very walls. All attempts of Byzantine emperors to save the Empire by political means, effecting a union of the Western and the Eastern churches, or enlisting the aid of the Western rulers, were doomed to failure. In 1430, Thessalonica was taken and on 11 May 1453, Constantinople fell. The once great empire ceased to exist.

After the fall of Constantinople, objects of Byzantine art were dispersed over a large territory. The artists and craftsmen of Byzantium sought refuge in foreign lands: some in Italy, others in Russia. Traditions of Byzantine art continued to develop on alien soil. Thus, in the Balkans we find frescoes and icons created by great artists who worked in the manner of late Byzantine painting. In Russia, the Byzantine tradition, which underwent complete transformation in the cultural atmosphere of a different country, greatly contributed to the flourishing of national art. Even the Turkish conquerors learnt from Byzantine craftsmen and architects, adopting Byzantine architectural forms and building techniques, and mastering the methods of Byzantine artisans.

The evolution of European art during the centuries which followed the fall of the Empire could not be properly understood without due regard to the artistic legacy left by Byzantium. The role of Byzantine art was not, by far, confined to that of a carrier of the antique traditions. Successful efforts to achieve the synthesis of the arts; a strong emotional tension; an interest in human psychology; an outstanding compositional mastery; a strong feeling of monumental form; a keen sense of colour; and a remarkable skill of conveying much by saying little—all these aspects of Byzantine art make it a great art in its own right, and give it a place of honour in the cultural history of mankind.

PLATES

1

1. Dish with the Triumph of the Emperor Constantius II. Late 4th century

2

3

2—5. Ewer with the muses. Circa 400

4

5

6

7

6—7. Bust of Julian the Apostate. 4th century

8—9. Medallion of the Emperor Constantius II. 340—350

8

9

10

10. Statue of the Good Shepherd. Late 4th century

11. Statue of the Good Shepherd. 4th century

11

12

12. Sarcophagus with scenes from the New Testament. 4th century

13

14

13—14. Relief with circus scenes. Circa 500

15

15. Polycandelon in the form of a basilica. 5th century

16. Polycandelon in the form of a disc. 6th century

16

17

17. Hanging lamp. 4th century

18

18. *Hanging lamp. 4th century*

19

19. Figurine of a bird and nestling. 4th—5th centuries
20. Fragment of a dish with circus scenes. 4th—5th centuries
21. Vessel for suspension in the shape of a fish. 4th century
22. Hanging lamp shaped as a camel. 4th century (?)

20

21

22

23. Dish with Christ holding a cross, with birds. 5th century

24. Fragment of a vessel with the Apostle Peter. 4th century

25. Fragment of a vessel with Abraham's Sacrifice. 4th century

23

24

25

26

26—29. Patera with scenes from the Old Testament. 4th century

27

28

29

30—31. Diptych with circus scenes. 5th century

32

33

32—34. *Leaf of the consular diptych of Areobindus. 506*

34

35

35. Portion of a diptych with scenes from a tragedy. 6th century

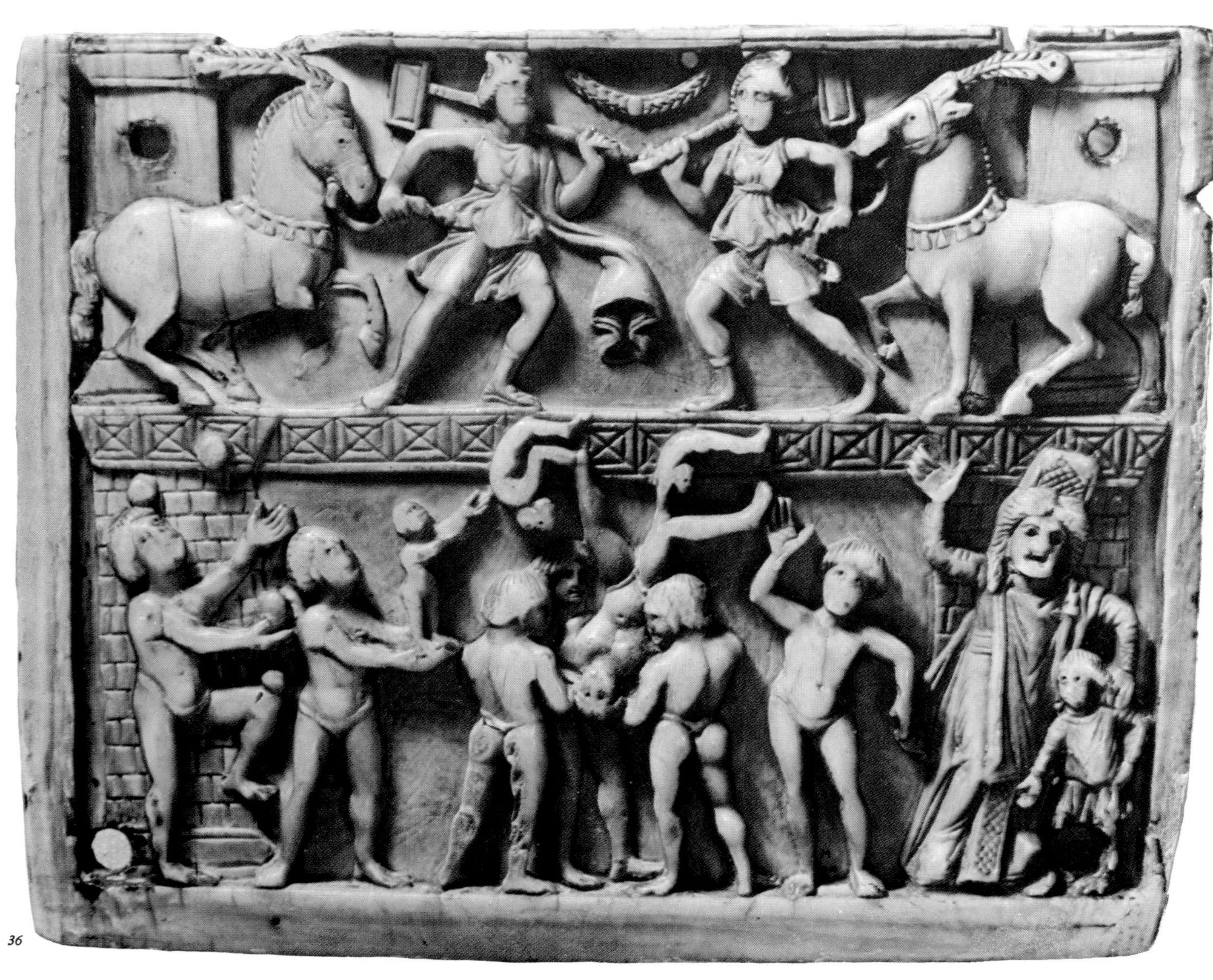
36

36. *Portion of the consular diptych of Anastasius. 517*

37

38

37—38. Portion of a diptych with scenes from the Life of Mary. 6th century

39

40

39—40. Pyxis with scenes from the Life of Joseph. 6th century

41—42. Pyxis with scenes from the Life of Jonah. 6th century

41

42

43

44

43—46. Pyxis with scenes from the Gospels. 6th century

45

46

47

48

47. Pyxis with scenes from the Life of Moses. 6th century
48—49. Pyxis with scenes from the Story of the Three Youths of Babylon. 6th century

49

50. *Portion of a diptych with scenes from the Life of the Virgin. 6th century*

51

52

51—52. Fragments of a pyxis with scenes from the Gospels. 6th century

53—54. Trulla (casserole) with a representation of a Nilometer. 491—518

53 54

55

56

55—56. Dish with a herdsman and his goats. 527—565

57

58

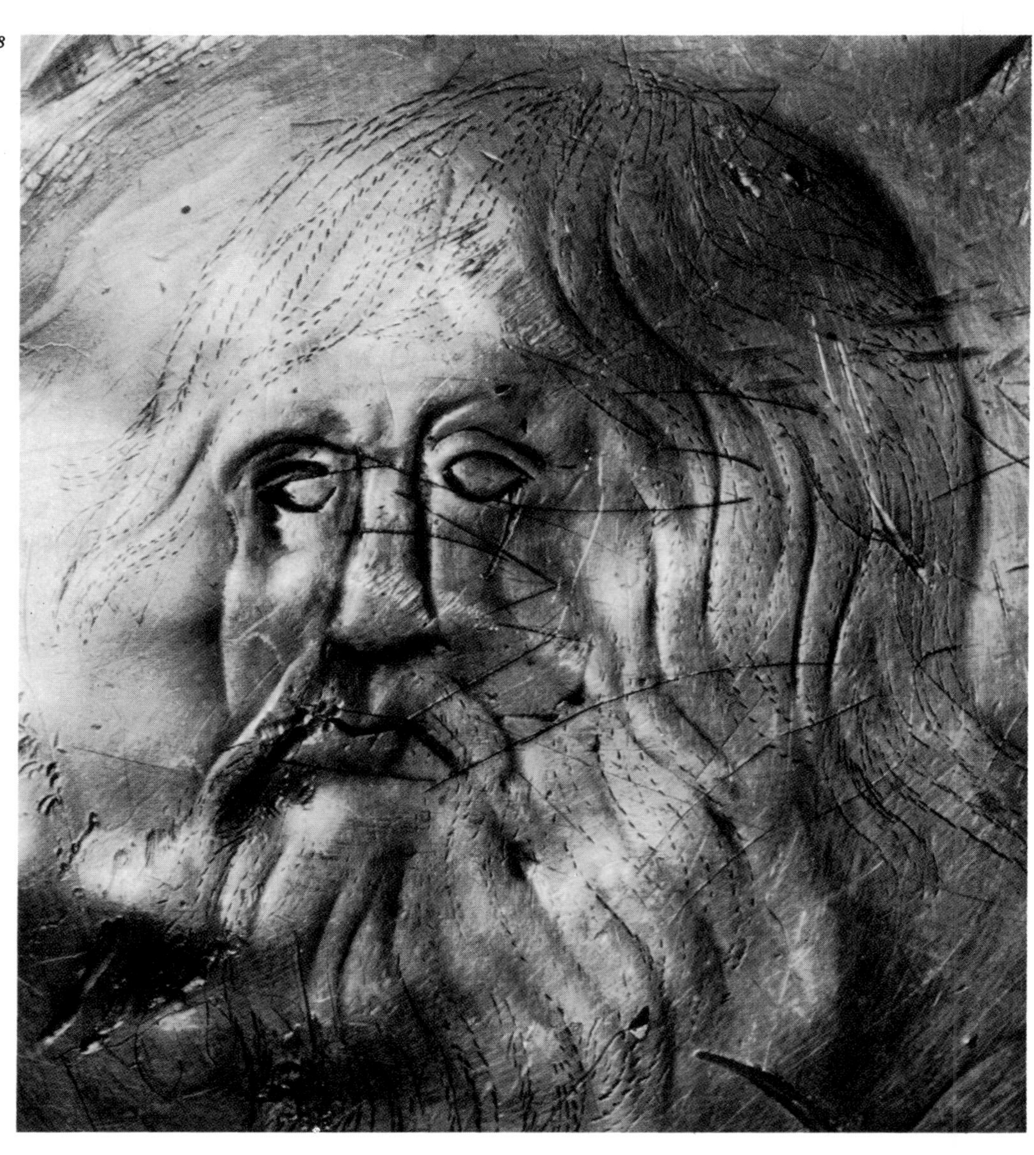

59

57—59. Dish with the scene of feeding a sacred serpent. 6th century

60

60—61. Dish with the scene of Athena deciding the quarrel of Ajax and Odysseus. 6th century

61

62

62—63. Ewer. 582—602

64

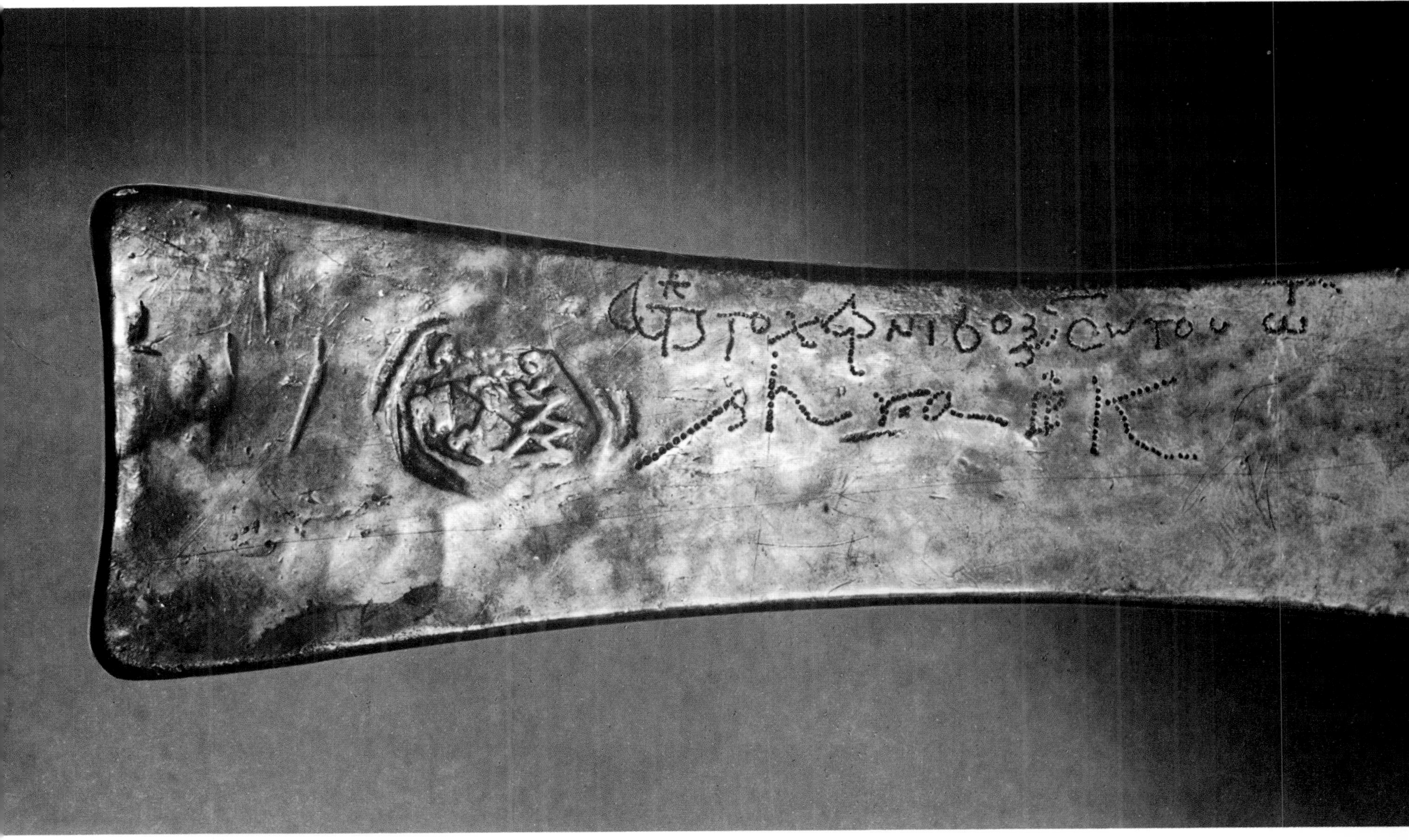

65

64—65. *Patera with a rosette. 582—602*

66

66—68. Paten of Bishop Paternus. 491—518

67

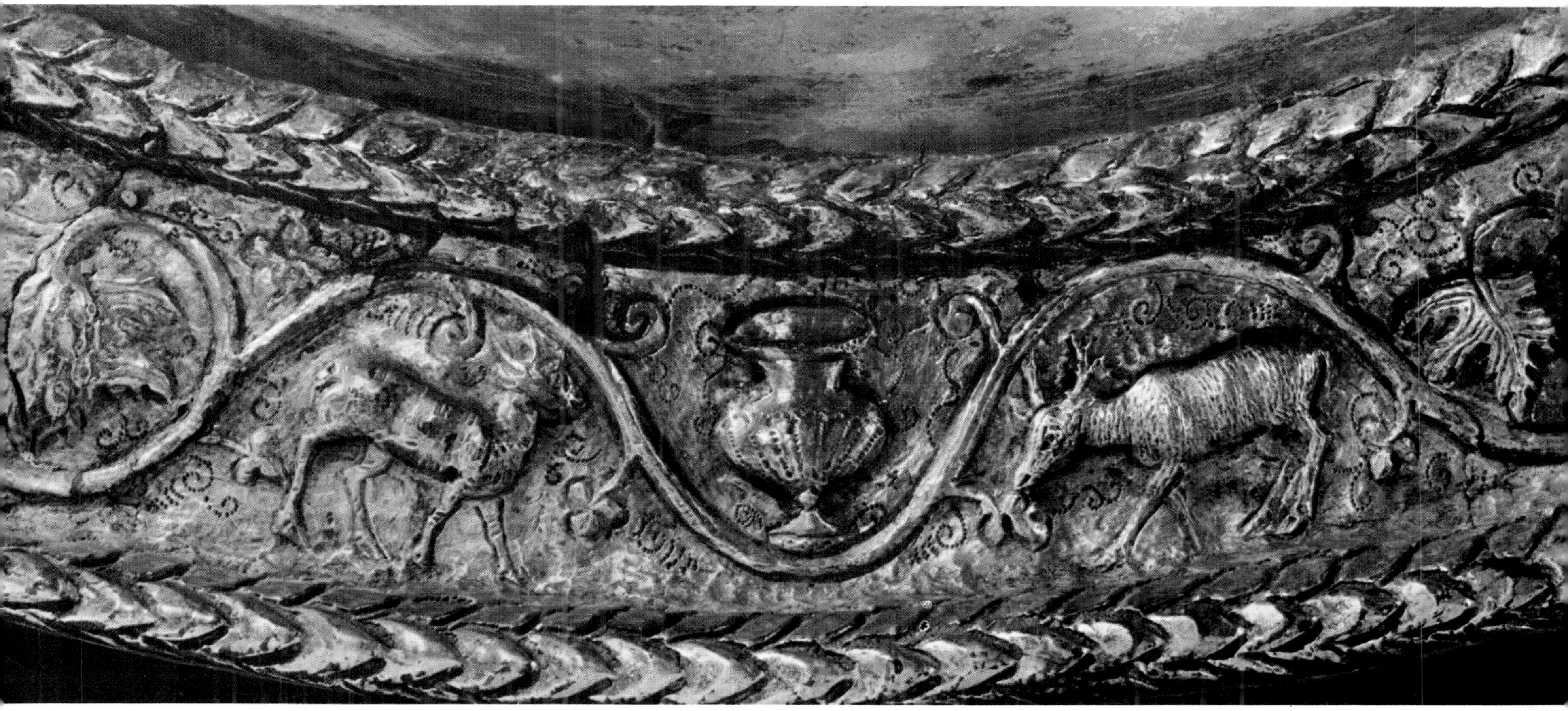

68

69. Dish decorated with a cross within a wreath, and fluting. 629—641

70. Amphora. 6th century

71. Dish with a rosette in a wreath of acanthus. 527—565

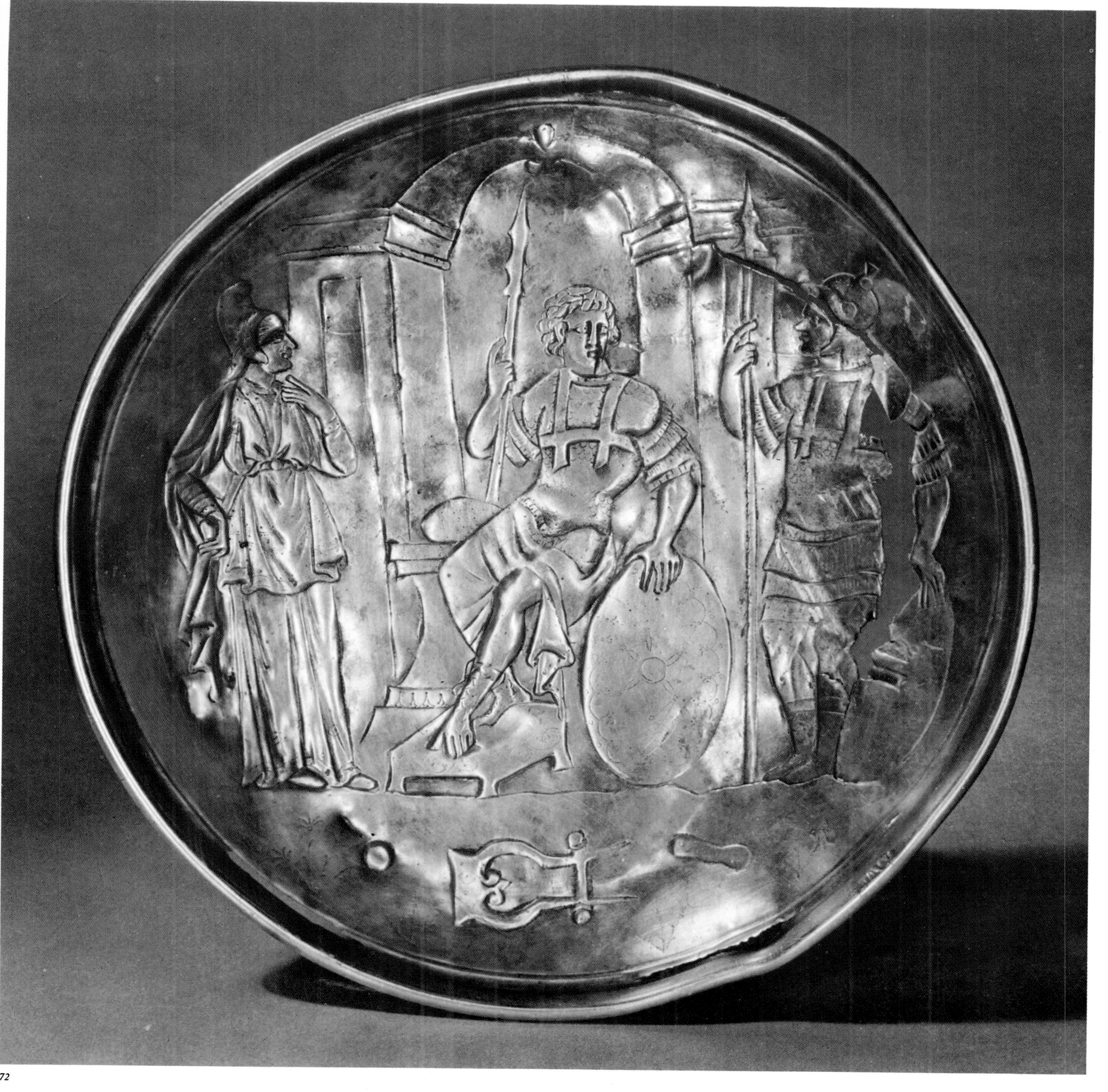

72

72. *Dish with Venus in the Tent of Anchises (?). Circa 550*

73

73—74. Dish with a horse under a tree. 527—565

75

75—77. *Reliquary. Circa 550*

76

77

78

78. *Paten with angels on either side of the cross. 6th century*

79

79. *Dish with an ornamental rosette. 651—668*

80. *Dish with an ornamental rosette. 629/30—641*

81

82

81. *Censer (?) with Christ and the Apostles. 6th century*

82. *Censer (?) with angels. 613—629/30*

83

83. *Dish with Meleager and Atalanta. 613—629*

84

84. Dish with Silenus and a Maenad. 613—629/30

85

86

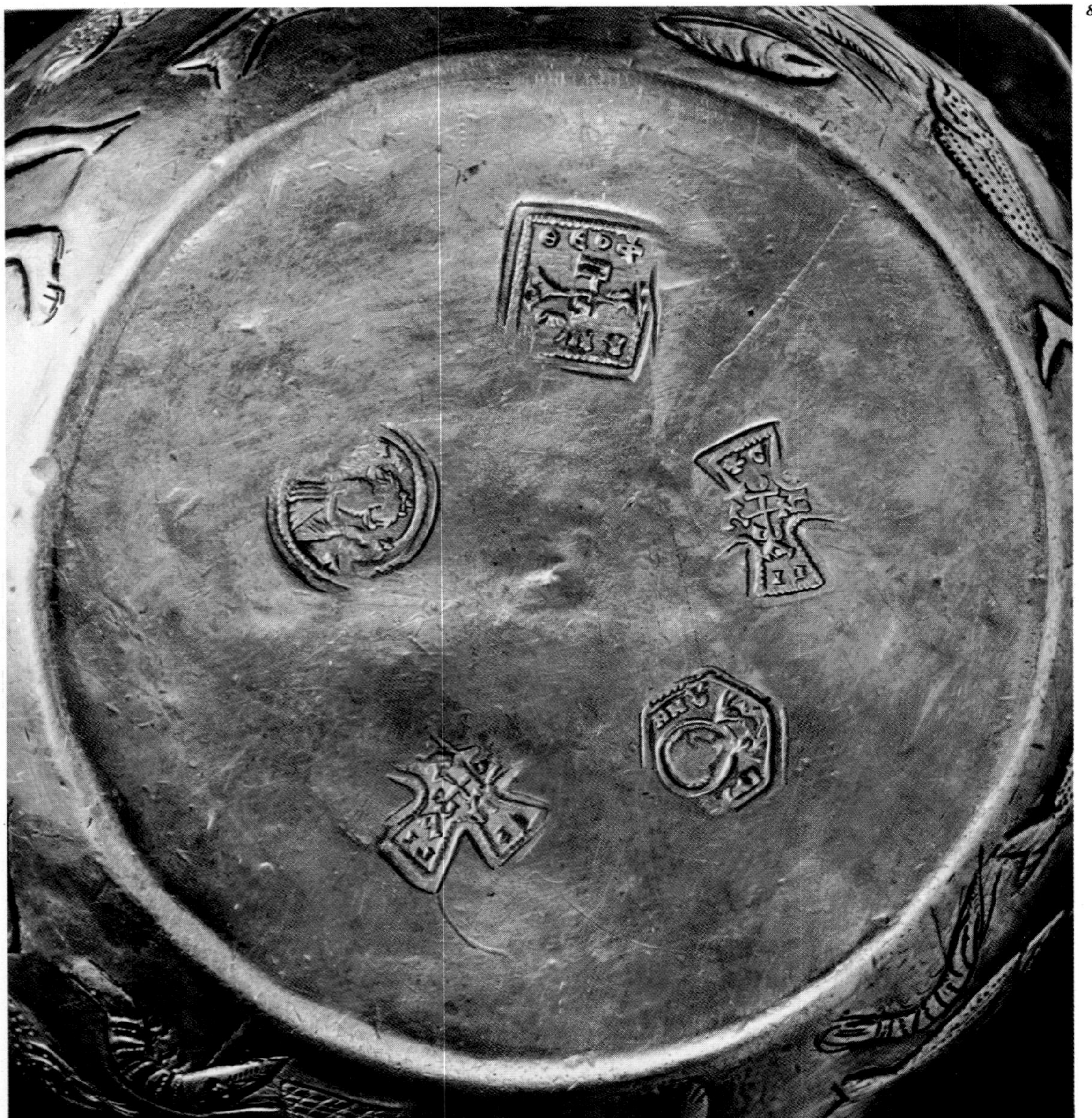

85—87. Trulla (casserole) with fishing scenes. 641—651

87

88

89

88—90. Ewer with Nereids. 641—651

91

91. Dish with an ornamental rosette. 527—565

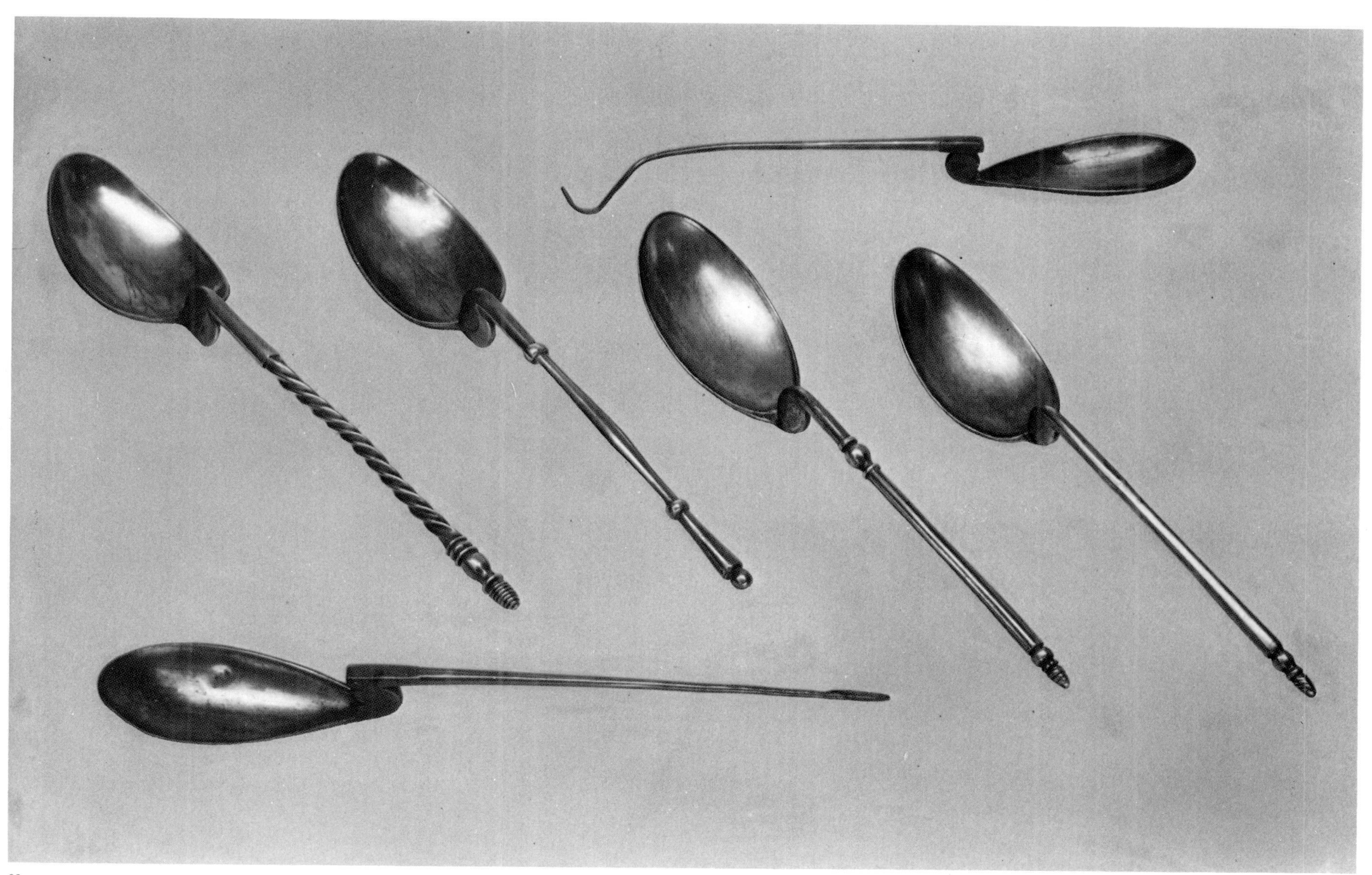

92

92. *Spoons. Late 4th—7th centuries*

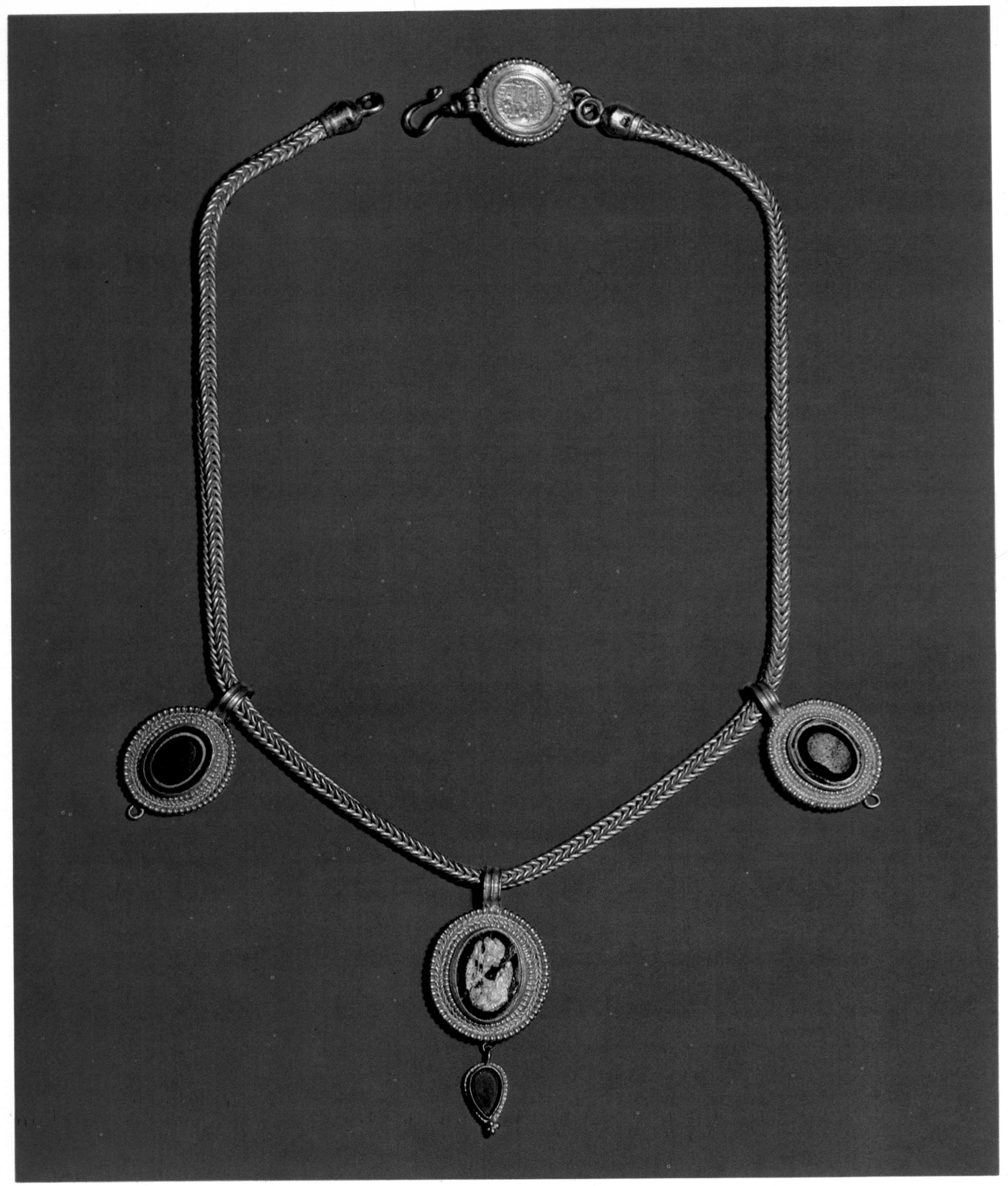

93—94. Chain with three pendants and a clasp made of a coin. 6th century

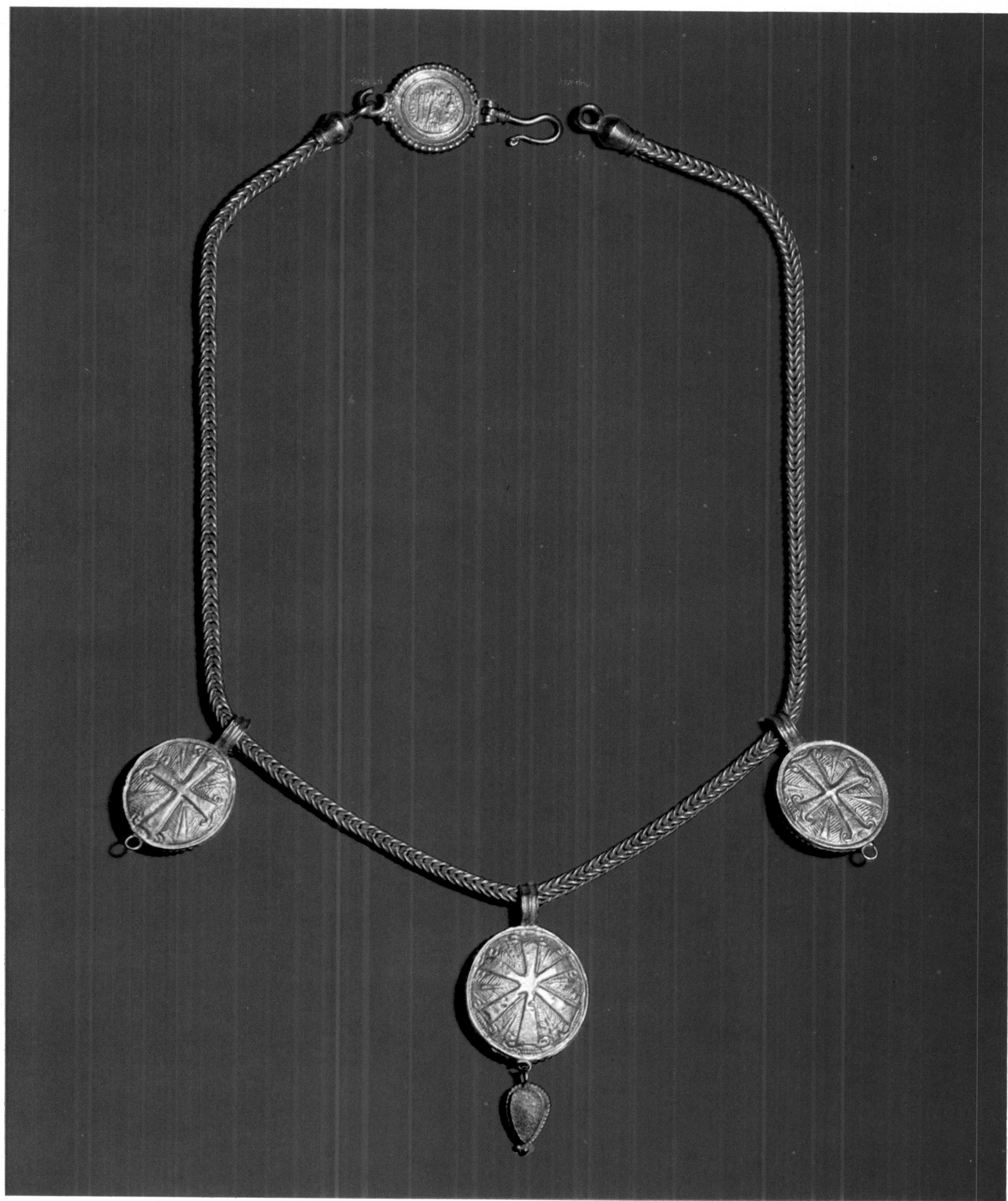

95. Chain with a medallion. Late 6th century

96. Rings. 7th century

97. Earrings. Late 6th century

96

97

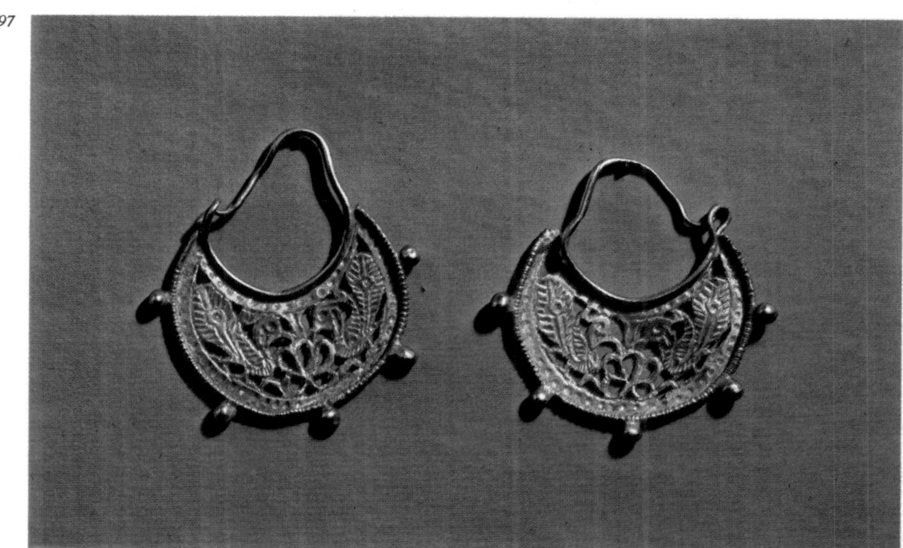

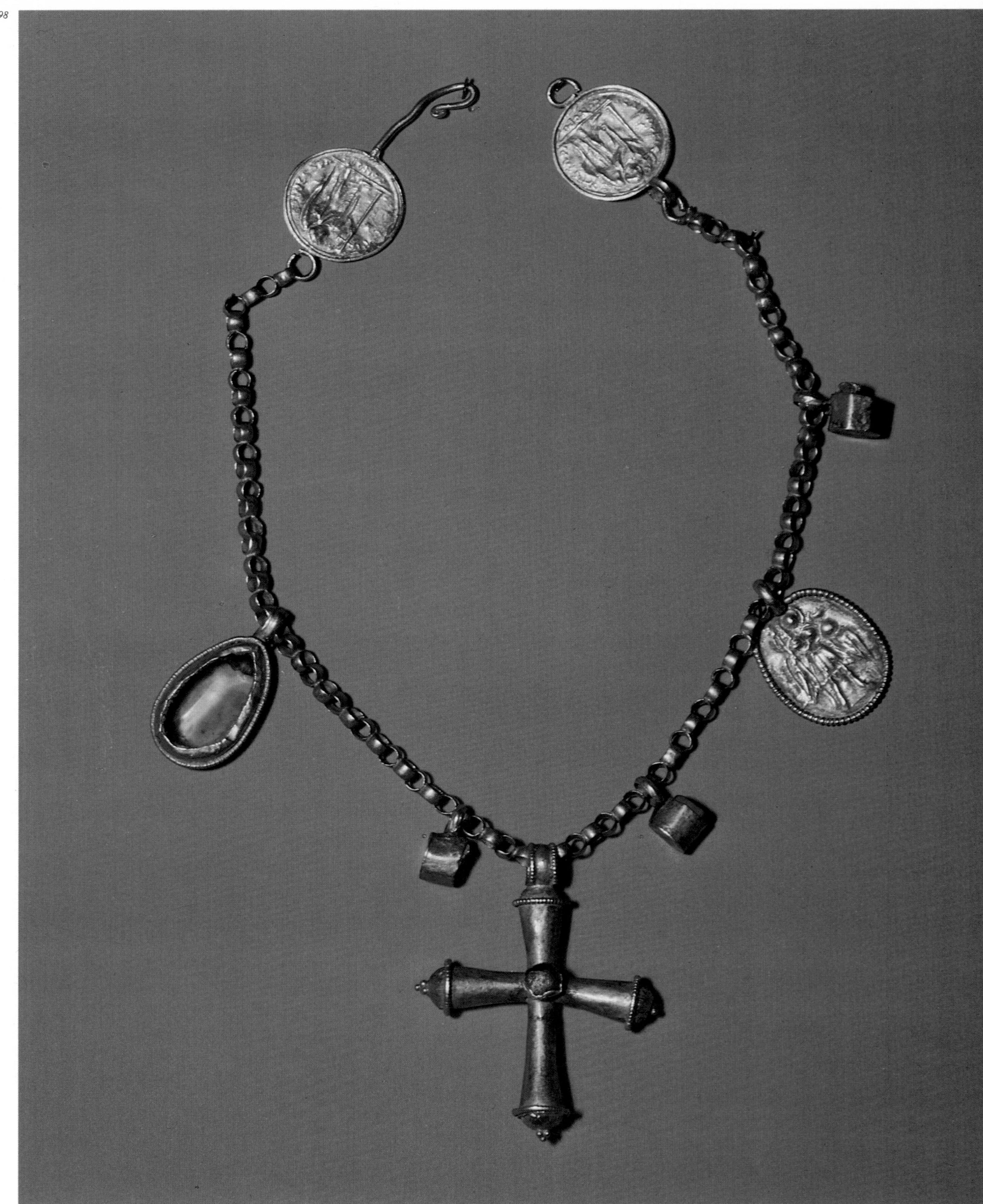

98. Chain with a cross and pendants. Late 6th century

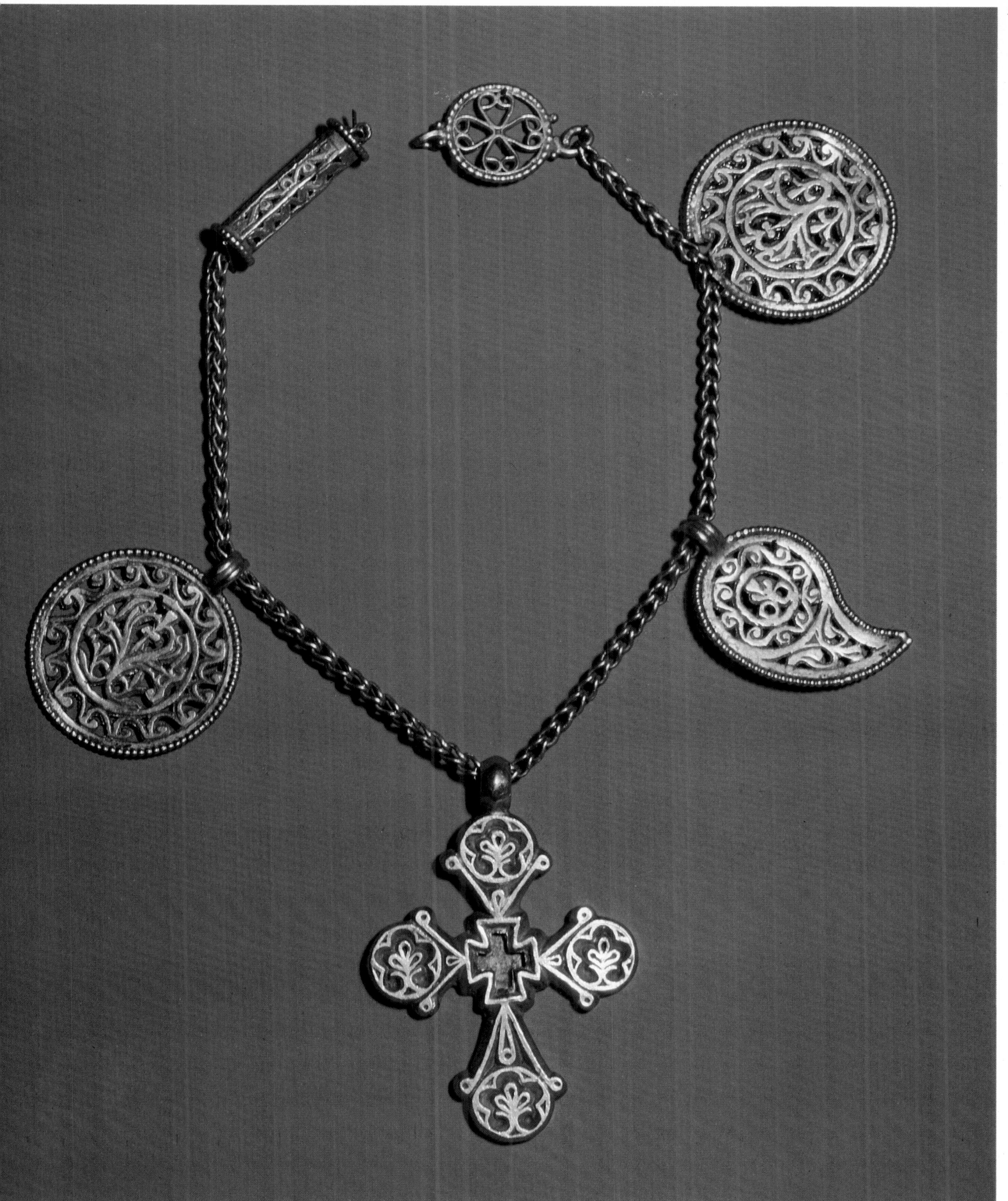

99. Chain supporting a cross and pendants. Late 6th century

100

100

102

100—101. Ring with the scene of a betrothal. 7th century

102. Bracelets. Late 6th century

103

104

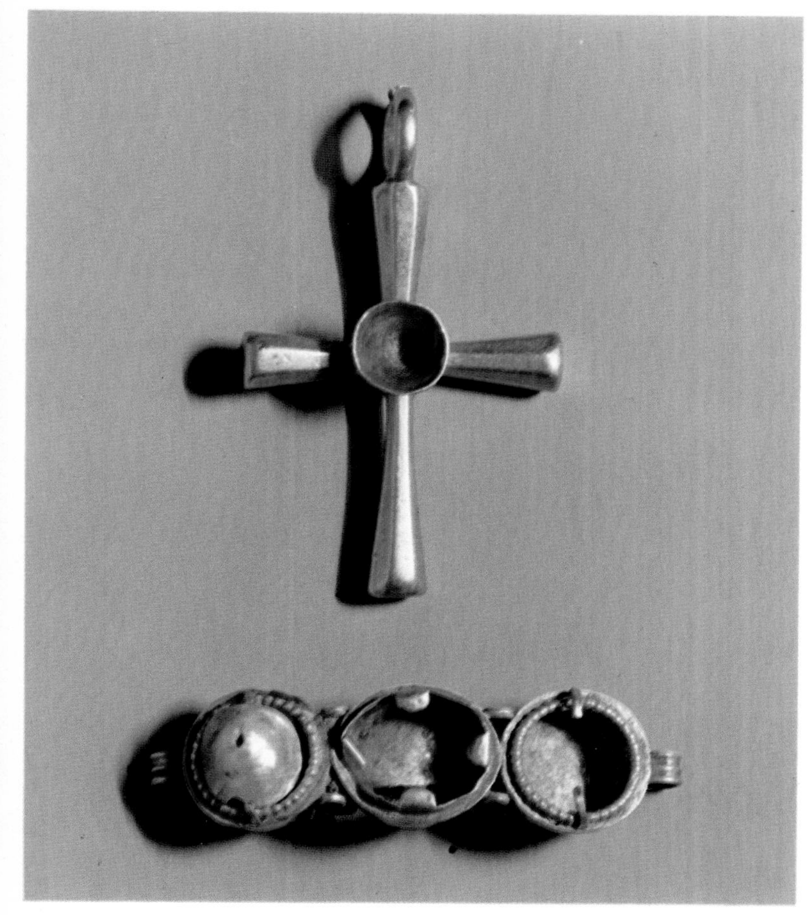

103. Rings. Late 6th century

104. Cross. Agraffe. Late 6th century

105. Buckle, tongue, and ornamental plaques from a belt. Late 6th century

105

106

107

108

106. Cameo with Christ Emmanuel. 6th century (?)
107. Cameo with the Annunciation. 6th century (?)
108. Cameo with the Annunciation. 6th century (?)
109. Icon of the Virgin and Child. 6th century

109

110

110—111. Icon of St John the Baptist. 6th century

112

112—113. Icon of Sts Sergius and Bacchus. 7th century

113

114. Icon of a male and female martyrs. 6th—7th centuries

115

116

115. Seal with Nike. 6th century

116. Seal with a goddess. 6th century

118

119

117. Seal with the Emperor Mauricius-Tiberius. 582—602

118. Seal with the Emperor Phocas. 602—610

119. Seal with Constans II and his son. 641—668

120. Textile. 7th—8th centuries

121

121. Plaque with St John the Baptist. 11th century (?)

122. Plaque with Christ Crowning the Emperor Constantine VII. Mid-10th century

ΚΩΝϹΤΑΝΤΙΝΟϹ ΕΝ ΘΩ
ΑΥΤΟΚΡΑ
ΤΩΡ
ΙϹ
ΧϹ
ΒΑϹΙΛΕΥϹ ΡΩΜΑΙΩΝ

123

124

123—127. Triptych with the Forty Martyrs and Warrior Saints. Early 11th century

126

128

129

128. Plaque with an angel. 11th century

129. Plaque with the Four Saints. 10th century

130

131

130—131. Casket with putti, centaurs and actors. 11th—12th centuries

13.

132. Casket with putti, maenads, and fighting soldiers. 11th century

133

133. *Casket with scenes from the Life of Adam and Eve. 11th century*

13

134. Casket with riders and gladiators. 11th—12th centuries

135. Casket with figures of warriors, actors, etc. 11th—12th centuries

136

136—139. *Diptych with the Twelve Feasts of the Church. 10th—11th centuries*

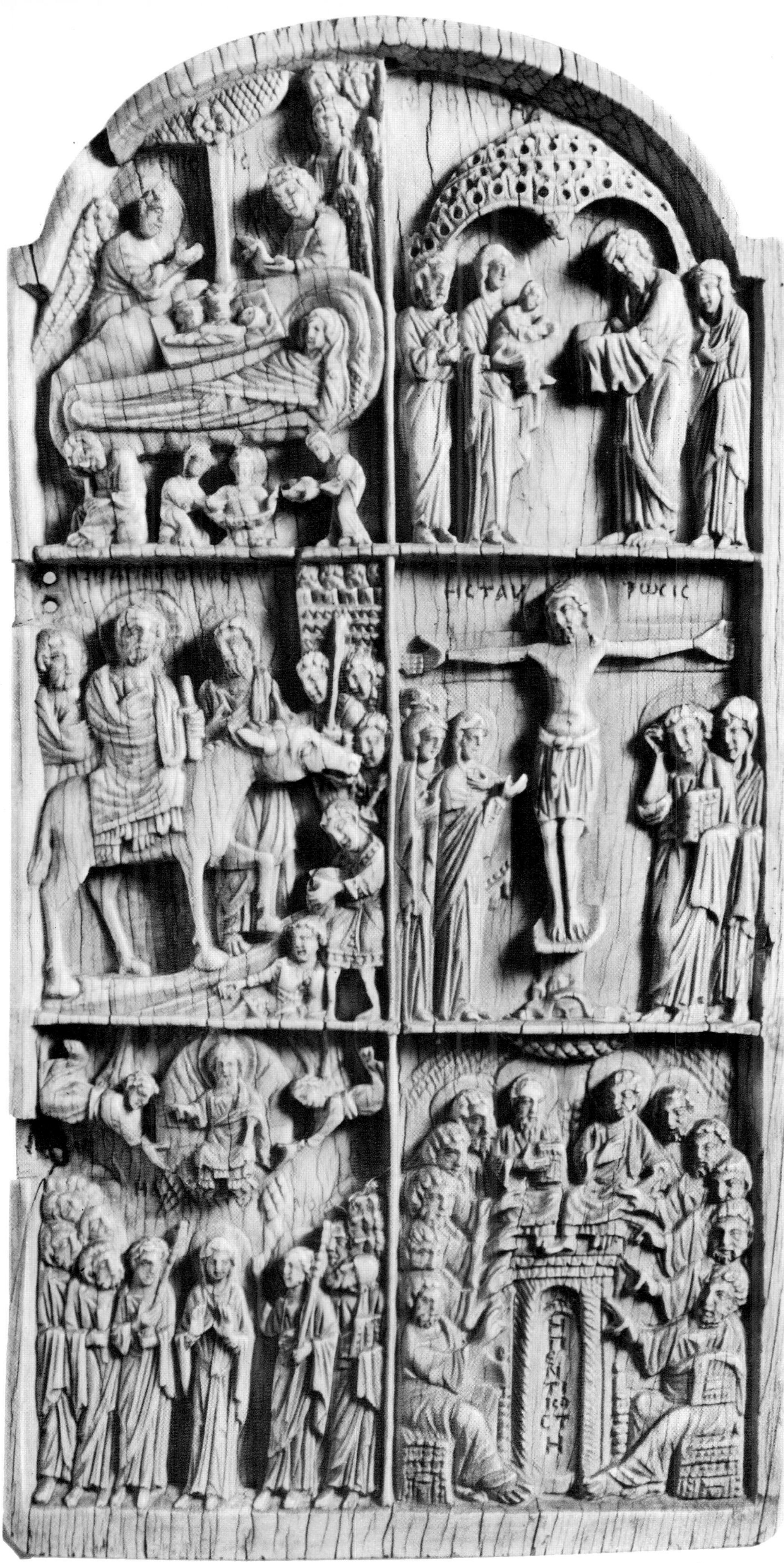

137

138

139

140. Plaque with six of the Twelve Feasts of the Church. 10th—11th centuries

141

142

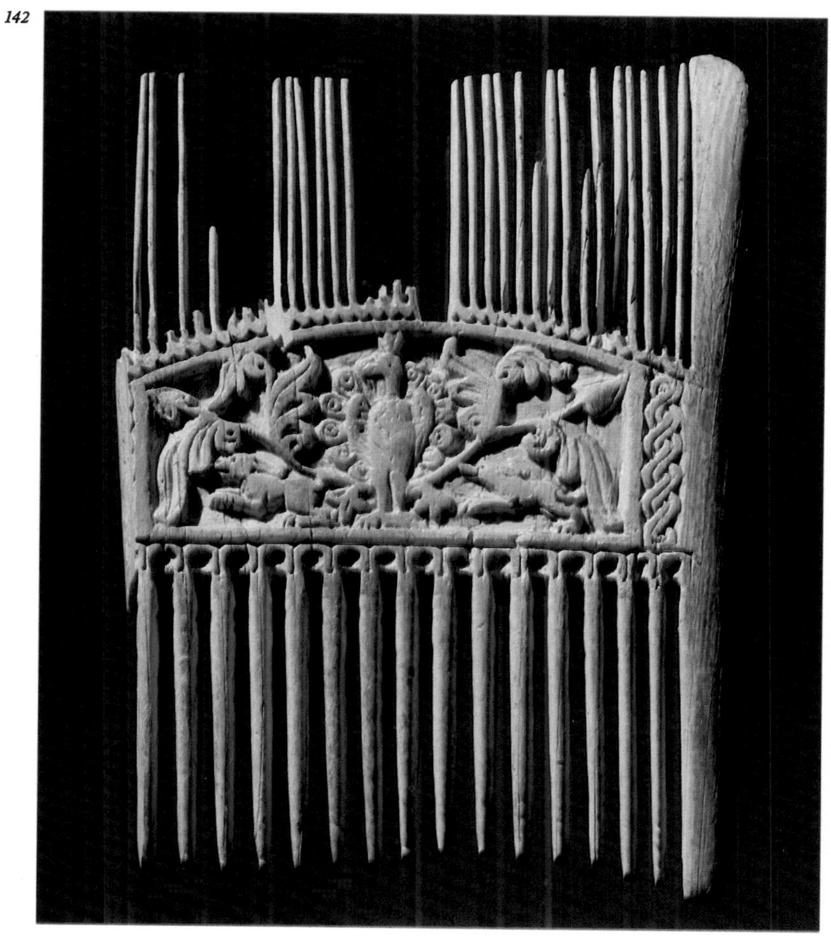

141—142. Comb with a peacock, and Heracles (Samson?) and the lion. 11th century

143. Plaque with the Crucifixion. 11th century (?)

144. Plaque with the Dormition. 11th century (?)

145

145—146. Icon of St Demetrius. 11th century (frame, 14th century)

ΔΗ
ΜΗΤΡΙ

147

147. Icon of the Deesis and Saints. 12th century

148

148. *Icon of the Crucifixion and Entombment. 11th—12th centuries*

149

149. Icon of Sts Theodore, George and Demetrius. 12th century

150

150. *Icon of Sts George and Demetrius. 11th—12th centuries*

151

152

151. Icon of the Annunciation. 12th century

152. Icon of St Demetrius or St George. 11th century

153

153. Chalice. 10th—11th centuries

154

157

154. *Cameo with Christ. 10th—11th centuries*

155—156. *Cameo with the Virgin and Child. 11th—12th centuries*

155

156

158

157—158. *Cameo with St Nicholas. 11th century*

159—160. *Cameo with Christ. 10th—11th centuries*

159

160

161

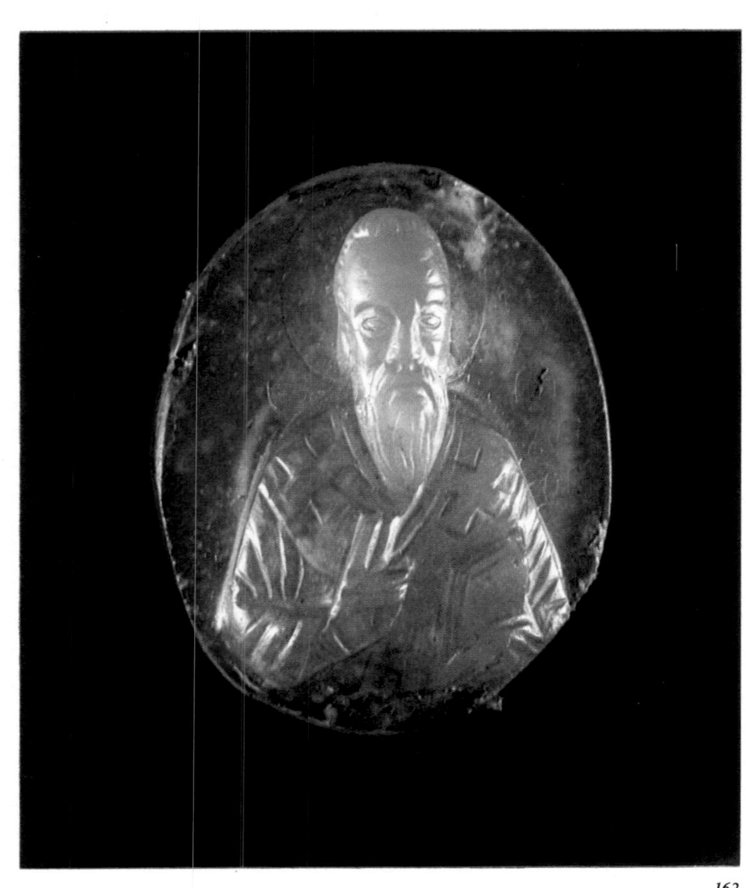

162

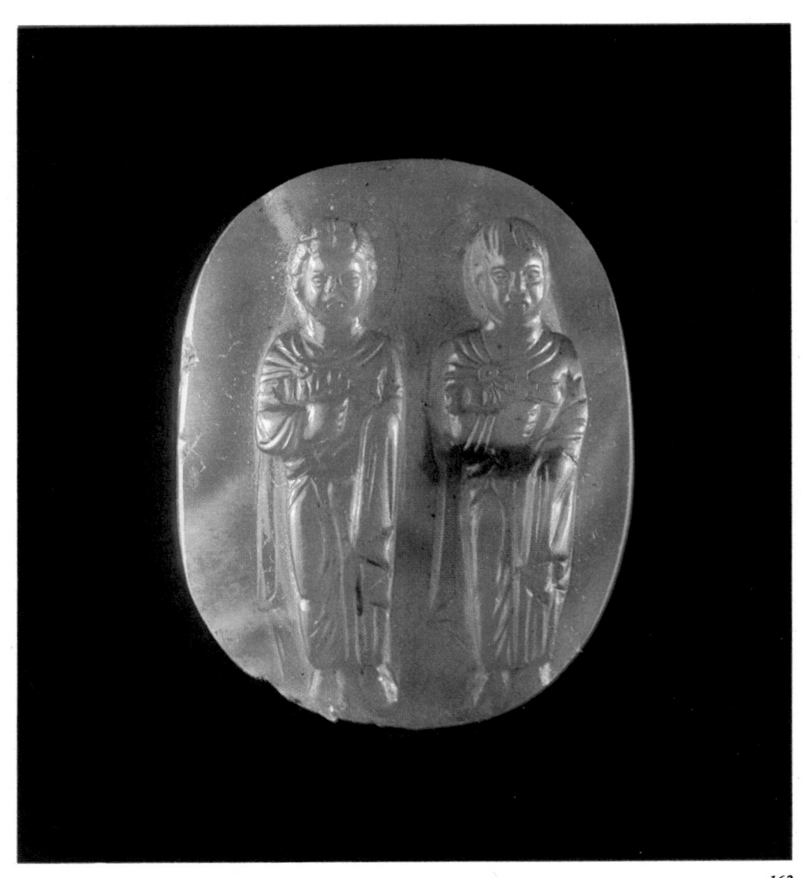

163

161. Cameo with Christ Enthroned. Late 11th—early 12th centuries

162. Cameo with St Basil. 10th century

163. Cameo with Sts George and Demetrius. 10th century

166

164

167

165

164—165. Cameo with a bust of Christ. Early 11th century

166. Cameo with the Virgin. 11th century

167. Cameo with Christ. 11th century

168

169

170

168—169. *Seal with two figures in imperial robes and the Ascent of Alexander the Great. 10th century*

170. *Seal with the Annunciation. 13th—14th centuries*

171. *Seal of the Cathedral of Hagia Sophia in Constantinople. 11th century*

171

172

173

172. Reverse of the seal with the Virgin and Saints: St Eustations and Saints. 11th—12th centuries

173. Seal with Daniel in the Den of Lions. 11th—12th centuries

174—175. Seal of Stauracius. 10th century

174

175

176

177

178

179

176. Cross with the Four Evangelists. 11th century
177. Reliquary with the Crucifixion. 11th century
178. Icon of the Crucifixion. 11th—12th centuries
179. Icon of the Virgin and Child. 10th century

180

181

182

180—181. Plaques with the Apostles James and Bartholomew. 10th—11th centuries

182. Icon of the Descent into Limbo (The Anastasis). 12th century

183

183. Plaque with St Peter. 12th century

184

185

184—185. Icon with scenes of the Descent into Limbo (The Anastasis), the Annunciation, Christ and Five Saints. 10th—11th centuries

186

188

187

186. Plaque with Christ Enthroned. 11th century

187. Plaque with Christ Crowning the Emperor Michael VII Ducas and the Empress Maria. 1076—81

188. Plaque with the Virgin and Child Enthroned. 11th century

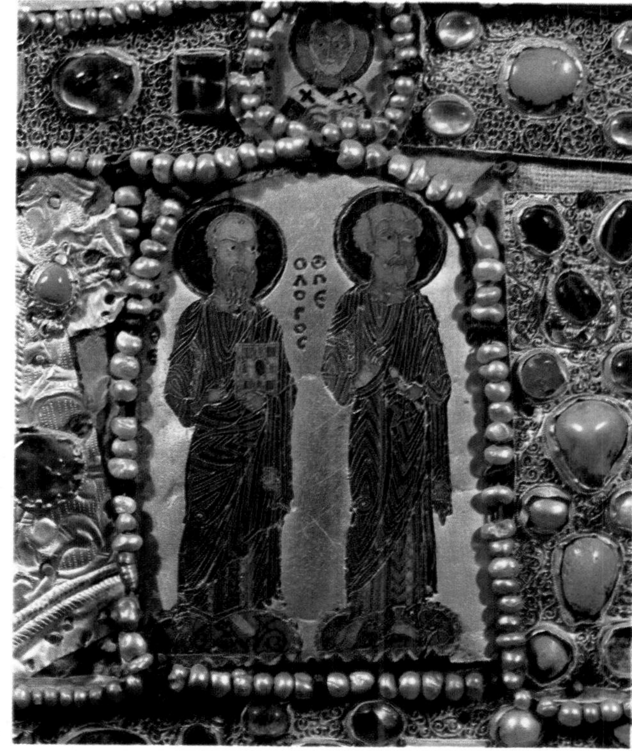
190

189

191

189. Cross with Constantine and Helen and the Four Prophets. 11th century

190—191. Two plaques with the Apostles. 11th century

192

192—195. *Composite icon with the Crucifixion, Christ, Saints, and Gospel scenes. Enamel plaques, 11th—12th centuries; silver plaques, 11th and 14th centuries*

ΙϹ ΧϹ
ΗϹΤΑΥ
ΡΩϹΗϹ

194

195

196

196. Icon of St Theodore Spearing the Dragon. 13th century

197

198

197—201. Triptych with the Deesis. 11th century

IC
XC

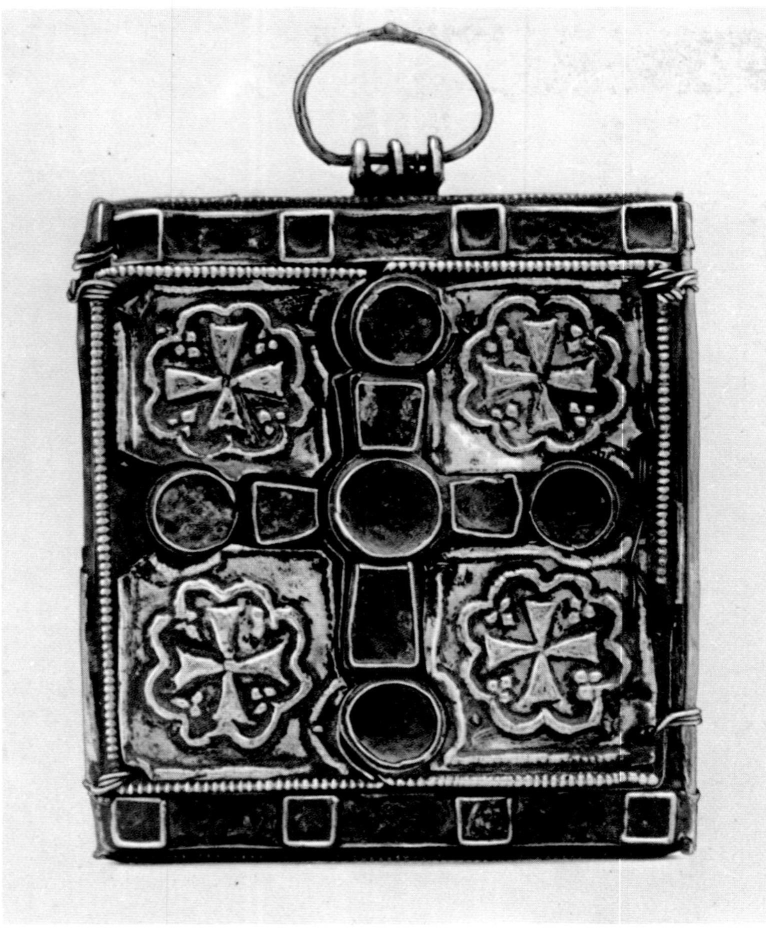

200

201

202. Reliquary (the so-called Philotheus' Staurothèque). 12th century

203

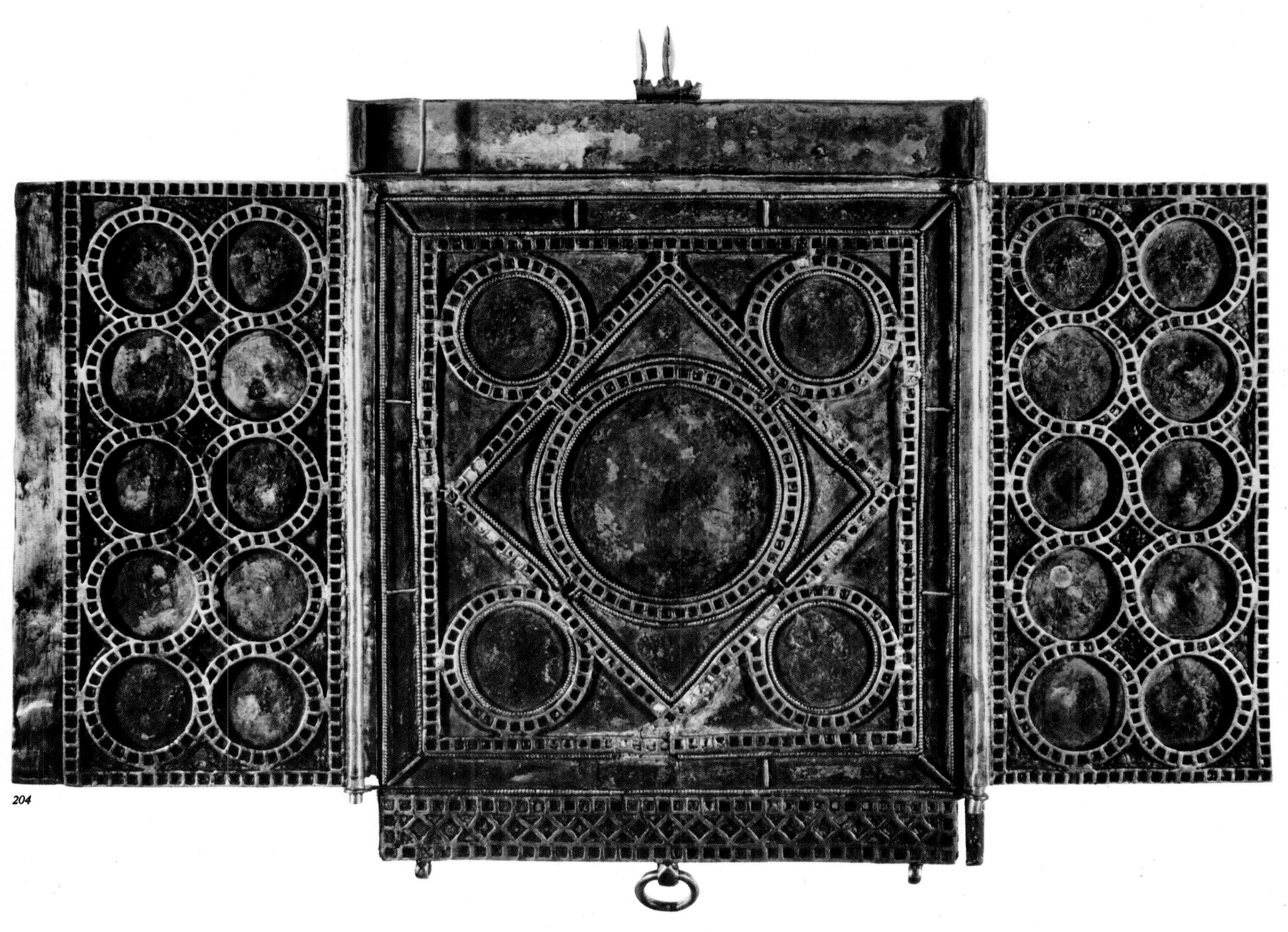

204

203—204. Reliquary with a leaved cross. 11th century

205—206. Reliquary in the form of a temple. 1059—67

ΑϹΙΩΑΝΝΗϹϹΕ
ΓΕΝΟΥϹΑΥ
ΤΩΡΕΙΑΝΦ
ΤΗΝΤΥΧΗΝ
ΥϹΤΟΡΑΦ

207—208. Staurothèque. Late 11th—early 12th centuries

209

210

209. Icon of Christ Enthroned. 12th century

210. Icon of Christ Enthroned and Saints. 12th—13th centuries

211. Cross with Christ, Saints and angels. Late 11th century

Ο ΑΓΙΟC
ΘΕΩΔΟΡΟC
IC
XC
ΑΠΟCΤΟΛ

212

212—214. Bowl with St Theodore, birds, animals and fishes. 11th century

213

215

216

215—217. Bowl of the bratina type with scale decoration. 12th century

218

219

218—219. Bowl with scenes under arches. 12th century

220

221

220—224. Lid from a vessel, with musicians, dancers and acrobats. 12th century

222

223

224

225

226

225—226. Vessel with a lid, decorated with hunters among ornament, and birds. 12th century

227

227. *Dish with a bird. 12th century*

228

228. *Dish with a fantastic creature fighting a serpent. 12th century*

229

229. Dish with a fantastic animal. 12th—13th centuries

230

230. *Dish with a fantastic animal. 12th century*

232

31

231. Dish with a hero killing a fantastic beast. 12th century

232. Bowl with a bird. 13th century

233

233. Icon of the Archdeacon Stephen. 11th century

234. Icon of St Pantaleon. 10th—11th centuries (?)

234

235

*235—236. Icon of the Virgin and Child (Our Lady of Vladimir).
First half of the 12th century*

238

237—238. *Icon of St Gregory the Thaumaturgus. 12th century*

239

239—241. Icon of the Apostle Philip and Sts Theodore and Demetrius. Late 11th—early 12th centuries

ΘΕ
ΟΔΩΡΟ

242

242. *Icon of Sts George, Theodore and Demetrius. 12th century*

243. *Icon of the Descent into Limbo (The Anastasis). 12th century*

244

244. Icon of the Pentecost. 12th century

245

245. Icon of the Transfiguration. 12th century

246

246. *Icon of St Nicholas. Late 13th—early 14th centuries*

247

247—248. Reliefs with the Apostles Peter and Paul. 12th century

249

249. Seal with Christ and the Empress Euphrosene. 1195—1203

250—251. Seal with the Emperor (?) David. 13th or 15th century

252. Ewer with fantastic birds. 13th century

250

251

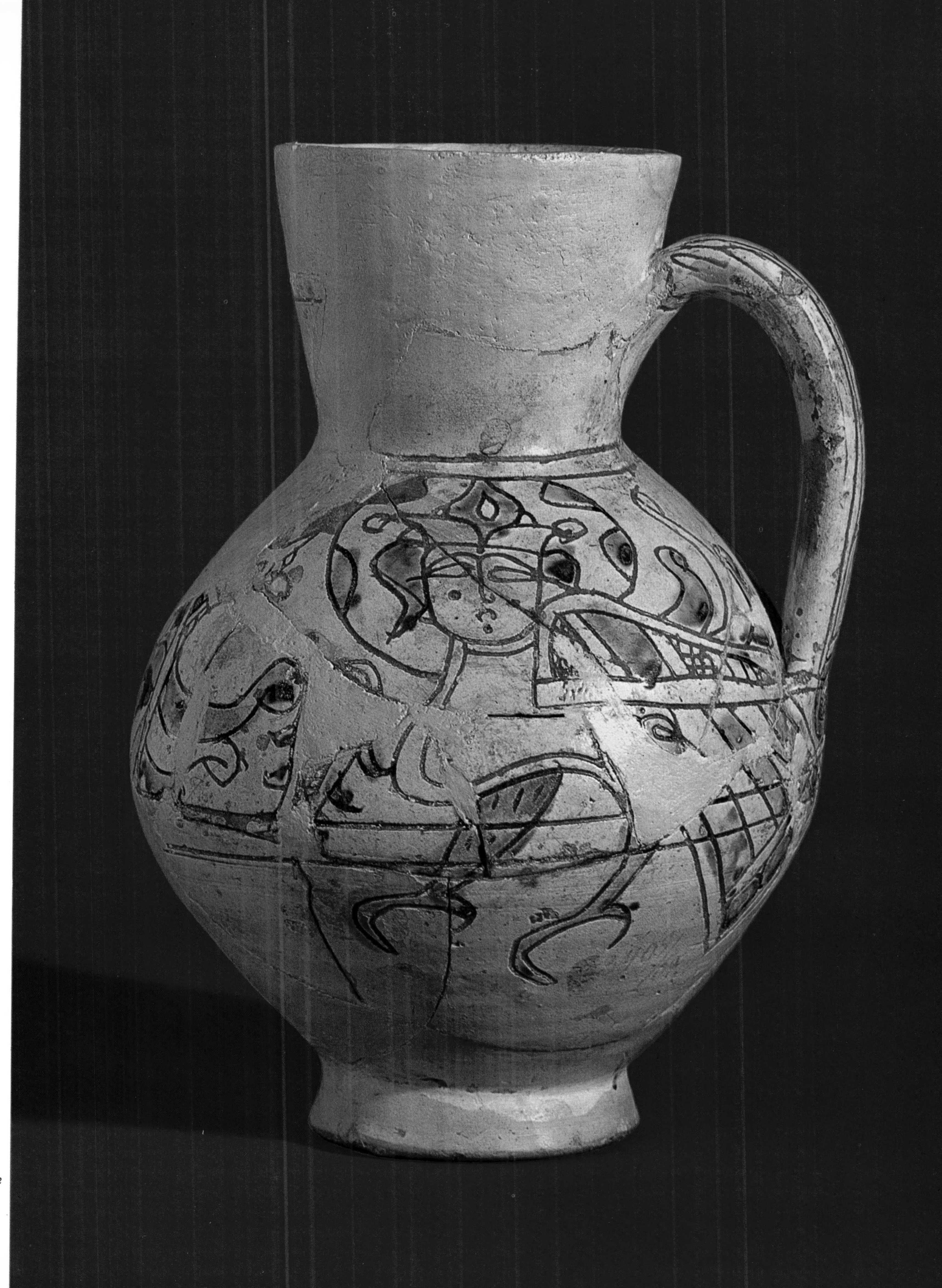

253—255. Helmet with the Deesis and Saints. 13th century

254

255

256

257

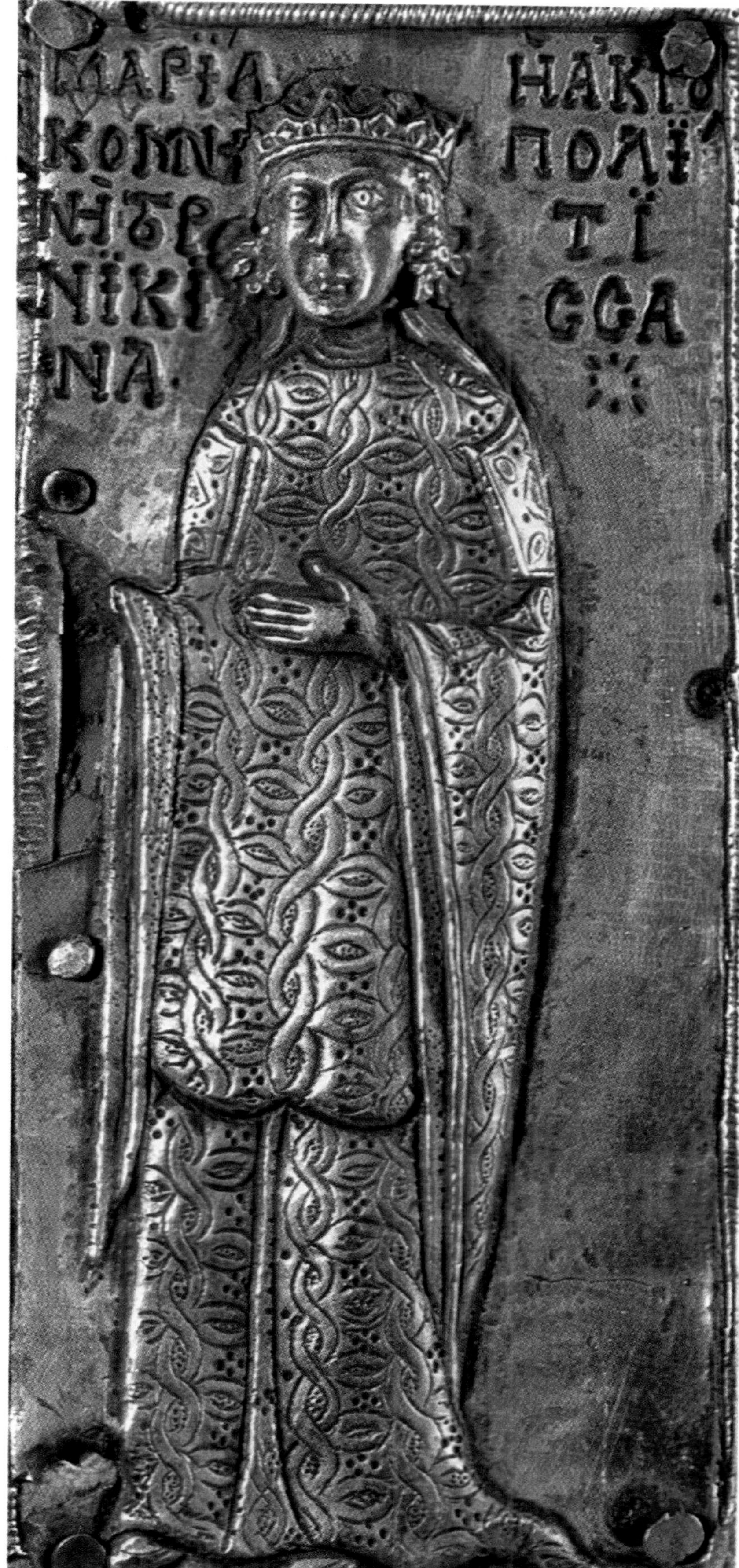

258

256—258. Icon of the Virgin and Child. 13th—14th centuries

259

260

259—260. Icon of the Virgin and Child. 13th century

261

261. *Icon of the Prophet Samuel. Late 13th century*

262

263

264

262. Icon of Christ Emmanuel. Late 13th century

263. Icon of the Four Saints. 14th century

264. Icon of St Theodore. Early 14th century

265. Relief with St Luke the Evangelist. Late 13th century

265

266

267

266—268. Icon of St George with scenes from his life. Late 12th—13th centuries

270

269. *Icon of Christ Pantocrator. 13th century*

270. *Icon of the Assembly of the Apostles. Early 14th century*

271

271. Icon of the Prophet Elijah in the Wilderness. 14th century

272—273. Icon of the Annunciation. First half of the 14th century

Ο ΑΡ ΓΑΒΡΙΗΛ

274—275. Icon of the Dormition. First half of the 14th century

276. Icon of the Virgin and Child, with Saints. 14th century

277. *Icon of St John the Baptist. 14th century*

279

278. Icon with six of the Twelve Feasts of the Church. 14th century

279. Icon of St John the Baptist. 14th century

280

280. Icon of the Raising of Lazarus. 14th century

281

281—284. Icon of Christ Pantocrator. 1363

285. *Icon of St Anastasia. 14th century*

287

286. *Base for a cross. 14th century (?)*

287. *Fragment of a triptych (?) with Gospel scenes. 14th century (?)*

288. *Icon of Our Lady of Pimen. Second half of the 14th century*

289

289. Icon of the Apostle Peter. Late 14th century

290. Icon of the Archangel Gabriel. Late 14th century

291. *Icon of the Apostle Paul. Late 14th century*

292

292—293. Icon of Abraham Entertaining the Three Angels. 15th century

293

294

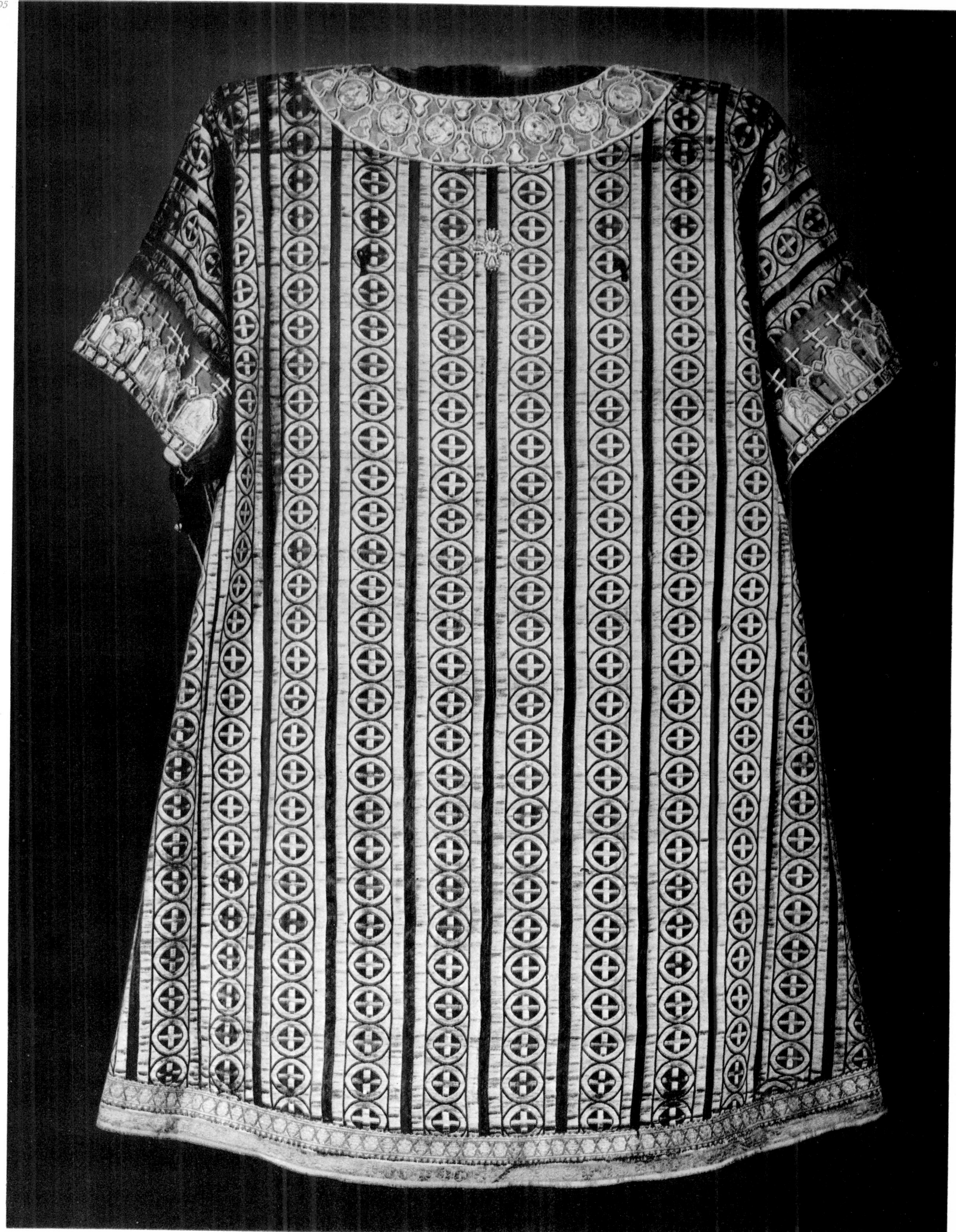

294—295. *Sakkos of the Metropolitan Peter. 1322*

296

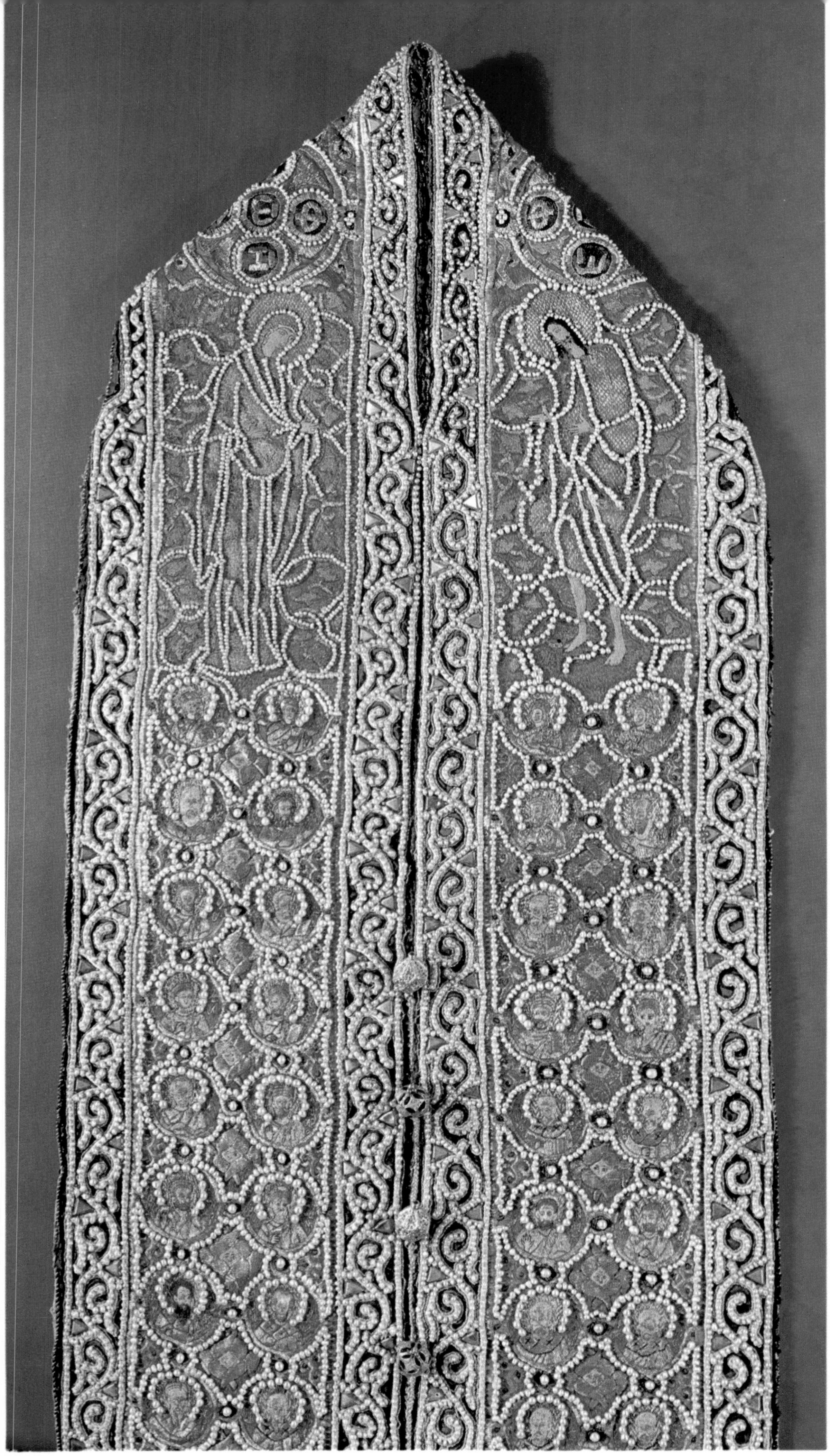

296—299. Epitrachelion of the Metropolitan Photius. 15th century

297

298

300

299

300—304. "Major" sakkos of the Metropolitan Photius. First half of the 15th century

301

302

305

305—307. "Minor" sakkos of the Metropolitan Photius. 14th—15th centuries

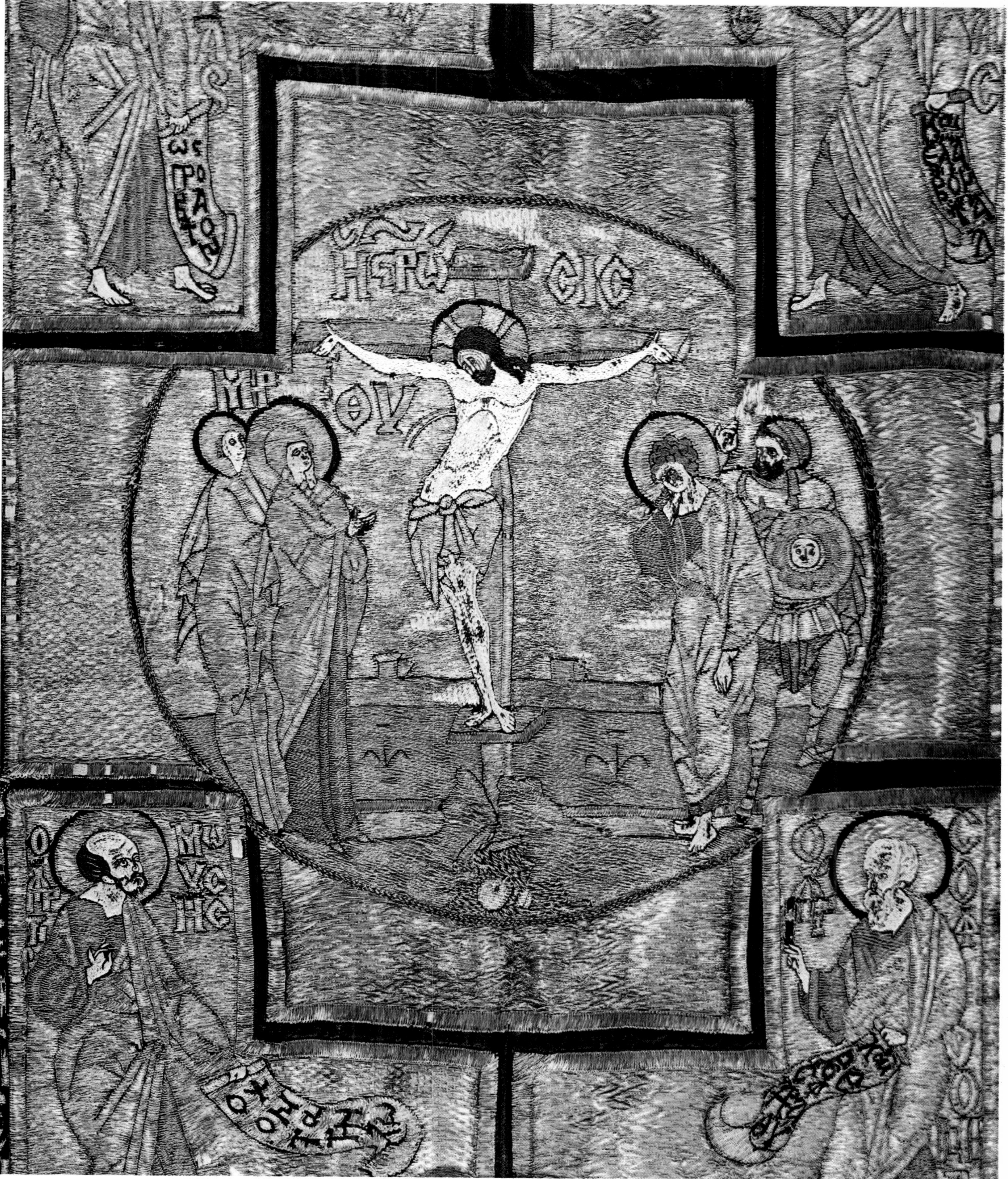

308

308—309. Sakkos of the Metropolitan Simon. Late 15th—early 16th centuries

310

311

310—314. Mount of the icon of Our Lady of Vladimir. 15th century

314

315—316. Icon of the Descent into Limbo (The Anastasis). 15th century

317

317—318. Icon of the Nativity of St John the Baptist. 15th century

319. Icon of St Gregorius Palamas. Late 14th—early 15th centuries

NOTES ON THE PLATES

1 DISH WITH THE TRIUMPH OF THE EMPEROR CONSTANTIUS II. Late 4th century

Silver gilt, niello

The dish is of the patera type, footless, decorated with turning on the rim. The reverse is plain, fitted with a ring for suspension. The Emperor is shown mounted. On the right is the figure of Nike crowning him with a palm branch. On the left is an attendant with a shield bearing a Chi-Rho monogram. Under the feet of the Emperor's horse is a shield with an umbo, belonging to a vanquished enemy. The representation is in *repoussé*. The manner of execution is linear. Some of the details are enriched with gilding or niello.

The Hermitage. Inv. No. 1820/79. Diameter 24.8 cm. Weight 660 gm.
Acquisitions 1892. Found in Kerch in 1891.

Niello and gilding have disappeared in several places. The reverse is considerably damaged, showing cracks.

The features of the Emperor show a resemblance to his profile representations on two other dishes from Kerch (Мацулевич, *Серебряная чаша*, табл. II, 3, 4; R. Delbrueck, *Spätantike Kaiserporträts*, Berlin—Leipzig, 1933, S. 146—147, Taf. 55, 56; Matzulewitsch, Taf. 24, 25).

LITERATURE: Мацулевич, *Серебряная чаша*; R. Delbrueck, *Spätantike Kaiserporträts*, Berlin—Leipzig, 1933, S. 147—151, Taf. 57, Abb. 45—47; Matzulewitsch, S. 95—100, Taf. 23; Peirce, Tyler, 1, p. 44, pl. 27; Банк, *Искусство Византии*, № 1, c. 121, 124, 127; Beckwith, *The Art*, p. 10, fig. 6; J. Doignon, «Le Monogramme cruciforme du sarcophage paléochrétien de Metz représentant le Passage de la Mer Rouge», *Cahiers archéologiques*, XIII, 1962, p. 82, fig. 12 ; P. Skubiszewski, *Czara Włocławska*, Poznań, 1965, rys. 30, str. 54 (Poznańskie towarzystwo przyjaciół nauk. Wydział historii i nauk społecznych. Prace komisji historii sztuki, t. VII, zeszyt 1); J. Deér, «Der Kaiser und das Kreuz», *Jahrbuch des Römisch-Germanischen Zentralmuseums*, Mainz, 1965, 12. Jahrgang, Taf. 49, Nr. 7; Grabar, *L'Age d'or*, p. 298, pl. 347; Delvoye, *L'Art byzantin*, p. 138, fig. 69; Buschhausen, *Ein byzantinisches Bronzekreuz*, S. 289; A. Grabar, *Christian Iconography. A Study of Its Origins*, Princeton University Press, 1968, p. 45, ill. 125; L. Inéral, «La Composition et le symbolisme de l'iconographie du Mausolée de l'Exode à El-Bagawat», *Rivista di Archeologia Christiana*, XLV, 1964, N. 1—4, Roma, p. 254, fig. 9; W. Wixom, "A Mystery Spoon from the Fourth Century", *The Bulletin of the Cleveland Museum of Art*, 1970, May, fig. 8, p. 145—148; Beckwith, *Early Christian and Byzantine Art*, p. 35, fig. 61; Angiolini Martinelli, *Linea e ritmo*, fig. 1, p. 21—24; Angiolini Martinelli, *Realtà e fantasia*, p. 57—58.

2—5 EWER WITH THE MUSES. *Circa* 400

Silver gilt

The ewer is tall, with a knob decorating the neck, and a low base. The bottom is flat; on the back are traces of a handle. The sides are ornamented with figures and scenes in *repoussé* disposed in three bands; the middle one shows the Muses with their attributes and the accompanying inscriptions giving their names in Greek. In the lower band are half-figures of a lion, a stag, a panther, a goat, a dog and a hare amid acanthus scrolls; in the upper band, a vine with clusters of grapes. The knob is decorated with a wreath of laurel leaves in *repoussé* work. The reverse of the bottom bears a rectangular control stamp with the representation of Tyche of Constantinople in a seated posture.

The Kremlin Armoury. Inv. No. 18167. Height 39 cm. Diameter of the base 11.3 cm. Weight 2 kg 250 gm. Acquisitions 1928. Found in a burial situated near the village of Bolshoy Kamenets in the upper reaches of the Sudzha (Kursk Region) in 1918 (?).

The upper portion of the neck and the handle are missing.

The shape of the ewer somewhat resembles that of a vessel found with the Traprain treasure, Scotland (A. Curle, *The Treasure of Traprain*, Glasgow, 1923, pl. VIII). A vase at the Museum at Cleveland (Volbach, *Silberarbeiten*, S. 25, 26, Taf. IV, 7) and a fragment of the Conceşti amphora (К. М. Скалон, «Об одном ранневизантийском серебряном кувшине из Молдавии», in: *Античная история и культура Средиземноморья и Причерноморья*, Л., 1968, c. 257, рис. 1, 3) may also be compared.

LITERATURE: Л. А. Мацулевич, *Погребение варварского князя в Восточной Европе*, М.—Л., 1934; Cruikshank Dodd, p. 236, fig. 84; Писарская, *Памятники*, c. 15, табл. I—IX; К. М. Скалон, «Об одном ранневизантийском серебряном кувшине из Молдавии», in: *Античная история и культура Средиземноморья и Причерноморья*, Л., 1968, c. 257, рис. 1, 3; Angiolini Martinelli, *Linea e ritmo*, fig. 2, p. 24—26; Angiolini Martinelli, *Realtà e fantasia*, p. 58.

6—7 BUST OF JULIAN THE APOSTATE. 4th century

Chalcedony

The Emperor is shown wearing a cloak fastened with a fibula on his left shoulder, and a bracelet round the wrist of his right hand. The cloak is edged with a band of lozenges. The pupils of the eyes were probably inlaid. Around the head runs a groove for the attachment of a metal diadem. The top of the head has a drill hole made for some unknown purpose. The head is worked in the round; the body is flat. The back has hardly been worked.

The Hermitage. Inv. No. ω 80. Height 9.2 cm.
Acquired in the second half of the 18th century.

Chipped in several places.

Iconographically (though not stylistically) comparable is the cameo in the collection of the Bibliothèque Nationale, Paris (R. Delbrueck, *Spätantike Kaiserporträts*, Berlin—Leipzig, 1933, S. 227—228, Taf. 121). Delbrueck does not accept the identification of the head as a portrait of Julian, and tends to date the cameo to the 5th century (E. Babelon, «Les Camées antiques de la Bibliothèque Nationale», *Gazette des Beaux-Arts*, 1899, 1, fig. 6).

LITERATURE: Банк, *Искусство Византии*, № 2, с. 121, 124, 127; В. Лихачева, «Халцедоновый бюст Юлиана Отступника»' *СГЭ*, 22, 1962, с. 18—21; P. Leveque, «De Nouveaux portraits de l'empereur Julien», *Latomus*, 1963, p. 74; О. Неверов, *Античные камеи в собрании Государственного Эрмитажа*, Л., 1971, № 107, с. 48, 95, ил. 107.

8—9 MEDALLION OF THE EMPEROR CONSTANTIUS II. 340—350

Gold

On the obverse is a bust of the Emperor Constantius II wearing a cloak over his cuirass; in his left hand Constantius holds a sphere surmounted by the figure of Nike. The inscription reads: *D*[ominus] *N*[oster] *Constantius Max*[imus] *Augustus*. On the reverse, Constantius and Constans are shown standing in a chariot drawn by six horses, each with a sphere in his left hand. On either side is a Nike crowning the Emperors with a wreath.
Above is an inscription reading: *DD* [Domini] *NN* [Nostri] *Constantius and Constans Augg* [Augusti]. Below are the Greek letters AN, an abbreviation for Antioch, the place of manufacture, a vessel full of coins, and two wreaths.

The Hermitage. Inv. No. 10002. Diameter 4.9 cm. Weight 41.89 gm.
Acquisitions 1899. Found with the hoard discovered on the choir in the church of the Kievo-Pecherskaya Lavra in 1898.

The medallion is slightly worn.

LITERATURE: Н. Петров, «Археологическая находка на хорах в великой церкви Киево-Печерской лавры», *Чтения в церковно-археологическом обществе при Киевской Духовной академии*, вып. II, Киев, 1899, с. 98; *Список старинных золотых и серебряных монет и медалей, принадлежащих Киево-Печерской лавре*, Киев, 1899, № 1, с. 4; F. Gnecchi, *I Medaglioni Romani*, v. 1, Milano, 1912, p. 29, tav. 10, *8*.

10 STATUE OF THE GOOD SHEPHERD. Late 4th century

Marble

The Good Shepherd is shown as a youth wearing a short belted tunic and boots. His right hand grasps the feet of a lamb he is carrying on his shoulders. The back of the statue is worked only at the sides; along the middle runs a rectangular projection resembling a pilaster. The modelling is flat.

The Hermitage. Inv. No. ω 215. Height 68.5 cm.
Acquired in 1912 through the agency of the Russian Ambassador and the Russian Archaeological Institute in Constantinople. Recovered from the ruins of a brick church at the village of Chinga situated in the neighbourhood of Panderma in Bithynia, Asia Minor. The statue seems to have been built into a wall.

The lower portion of the figure, and the left arm from the elbow, are missing. Pieces are broken from the nose and one of the lips of the shepherd, and from the lamb's fore legs; the back of the lamb is cut away at the top, probably to fit it into its place in the wall.

For related objects, see G. Mendel, *Catalogue des sculptures grecques, romaines et byzantines*, t. 2, Constantinople, 1914, Nos 648—650, p. 412—420; V. Elbern, «Aus heidnischer und christlicher Spätantike. Zwei Neuerwerbungen für die frühchristlich-byzantinische Sammlung», *Berliner Museen*, N. F., 13, 1963, S. 12—22, Abb. 1—4. A number of parallels will be found listed in the latter work.

LITERATURE: G. Collwitz, *Kunstwerke aus dem Besitz der Universität Freiburg im Breisgau*, Freiburg i. B., 1957, S. 12; Th. Klauser, «Katalog der Kaiserzeitlichen Schaftträger-Statuen», *Studien zur Entstehungsgeschichte der christlichen Kunst*, 1. Jahrbuch, 1958, Anhang A, S. 45, Nr. 17; Банк, *Искусство Византии*, № 12, с. 121, 124, 127; J. A. Gaya Nuño, *Historia y guia de los museos de España*, Madrid, 1955, p. 46; V. Elbern, «Aus heidnischer und christlicher Spätantike. Zwei Neuerwerbungen für die frühchristlich-byzantinische Sammlung», *Berliner Museen*, N. F., 13, 1963, S. 12—22, Abb. 11.

11 STATUE OF THE GOOD SHEPHERD. 4th century

Marble

The statue shows the Good Shepherd as an old man in a short belted tunic, carrying a lamb on his shoulders. The back is treated summarily. The statue is executed in high relief and shows plastic modelling.

The Hermitage. Inv. No. ω 212. Height 34 cm.
Acquisitions 1912. Formerly in the Pats collection, where it came from the Łazienki Palace, Warsaw.

The arms and the legs of the shepherd are missing, as well as the head and legs of the lamb of which only fragments have survived.

LITERATURE: Банк, *Искусство Византии*, № 11, с. 121, 124, 127.

12 SARCOPHAGUS WITH SCENES FROM THE NEW TESTAMENT. 4th century

Marble

The sarcophagus is rectangular in shape; the front panel shows the New Testament scenes, executed in relief; the subjects are the Raising of Lazarus, the Healing of the Woman Diseased with an Issue of Blood, the Healing of the Blind, the Virgin between the Apostles Peter and Paul, St. Peter Taken Prisoner, and Peter Striking the Rock. The figures are disposed in two rows, the front and the back one.

The Hermitage. Inv. No. ω 1209. Height 55.5 cm. Length 230 cm. Width 67 cm.
Acquisitions 1885. Formerly in the Basilewsky collection, where it came from Cahors, France. According to tradition, it served as a shrine for the relics of Bishop Desiderius who died in the 7th century.

Cracks and small losses of stone in several places. The relief is much worn.

For related objects, see G. Stulfauth, *Die Apokriphen Petrusgeschichten in der altchristlichen Kunst*, Berlin—Leipzig, 1925, Abb. 18—20, 22, 23.

LITERATURE: Darcel, Basilewsky, p. 1, N° 1; Банк, *Искусство Византии*, № 13, с. 121, 124, 127; H. von Schoenebeck, «Die christliche Sarkophagplastik unter Konstantin», *Römische Mitteilungen*, 51, 1936, S. 320; L. d'Alauzier, «Le Sarcophage de Saint-Didier», *Bulletin de la Société des études littéraires, scientifiques et artistiques du Lot*, LXXXVIII, 1967, fasc. 4, p. 197—210, fig. 2.

13—14 RELIEF WITH CIRCUS SCENES. *Circa* 500

Marble

The rectangular marble slab is carved with circus scenes executed in relief, and with a cross in very low relief, almost engraved, at the back. Corniced at top and bottom. The central portion shows two symmetrically arranged groups of an acrobat and a bear; on the right is a group of two men, a boar and a dog; on the left, a man riding a bull, a bear, and a boar. Along the top runs a groove. The piece is likely to have been used as a chancel-screen in a church.

The Hermitage. No. ω 224. Height 65 cm. Length 157 cm. Thickness 15 cm.
Acquisitions 1919. Formerly in the Academy of Arts, Petrograd. One of the marbles brought by Admiral Spiridov from the islands in the Aegean Sea in 1774.

The bottom right-hand corner is missing; the foot of the acrobat in the scene right of the centre is missing, too. Chipped in several places.

For related objects, see И. Велков, «Релиеф с циркови игри от София», *Известия на Българската Археологически Институт*, т. 1 (1921—1922), табл. IV.

LITERATURE: Г. Трей, *Указатель скульптурного отделения музея Академии художеств*, Спб., 1871, № 759; Л. А. Мацулевич, «Рельеф с цирковыми сценами в Эрмитаже», *SK*, II, 1928, с. 139—148, табл. XVIII—XX; Банк, *Искусство Византии*, № 14, с. 121, 124, 127; Dekan, *Herkunft und Ethnizität*, Abb. 127.

15 POLYCANDELON IN THE FORM OF A BASILICA. 5th century

Bronze

The polycandelon has the form of a basilica with a semicircular apse, and the episcopal chair inside. The base is fitted with ten brackets shaped as dolphins and terminating in rings for the support of the lamps. The titles on the gabled roof are shown by engraved lines. At either extremity of the roof is a ring for the attachment of a suspension chain. There is a cross over the entrance door.

The Hermitage. Inv. No. ω 71. Height 26 cm. Length 34 cm. Width 17 cm.
Acquisitions 1885. Formerly in the Basilewsky collection. Found in a vault near Orléansville, Algiers.

The cross on the chair and part of the cross on the lunette are missing. Rings are missing from two of the brackets. Small losses of metal.

LITERATURE: G. B. de Rossi, «Notizie. Vetri cimeteriali inediti nel Museo del Signore conte della Guerardesca», *Bollettino di Archeologia Cristiana*, 1866, p. 15—16; Peigne-Delacourt, «Porte-lampes du Ve siècle de l'ère chrétienne représentant une basilique», *Revue de l'art chrétien*, X, 1866, p. 536—548; Darcel, Basilewsky, p. 8, N° 37, pl. IV; A. Michel, *Histoire de l'art*, v. 1, Paris, 1905, p. 60, 102; Leclercq, *Manuel*, p. 559—563; Volbach, *Metallarbeiten*, Nr. 46, S. 52; Банк, *Искусство Византии*, № 9, с. 121, 124, 127; Grabar, *L'Age d'or*, pl. 379.

16 POLYCANDELON IN THE FORM OF A DISC. 6th century

Bronze

The polycandelon is an openwork disc with twelve flat spokes radiating from the circle in the centre; six of the spokes terminating in rings, alternate with six others terminating in a floral motif, and having a cross in the middle. The disc is suspended by three chains from a vertical disc in openwork with a six-pointed star in the centre.

The Hermitage. Inv. No. ω 39. Length of chain 21.5 cm. Maximum diameter 22.8 cm. Diameter of the smaller disc 10.2 cm.
Acquisitions 1885. Formerly in the Basilewsky collection. In all probability, it comes from Calabria, S. W. Italy.

The bronze is patinated.

For related objects, see *ОАК за 1913—1915 гг.*, Пг., 1918, рис. 84, с. 56; Ross, *Catalogue*, 1, Nos. 42—44, pl. XXX, XXXI. A number of other parallels will be found listed in the latter work. For objects showing a more distant resemblance to No. 16, see C. Gómez-Moreno, *Medieval Art from Private Collections. A Special Exhibition at the Cloisters. October 30, 1968—January 5, 1969. The Metropolitan Museum of Art*, 1968, No. 83.

LITERATURE: Rohault de Fleury, *La Messe*, v. 6, Paris, 1898, p. 12, tabl. CLXXXIX; Leclercq, *Manuel*, p. 563, fig. 369.

17 HANGING LAMP. 4th century

Bronze

The lamp has two projecting spouts for the wicks. The spouts are round, with a scalloped lip around the opening; the handle shaped as a lily. On either side of the body is a Chi-Rho monogram in relief.

The Hermitage. Inv. No. ω 44. Height 11.3 cm. Total length 22.5 cm.
Acquisitions 1885. Formerly in the Basilewsky collection.

The lid is missing; three petals are broken from the lily-shaped handle.

For related objects, see Dalton, *Catalogue*, Nos. 501, 502, p. 101, pl. XXVII; *Early Christian and Byzantine Art Exhibition*, Nos. 238, 239, p. 62; Ross, *Catalogue*, 1, No. 30, p. 29—32, pl. XXV.

LITERATURE: Darcel, Basilewsky, p. 7, N° 32, pl. III; Банк, *Искусство Византии*, № 5, с. 121, 124, 127; Ross, *Catalogue*, 1, p. 31—32.

18 HANGING LAMP. 4th century

Bronze

The lamp has two suspension chains, one attached to the top near the opening through which the lamp was filled, the other to the handle shaped as a griffon's head. On either side of the body is a Chi-Rho monogram in relief. The projecting spout for the wick is six-sided. The bottom is small and has a conoid shape.

The Hermitage. Inv. No. ω 48. Height 15 cm. Total length 22 cm.
Acquisitions 1885. Formerly in the Basilewsky collection.

The bronze is patinated; the spout is broken through.

For related objects, see Dalton, *Catalogue*, Nos. 501, 502, p. 101, pl. XXVII; *Early Christian and Byzantine Art Exhibition*, Nos. 238, 239; Ross, *Catalogue*, 1, p. 31—32; Marvin C. Ross, "Byzantine Bronzes", *Art in Virginia*, 1970, 10, No. 2, p. 35; M. Tatič-Djurič, «Une Lampe de la basse antiquité conservée au Musée National de Belgrad», *Жива антика*, 1960, год. X, 238—248, сл. 1.

LITERATURE: Darcel, Basilewsky, p. 8, N° 36, pl. III; Leclercq, *Manuel*, p. 564, fig. 371; Банк, *Искусство Византии*, № 6, с. 121, 124, 127.

19 FIGURINE OF A BIRD AND NESTLING. 4th—5th centuries

Bronze

The figurine is cast solid. Its function is obscure. The bird has a ball in its half open beak. The feathering is indicated by engraving. The eyes are shown by three concentric circles.

The Hermitage. Inv. No. ω 38. Height 7.5 cm. Length 13.5 cm.
Acquisitions 1885. Formerly in the Basilewsky collection.

The bronze is patinated.

For related objects, see Volbach, *Metallarbeiten*, Nr. 42, S. 50, Taf. VIII; J. Strzygowski, *Koptische Kunst*, Wien, 1904, Nr. 1941, S. 292—293, Taf. XXXIII; Marvin C. Ross, "Byzantine Bronzes", *Art in Virginia*, 1970, 10, No. 2, p. 34.

LITERATURE: Банк, *Искусство Византии*, № 10, с. 121, 124, 127; Т. Б. Вирсаладзе, «Фресковая роспись в церкви Архангелов села Земо-Крихи», *Ars Georgica*, 6, 1963, с. 161.

20 FRAGMENT OF A DISH WITH CIRCUS SCENES. 4th—5th centuries

Clay, reddish-brown glaze

The fragment is a piece from a rectangular vessel with a relief representation of a scene of a contest with animals in the arena (?), enclosed in a rectangular frame; in the centre is a man holding a horse by the bridle;

he has a spear in his left hand; facing him are a goat, and a bear standing up on its hind legs. Below is seen the upper part of a human figure, and an animal leaping.
The reverse of the bottom shows traces of a foot.

The Hermitage. Inv. No. X 339. 32.5 × 15 cm.
Acquisitions 1915. Received from the Archaeological Commission. Found at Chersonese.

The fragment is triangular in shape. There is a detached piece with a recumbent figure upon a couch.

A similar subject is represented on a dish described by H. Fuhrmann («Studien zu den Consulardiptychen verwandten Denkmälern», *Römische Mitteilungen*, 55, 1940, S. 99, Taf. 12).

21 VESSEL FOR SUSPENSION IN THE SHAPE OF A FISH. 4th century

Bronze

The vessel may have served as a lamp. The chain is attached to a ring on top of the suspension hoop. The scales are shown by engraving.

The Hermitage. Inv. No. ω 37. Height (without the hoop) 5 cm. Width 10.6 cm.
Acquisitions 1885. Formerly in the Basilewsky collection.

The bronze is patinated.

LITERATURE: Банк, *Искусство Византии*, № 8, с. 121, 124, 127.

22 HANGING LAMP SHAPED AS A CAMEL. 4th century (?)

Bronze

The lamp has two spouts above the fore legs of the camel; the suspension chain is attached to the saddle. The hair is indicated by dots.

The Hermitage. Inv. No. ω 119. Height 9.9 cm. Length 11.2 cm.
Acquisitions 1896. Formerly in the Martin collection.

The bronze is patinated.

For related objects, see J. Strzygowski, *Koptische Kunst*, Wien, 1904, Nr. 9143, S. 293, Abb. 324.

LITERATURE: Банк, *Искусство Византии*, № 7, с. 121, 124, 127.

23 DISH WITH CHRIST HOLDING A CROSS, WITH BIRDS. 5th century

Clay, reddish-brown glaze

The dish is circular in shape; the central portion is engraved with a full-length figure of Christ holding a large cross. Around the figure are three doves. The ring foot is low.

The Hermitage. Inv. No. X 385. Diameter 38.5 cm. Height 5.4 cm.
Acquisitions 1907. Received from the Archaeological Commission. Found at Chersonese in 1904.

Restored from a multitude of small fragments; the lacunae filled with plaster.

For related objects, see Leclercq, *Manuel*, p. 539, fig. 359; G. Jacopi, «L'antro di Tiberio a Sperlugo. Patera Filtile protocristiana», in: *I monumenti Romani*, t. 4, Roma, 1963, p. 157—159, fig. 157, 158.

LITERATURE: *ОАК за 1904 г.*, 1907, с. 53, рис. 74 а, б; *ИАК*, XX, 1906, с. 36, рис. 12 а, б; С. Беляев, «Об одном блюде из Херсонеса», *СГЭ*, 37, 1973, с. 47.

24 FRAGMENT OF A VESSEL WITH THE APOSTLE PETER. 4th century

Glass, gold foil

The representation is engraved on a piece of gold foil placed between two layers of glass. On either side of the head is an inscription reading: *Petrus*.

The Hermitage. Inv. No. E 2038. Diameter 9.3 cm.
Acquisitions 1885. Formerly in the Basilewsky collection. Found in the catacombs of Rome.

The border is missing.

LITERATURE: G. B. de Rossi, «Notizie. Vetri cimeteriali inediti nel Museo del Signore conte della Guerardesca», *Bollettino di Archeologia Cristiana*, 1863, p. 25, 30, N. 4; Darcel, Basilewsky, p. 9, N° 40, pl. V, 1; H. Vopel, *Die altchristlichen Goldgläser*, Freiburg i. B., 1899, Nr. 314, S. 107; Банк, *Искусство Византии*, № 3, с. 121, 124, 127.

25 FRAGMENT OF A VESSEL WITH ABRAHAM'S SACRIFICE. 4th century

Glass, gold foil

The scene is engraved on a piece of gold foil placed between two layers of glass.

The Hermitage. Inv. No. E 2037. Diameter 9.5 cm.
Acquisitions 1885. Formerly in the Basilewsky collection. Found in the catacombs of Rome.

The border is missing.

LITERATURE: G. B. de Rossi, «Notizie. Vetri cimeteriali inediti nel Museo del Signore conte della Guerardesca», *Bollettino di Archeologia Cristiana*, 1868, p. 32—33; Darcel, Basilewsky, p. 9, N° 41, pl. V; H. Vopel, *Die altchristlichen Goldgläser*, Freiburg i. B., 1899, Nr. 181, S. 61, 102; Банк, *Искусство Византии*, № 4, с. 121, 124, 127.

26—29 PATERA WITH SCENES FROM THE OLD TESTAMENT. 4th century

Glass

The patera is engraved with scenes from the Old Testament. The central medallion shows Abraham's Sacrifice; it is encircled by a broad band with scenes illustrating the subjects of Jonah Being Cast Forth into the Sea, Jonah under the Gourd, the Fall of Man, the Raising of Lazarus, Peter Brings Water out of the Tree (?), Daniel in the Den of Lion's, the Three Youths in the Fiery Furnace, Susanna. The scenes are accompanied by Latin inscriptions in two different scripts.

The Hermitage. Inv. No. ω 73. Diameter 23 cm.
Acquisitions 1885. Formerly in the Basilewsky collection. Found near Doclea in the neighbourhood of Podgorica (the present-day Titograd, Yugoslavia) in 1870.

Restored; pieces broken from the edge.

There is a certain affinity in shape, technique and the choice of subjects between this patera and the dish found at Arras, France. Stylistically, however, they are different (Coche de la Ferté, *L'Antiquité*, N° 54, p. 57, 109—110).

LITERATURE: *Bulletin de la Société Nationale des Antiquaires de France*, 1873, p. 71—73; G. B. de Rossi, «L'Insigne piatto vitreo de Podgoritza oggi nel museo Basilewsky in Parigi», *Bollettino di Archeologia Cristiana*, 1877, p. 77—85, tav. V, VI; Le Blant, *Etudes sur les sarcophages chrétiens antiques de la ville d'Arles*, Paris, 1878, p. XXVIII—XXX, pl. 35; O. Wulff, *Altchristliche und Byzantinische Kunst. Nachtrag*, Potsdam, 1936, S. 8; Coche de la Ferté, *L'Antiquité*, p. 110; P. Levi, "The Podgoritza Cup", *The Heytrop Journal*, IV, 1963, p. 55—60; *Эрмитаж*, 1965, № 73.

30—31 DIPTYCH WITH CIRCUS SCENES. 5th century

Ivory

Both the leaves of the diptych are covered with scenes of contests between venatores and lions, or panthers, in the arena. Different ethnical types are rendered. The tunics of the venatores are identical in style, but bear different devices sewn on to the front or the back as distinguishing marks of the different *scholae* they belong to. In the right leaf, the line of the soil is indicated under each man, while in the left it is shown only under the bottom group. This suggests that the leaves were executed by different masters. The back panel is slightly hollowed, and bordered with an incised line.

The Hermitage. Inv. No. ω 10. Height 33 cm. Width of each leaf 10.5 cm.
Acquisitions 1885. Formerly in the Basilewsky collection.

Part of the left-hand leaf (left side) was lost, and re-created in 1869. The ornamental border on the right-hand leaf has been cut away almost entirely.

LITERATURE: Darcel, Basilewsky, p. 11, N° 45, pl. VI; Delbrueck, *Die Consulardiptychen*, Nr. 60, S. 30, Taf. 60; Peirce Tyler, 1, p. 79, tabl. 122; А. Банк, «Диптих с изображением цирковых сцен», in: *Сокровища Эрмитажа*, М.—Л., 1949, с. 123—126; Volbach, *Elfenbeinarbeiten*, Nr. 60, S. 52—54, Taf. 32; *Masterpieces*, No. 23, p. 17; Talbot Rice, *The Art*, p. 295, fig. 35; Банк, *Искусство Византии*, № 15—19, с. 121, 124, 127; Ross, *Catalogue*, 1, p. 3; *Эрмитаж*, Л., 1964, № 34.

32—34 LEAF OF THE CONSULAR DIPTYCH OF AREOBINDUS. 506

Ivory

The piece is the right-hand leaf of the diptych. It is carved with the scene of the consul Areobindus presiding in the circus. In his right hand is the *mappa* with which the signal for the beginning of the games is given; and in his left, a sceptre topped with a group of the Emperor Anastasius handing to a consul a scroll, the symbol of his office. Behind the throne are two guards. Above is a Latin inscription which reads: *Fl*[avius] *Areob*[indus] *Dagal*[aifus] *Areobindus V*[ir] *I*[llustris]. The throne rests on legs shaped as figures of lions. The corners of the seat are decorated with figures of Victories holding plaques with representations of consuls. Below the foot of the throne is a group of ten spectators; the bottom part of the leaf is carved with circus scenes, bear-hunt, etc.

The Hermitage. Inv. No. ω 12. Height 37.6 cm. Width 14 cm.
Acquisitions 1885. Formerly in the Basilewsky collection.

Pieces of considerable size were lost and re-created in the left-hand part of the leaf as well as part of the figure of the Emperor in the group topping the sceptre: heads of the first, second, fourth and fifth spectators, and some other details.

For related objects, see Volbach, *Elfenbeinarbeiten*, Nr. 8—10.

LITERATURE: Delbrueck, *Die Consulardiptychen*, Nr. 12, S. 114, Taf. 12; Volbach, *Elfenbeinarbeiten*, Nr. 11, S. 33, Taf. 5; Банк, *Искусство Византии*, № 21, с. 121, 124, 127; I. Husar, «Antike Grundlagen der frühmittelalterlichen Ästhetik», *Das Altertum*, XV, 1969, H. 2, S. 100.

35 PORTION OF A DIPTYCH WITH SCENES FROM A TRAGEDY. 6th century

Ivory

The ivory once formed a portion of the right-hand leaf of a five-part diptych. It is carved with scenes arranged in two rows against arcaded backgrounds. Above is a tragic actor who, having just divested himself of a female mask, is greeting the public; and three men of the chorus (the scene represented being probably from *Medea*). Below is the leader of the chorus (?) with two boys and two men.

The Hermitage. Inv. No. ω 15. Height 14 cm. Width 7.3 cm.
Acquisitions 1885. Formerly in the Basilewsky collection.

Losses of ivory in the top part of the frame, and in the band separating the two rows. Three holes in the background; cracks; the relief is worn.

LITERATURE: Darcel, Basilewsky, p. 7, N° 31; Delbrueck, *Die Consulardiptychen*, Nr. 53, S. 208; Peirce, Tyler, 2, p. 63, tabl. 12 a; Volbach, *Elfenbeinarbeiten*, Nr. 53, S. 50, Taf. 28; Банк, *Искусство Византии*, № 23, с. 121, 124, 127.

36 PORTION OF THE CONSULAR DIPTYCH OF ANASTASIUS. 517

Ivory

The lower part of a leaf from the consular diptych of Anastasius is decorated with circus scenes carved in relief against an architectural background. In the upper register are two Amazons bringing horses into the arena; in the centre of the bottom register is a group of acrobats performing; on the left is a juggler; on the right, a scene from a tragedy.

The Hermitage. Inv. No. ω 263. Height 10.5 cm. Width 12.5 cm.
Acquisitions 1924. Formerly in the Museum of the Stieglitz School of Art and Design, Leningrad, for which it was purchased in Vienna in 1886. Comes from the Castellani collection, Rome. It was first recorded in Limoges.

Pieces have been sawn out of the top edge. Four round holes have been drilled in the corners of the fragment, two on either side.

For related objects, see Volbach, *Elfenbeinarbeiten*, Nr. 17, 18, 21.

LITERATURE: Delbrueck, *Die Consulardiptychen*, Nr. 18, S. 125, Taf. 18; Peirce, Tyler, 2, p. 63, tabl. 13 c; Volbach, *Elfenbeinarbeiten*, Nr. 19, S. 36, Taf. 9; Банк, *Искусство Византии*, № 20, с. 121, 124, 127.

37—38 PORTIONS OF A DIPTYCH WITH SCENES FROM THE LIFE OF MARY. 6th century

Ivory

These portions together formed part of a multiple diptych. The scenes represented are the Annunciation to St Anne and the Visitation. Traces of colour remain. The background is painted with gold stars. The top edge of the fragment with the Annunciation is carved with dentil ornament.

The Hermitage. Inv. Nos. ω 300, 301. Height 10.3 cm. Width 6.9 cm (each fragment).
Acquisitions 1921. Formerly in the Botkin collection. The portions once formed part of the Murano diptych now in the Museo Nazionale, Ravenna.

In cutting the diptych, the bands separating the panels have been destroyed. The relief is badly worn.

On other parts of the same diptych, see Volbach, *Elfenbeinarbeiten*, Nr. 125—128.

LITERATURE: J. Strzygowski, «Zwei weitere Stücke der Marientafel zum Diptychon von Murano», *BZ*, VIII, 1899, S. 678—681; Айналов, *Эллинистические основы*, с. 205; J. Strzygowski, «Hellenistische und koptische Kunst in Alexandria», *Bulletin de la Société Archéologique d'Alexandrie*, 1902, N° 5, p. 87, fig. 65—66; *Собрание М. П. Боткина*, Спб., 1911, с. 44—45, табл. 55; Мацулевич, *Византийские резные кости*, с. 43—47; Volbach, *Elfenbeinarbeiten*, Nr. 129, S. 89, Taf. 68; J. Lafontaine-Dosogne, *Iconographie de l'Enfance de la Vierge dans l'Empire byzantin et en Occident*, t. 1, Paris, 1964, p. 70, fig. 40; *Propyläen Kunstgeschichte*, Taf. 92 a, b; K. Weitzmann, "Ivory Sculpture of the Macedonian Renaissance", *Kolloquium über Frühmittelalterliche Skulptur. 1970. Vortragstexte*, Mainz, 1971, S. 12, Taf. 17 a, b.

39—40 PYXIS WITH SCENES FROM THE LIFE OF JOSEPH. 6th century

Ivory

The pyxis is round in shape; the scenes executed in high relief illustrate the Bible story of Joseph: Joseph Dines with His Brethren, and the Finding of the Cup in Benjamin's Sack.

The Hermitage. No. ω 8. Height 7.7 cm. Diameter 9.5 cm.
Acquisitions 1885. Formerly in the Basilewsky collection.

The bottom is missing. The body is mounted on wood. Some cracks and losses of ivory.

Volbach suggested a comparison with the Old Testament scenes on Maximian's Chair at Ravenna (Volbach, *Elfenbeinarbeiten*, Nr. 140), and with two other pyxides (*ibid.*, Nr. 105, 182) from the point of view of style.

LITERATURE: Peirce, Tyler, 2, p. 62, tabl. 9 d; Volbach, *Elfenbeinarbeiten*, Nr. 191, S. 117, Taf. 95; Банк, *Искусство Византии*, № 27, 28, c. 121, 124, 127.

41—42 PYXIS WITH SCENES FROM THE LIFE OF JONAH. 6th century

Ivory

The pyxis is round in shape, with scenes executed in high relief. The subject of the scenes is the history of Jonah: Jonah Being Cast Forth into the Sea, Jonah under the Gourd; the spaces between the scenes are carved with figures of angels.

The Hermitage. No. ω 6. Height 7.8 cm. Diameter 11.5 cm.
Acquisitions 1885. Formerly in the Basilewsky collection. Comes from the church of S. Ambrogio in Milan.

A heart-shaped patch where the lock used to be (?). A piece is broken from the edge. Some cracks. The lid and the bottom are missing.

Volbach compares the pyxis to the Murano diptych (Volbach, *Elfenbeinarbeiten*, Nr. 125).

LITERATURE: Dacel, Basilewsky, N° 28, p. 5, pl. XII; Volbach, *Elfenbeinarbeiten*, Nr. 175, S. 110—111, Taf. 89; Банк, *Искусство Византии*, № 29—31, c. 121—124, 127; Dekan, *Herkunft und Ethnizität*, Abb. 133.

43—46 PYXIS WITH SCENES FROM THE GOSPELS. 6th century

Ivory, bronze

The pyxis is round in shape, with a lock and a bronze lid (probably a later addition?) worked in *repoussé* with representations of the Apostles Peter and Paul standing on either side of the cross. The body of the pyxis is carved with scenes showing Christ and the Samaritan Woman at the Well; the Healing of the Woman Diseased with an Issue of Blood; the Healing of the Blind Man of Jericho; the Healing of the Man Sick of the Palsy; the Raising of Lazarus, and the Healing of the Man Possessed with a Devil. The fastening devices by which the bottom and the lid are attached to the body, are made of copper.

The Hermitage. Inv. No. ω 5. Height (with the lid on) 9.5 cm. Diameter 11.8 cm.
Acquisitions 1885. Formerly in the Basilewsky collection, where it came from the Hahn collection, Hanover.

A number of cracks of different length, mainly in the upper portion; some holes; the edge damaged in places, and reinforced with copper plates.

For related pyxides see Volbach, *Elfenbeinarbeiten*, Nr. 130, 163, and others. For parallels for the lid, see A. Grabar, «Un Reliquaire provenant d'Isaurie», *Cahiers archéologiques*, XIII, 1962, fig. 4.

LITERATURE: Darcel, Basilewsky, p. 6, N° 20, pl. II; Peirce, Tyler, 2, p. 62—63, tabl. 11 b; Volbach, *Elfenbeinarbeiten*, Nr. 179, S. 112, Taf. 90; Банк, *Искусство Византии*, № 24—26, c. 121, 124, 127; W. F. Volbach, «Zur Lokalisierung frühchristlicher Pyxiden», *Festschrift Fr. Gerke*, Baden-Baden, 1962, S. 85, Abb. 7.

47 PYXIS WITH SCENES FROM THE LIFE OF MOSES. 6th century

Ivory

The pyxis is roughly elliptical in shape; it is carved with scenes from the life of Moses: Moses Receives the Tables of the Law, Moses Striking the Rock, and the Bringing of Offerings.

The Hermitage. Inv. No. ω 9. Height 8.4 cm. Diameter 11.6 cm.
Acquisitions 1885. Formerly in the Basilewsky collection.

The side is split and reinforced with a copper plaque. Some round holes. The surface has minor damages all over. The wooden bottom is modern. Traces of the fastening pieces by which the lid and the lock were attached to the body.

Volbach suggests a comparison with the Old Testament scenes on Maximian's Chair at Ravenna (Volbach, *Elfenbeinarbeiten*, Nr. 140). See also Weitzmann, *Catalogue*, No. 18, pl. XVI—XVII.

LITERATURE: Darcel, Basilewsky, p. 6, N° 29; Peirce, Tyler, 1, p. 96, tabl. 163 b; Volbach, *Elfenbeinarbeiten*, Nr. 190, S. 117, Taf. 95; Банк, *Искусство Византии*, № 32, c. 121, 124, 127; Weitzmann, *The Survival*, p. 59, fig. 30; Weitzmann, *Catalogue*, p. 32, 35, pl. XVII, fig. 13.

48—49 PYXIS WITH SCENES FROM THE STORY OF THE THREE YOUTHS OF BABYLON. 6th century

Ivory

The pyxis is circular in shape, with a conical ivory lid. It is carved with reliefs representing the Three Youths in the Fiery Furnace, and the Three Youths before Nebuchadnezzar. Below the square lock is a cross within a laurel wreath.

The Hermitage. Inv. No. ω 7. Height (without the lid) 9 cm. Diameter 12.2 cm.
Acquisitions 1885. Formerly in the Basilewsky collection, where it came from the Hahn collection, Hanover.

The missing pieces of the bottom have been replaced by new ones. Cracks and small holes. The lid is split; the fastening pieces on the lid are made of copper. The lock is modern.

Volbach compares the pyxis to a diptych (Volbach, *Elfenbeinarbeiten*, S. 82, Nr. 125) and to another stylistically related pyxis (*ibid.*, Nr. 174).

LITERATURE: Darcel, Basilewsky, p. 5, N° 27, pl. II; Volbach, *Elfenbeinarbeiten*, Nr. 178, S. 112, Taf. 90; Дьяконова, *Искусство Востока*, № 21, с. 121—123.

50 PORTION OF A DIPTYCH WITH SCENES FROM THE LIFE OF THE VIRGIN. 6th century

Ivory of a very dark shade

The rectangular plaque once formed part of a diptych. It is carved with the Annunciation in the top register, and with the Proof of the Virgin, in the bottom register. The two scenes are separated by a broad band on which are two doves confronted with a cross with flaring arms between. The right margin and the lower edge are adorned with a rope-like pattern. The top edge is decorated with a row of guttae.

The Pushkin Museum of Fine Arts. Inv. No. П 2 б. 326. Height 24 cm. Width 9.5 cm.
Acquisitions 1932. Formerly in the History Museum, Moscow, where it came from the Uvarov collection. Purchased in Kazan.

A small piece is missing from the upper part. Four round holes along the left side. The relief is worn.

For related objects, see Volbach, *Elfenbeinarbeiten*, Nr. 132. Volbach is of the opinion that the diptych may have been manufactured in the Caucasus.

LITERATURE: А. С. Уваров, «Церковный диптих V века», in: *Сборник мелких трудов*, т. 1, М., 1910. с. 107—119, табл. LXXXIV, № 121; D. Aïnalov «Un Fragment d'évangéliaire du VIe siècle de la collection V. N. Khanenko», *Byzantion*, I, 1924, p. 68—71, fig. 4; Volbach, *Elfenbeinarbeiten*, Nr. 132, S. 89, Taf. 68; W. F. Volbach, «Zur Lokalisierung frühchristlicher Pyxiden», *Festschrift Fr. Gerke*, Baden-Baden, 1962, S. 85.

51—52 FRAGMENTS OF A PYXIS WITH SCENES FROM THE GOSPELS. 6th century

Ivory

The two fragments of a pyxis are carved with the Entry into Jerusalem and another scene, probably representing Christ in the act of working a miracle.

The Pushkin Museum of Fine Arts. Inv. No. П 2 б. 327. Height 8.5 cm. Diameter approximately 12 cm.
Acquisitions 1932. Formerly in the History Museum, Moscow. Found in the Ozorukovo barrow (North Ossetia), containing a find of a coin of Chosroes (543), in 1893.

The figures of Christ and a bearded apostle have been preserved; on the smaller fragment is the miraculous healing. Traces of colouring remain.

The Echmiadzin Gospels cover may be compared (Volbach, *Elfenbeinarbeiten*, Nr. 142). Volbach thinks that the pyxis may have been manufactured in the Caucasus.

LITERATURE: Д. В. Айналов, «Обломки пиксиды и другие древности из Озоруковского могильника, находящиеся в Историческом музее», *Археологические известия и заметки*, II, 1894, с. 1—8, рис. I; Айналов, *Эллинистические основы*, с. 203—205, рис. 42; Volbach, *Elfenbeinarbeiten*, Nr. 189, S. 116, Taf. 94; W. F. Volbach, «Zur Lokalisierung frühchristlicher Pyxiden», *Festschrift Fr. Gerke*, Baden-Baden, 1962, S. 85, Abb. 6.

53—54 *TRULLA* (CASSEROLE) WITH A REPRESENTATION OF A NILOMETER. 491—518

Silver

The *trulla* is round, with a broad flat rim, and a straight handle; it rests on a ring foot. The edge of the rim is ornamented with a rope pattern. At the centre is a medallion showing a scene executed in relief, of two erotes measuring the height to which the Nile has risen. The medallion is surrounded by a frieze of incised vases and rosettes. The rim is decorated with *repoussé* animals, birds and fishes against a Nilotic landscape. On the handle is a figure of Neptune with a trident, one foot resting on the back of a dolphin. The reverse of the handle bears four control stamps of the reign of the Emperor Anastasius.

The Hermitage. Inv. No. ω 2. Diameter 24.2 cm. Diameter of bottom 11.2 cm. Length of handle 12 cm. Weight 958.4 gm.
Acquisitions 1859. Received from the Archaeological Commission. Purchased in Perm. Said to have been found at a distance of 18 km from Cherdyn.

A dent and a fracture in the rim right of the handle. Several dents in the body. A drill hole at the end of the handle.

Another *trulla* in the Hermitage collection (see No. 85) has a similar representation of Neptune; also see Matzulewitsch, S. 72—75, Abb. 7, 8; N. Zori, "The House of Kyrios Leontis at Buth Shean", *Israel Exploration Journal*, 16, 1966, No. 2, p. 123.

LITERATURE: Rosenberg, S. 630—631; Matzulewitsch, S. 75—80, Taf. 16, Abb. 9—11; Peirce, Tyler, 2, p. 88, tabl. 44 a; Банк, *Искусство Византии*, № 33, 34, с. 121, 124, 127; Volbach, *Frühchristliche Kunst*, S. 92—93, Taf. 252; Cruikshank Dodd, No. 1, p. 52—53; Volbach, *Silberarbeiten*, S. 63, Taf. 1, 2; Ross, *Catalogue*, 1, p. 7—9; Angiolini Martinelli, *Linea e ritmo*, fig. 3, p. 26; Angiolini Martinelli, *Realtà e fantasia*, p. 50—51.

55—56 DISH WITH A HERDSMAN AND HIS GOATS. 527—565

Silver

The dish is flat and rests on a ring foot. The *repoussé* decoration shows a goatherd seated facing right on a sort of a crude stone bench, with a dog at his feet. In the right portion of the scene are two goats. The border is decorated with a band of slightly curling acanthus leaves in relief, and edged with a thin band of rope pattern. The reverse is engraved with four ornamental compositions of acanthus scrolls issuing from a vase and terminating in rosettes. The bottom is marked with five control stamps of the reign of the Emperor Justinian.

The Hermitage. Inv. No. ω 277. Diameter 23.8 cm. Diameter of the ring foot 9 cm. Weight 1380 gm. Acquisitions 1908. Found with the Klimovo treasure (Solikamsk District of the Perm Province), containing a number of other Byzantine and Sassanian objects, in 1907.

Two small holes in the border. A dent and a break in the foot. The edge notched in several places.

LITERATURE: Rosenberg, S. 698—699; Matzulewitsch, S. 112—113, Taf. 31, 32; Maculevič, *Argenterie*, p. 293, N° 4, tabl. XLV; А. Банк, «Византийское блюдо с изображением пастуха», in: *Сокровища Эрмитажа*, М.—Л., 1949, с. 119—122; J. Beckwith, *The Andrews Diptych*, London, 1958, p. 22; Банк, *Искусство Византии*, № 43—45, с. 122, 125, 128; Talbot Rice, *The Art*, p. 296—297, pl. 42; Cruikshank Dodd, No. 9, p. 70; Beckwith, *The Art*, p. 42—43, fig. 53; G. Mathew, *Byzantine Aesthetics*, London, 1963, p. 77, fig. 11; *L'Art byzantin*, p. 408; *Эрмитаж*, Л., 1964, № 35; Beckwith, *Early Christian and Byzantine Art*, p. 42—43, fig. 78; H. Stern, *L'Art byzantin*, Paris, 1965, p. 33, fig. 40; Weitzmann, *Studies*, p. 132—133, fig. 107; Angiolini Martinelli, *Linea e ritmo*, fig. 4, p. 27—28; Angiolini Martinelli, *Realtà e fantasia*, p. 52—53.

57—59 DISH WITH THE SCENE OF FEEDING A SACRED SERPENT. 6th century

Silver gilt

The dish is circular in shape. The bottom shows traces of a ring foot. The dish is worked in *repoussé* with a kneeling maenad holding a kantharos from which she feeds a serpent emerging from a cist. The segment in the lower portion of the dish displays the attributes of the cult: a bowl, a diptych, and a branch. The background is partially gilt. The reverse is engraved with the head of an old man (the personification of the Ocean?) surrounded by a frieze of sea-monsters.

The Hermitage. Inv. No. ω 285. Diameter 26 cm. Weight 987 gm.

Acquisitions 1911. Gift of M. Shcherbatova. Formerly in the collection of G. Stroganov who acquired it in Russia in 1873.

The ring foot is missing, the dish is broken through and scratched in several places. A small hole in the upper part near the rim. The background gilding remains only in the middle.

LITERATURE: Л. Стефани, «Кормление змей при орфических таинствах», *Записки Академии наук*, XXV, 1874, прилож. 3; Н. Макаренко, «Несколько предметов из собрания графа Г. С. Строганова», *Старые годы*, 1911, 10, с. 36, табл. I; Matzulewitsch, S. 58—60, Taf. 33; Банк, *Искусство Византии*, № 50, 51, с. 122, 125, 128; Angiolini Martinelli, *Linea e ritmo*, fig. 5, p. 28—29; Angiolini Martinelli, *Realtà e fantasia*, p. 57.

60—61 DISH WITH THE SCENE OF ATHENA DECIDING THE QUARREL OF AJAX AND ODYSSEUS. 6th century

Silver

The dish, circular in shape, rests on a low ring foot and is decorated with the scene of the quarrel between Ajax and Odysseus, in *repoussé* work. In the centre of the composition is the figure of Athena with Ajax and Odysseus on either side. Above is a half-figure of a shepherd (?) emerging from some hills. In the lower portion of the dish lies the armour of Achilles. The reverse is engraved with four ornamental compositions showing vine scrolls issuing from vases, birds (ducks, ibises, etc.) and fruits (pears, apples, pomegranates, etc.).

The Hermitage. Inv. No. ω 279. Diameter 26.6 cm. Diameter of the ring foot 10.8 cm. Weight 1219 gm. Acquisitions 1925. Formerly in the collection of S. Stroganov. Found near the village of Sludka in the Perm Province in 1780 (?).

There is a resemblance between the armour in our piece and in the scenes from the life of David on the silver dishes found with the Cyprus treasure (Cruikshank Dodd, Nos. 58, 61, 63).

LITERATURE: Matzulewitsch, S. 54—58, Taf. 35, Abb. 6; Beckwith, *Two Exhibitions*, p. 338, fig. 8; Talbot Rice, *The Art*, p. 306, pl. 74; Банк, *Искусство Византии*, № 46, 47, с. 122, 125, 128; Weitzmann, *The Survival*, p. 47, fig. 2; Volbach, *Silberarbeiten*, S. 30; *L'Art byzantin*, p. 408; Angiolini Martinelli, *Linea e ritmo*, fig. 6, p. 50—52.

62—63 EWER. 582—602

Silver gilt

The body of the ewer is eight-sided. One end of the handle is attached to the back of the ewer in the middle part of the body; the other is joined to the rim by a lunate lip decorated with heads of fishes; there is a thumb-piece ornamented with the head and front part of an animal. The base of the handle is adorned with a mask in *repoussé*. The base of the ewer has the form of an octofoil rosette; the reverse bears five control stamps of the reign of the Emperor Mauricius-Tiberius.

The Hermitage. Inv. No. ω 826. Height (with the handle) 28 cm. Diameter of the base 9.6 cm. Weight 1364 gm.
Acquisitions 1914. Received from the Archaeological Commission. Part of the hoard discovered at the village of Malaya Pereshchepina in the Poltava Province in 1912.

The handle composed of two separate pieces has been soldered on to the body anew. A crack along one of the ribs which is slightly crushed; a dent and a break in the body; a horizontal crack along the rim. Very little gilding remains.

LITERATURE: Бенешевич, *Надписи*, с. 106—107, рис. 5; Бобринский, *Перещепинский клад*, с. 2, табл. IV, рис. 6 а—г; Rosenberg, S. 692—693; Matzulewitsch, S. 6. 82—85, Taf. 18, Abb. 15—17; Банк, *Искусство Византии*, № 56, 57, с. 122, 125, 128; Cruikshank Dodd, No. 31, p. 120; Б. И. Маршак, К. М. Скалон, *Перещепинский клад*, Л., 1972, с. 5.

64—65 PATERA WITH A ROSETTE. 582—602

Silver gilt

The patera has a flat border opening outwards and a short flat handle slightly widening towards the end. The inside decoration has for its central motif an ornamental rosette surrounded by an ivy *rinceau*. It is encircled by a band of lobe-shaped depressions with *repoussé* shells in the inside. The border is decorated with a band of egg-and-tongue ornament. In places, traces of gilding are seen. The patera rests on a ring foot. The reverse of the bottom bears four Byzantine control stamps of the reign of the Emperor Mauricius-Tiberius; on the reverse of the handle is a fifth stamp, and a dotted inscription referring to the total weight of the patera and the ewer accompanying it (see No. 62); the term ΧΕΡΝΙΒΟΞΕϹΤΟΝ, employed here, is used to designate a washing-set consisting of a basin and ewer and designed for the ablutions of a bishop during the Lavatory.

The Hermitage. Inv. No. ω 825. Height 7.2 cm. Length (with the handle) 38.5 cm. Diameter 25.5 cm. Weight 1264 gm.
For data on acquisition and provenance, see No. 62.

The edge fractured in many places; small holes in the body.

LITERATURE: Бенешевич, *Надписи*, с. 104—105, рис. 3, 4; Бобринский, *Перещепинский клад*, с. 2, табл. II, рис. 2 а—г; Rosenberg, S. 690—691; Matzulewitsch, S. 7, 80—83, Taf. 17, Abb. 13—14; Банк, *Искусство Византии*, № 58, 59, с. 122, 125, 128; Cruikshank Dodd, No. 30, p.118—119.

66—68 PATEN OF BISHOP PATERNUS. 491—518

Silver gilt, pastes, gems

The paten, with a deep bowl and a broad border, rests on a ring foot. In the centre is a Chi-Rho monogram and the letters A and Ω surrounded by a gilt band with an incised Latin inscription reading: *Ex antiquis renovatum est per Paternum reverentiss* [imum] *Episc* [opum] *nostrum amen*, which means: "Restored from the antique by Paternus, our reverend bishop. Amen". Round the rim framed on either side by a rope pattern is a vine scroll with birds, animals, vases and baskets of fruit in *repoussé*. On top of the ornament are soldered oval and cruciform settings for jewels and pastes. The ornament is gilt. The reverse of the bottom bears four control stamps of the reign of the Emperor Anastasius. On the inside of the base is a dotted inscription referring to the weight of the silver and gold used in the manufacture of the dish.

The Hermitage. Inv. No. ω 827. Diameter 61 cm. Diameter of the base 31.8 cm. Height of the ring foot 1.8 cm. Weight 6224 gm.
For data on acquisition and provenance, see No. 62.

The paten is restored from a number of fragments, soldered together and mounted on a metal frame. Pieces are missing from the left bottom part. Jewels and paste from the settings are also missing.

Patens found in Antalya, Turkey, may be compared (*Handbook of the Byzantine Collection. Dumbarton Oaks*, Washington, 1967, Nos. 63—65, p. 18—19).

NOTES: (1) Paternus was bishop of the town of Tomi (Constanța) in the first quarter of the 6th century. (2) There are two different interpretations of the word *renovatum*: some of the authorities understand it as referring to the fact that the dish was partially reconstructed; others are of the opinion that the word conveys the idea of the dish being made of old materials.

LITERATURE: Бенешевич, *Надписи*, с. 108, рис. 6—11; Бобринский, *Перещепинский клад*, с. 1—2, табл. I, рис. 1 а—г; Rosenberg, S. 632—633; Matzulewitsch, S. 5, 101—107, Taf. 26, 27, Abb. 21, 22; *Masterpieces*, No. 28, pl. 18—19; Talbot Rice, *The Art*, p. 293; Банк, *Искусство Византии*, № 54, 55, с. 122, 125, 128; Cruikshank Dodd, No. 11, p. 54—55; Beckwith, *The Art*, p. 45, fig. 57; Volbach, *Silberarbeiten*, S. 29—30; V. Elbern, «Der eucharistische Kelch im frühen Mittelalter», *Zeitschrift des deutschen Vereins für Kunstwissenschaft*, XVII, 1963, S. 174—175, Fig. 115; *L'Art byzantin*, p. 497; Rodu Vulpe, Jon Barnea, «Romanii la Durarea de Jos», *Din Istoria Dobrogei*, II, 1968, București, fig. 62; *Propyläen Kunstgeschichte*, Taf. 70 a, S. 190, 194—195; Beckwith, *Early Christian and Byzantine Art*, p. 43, 53, fig. 79; Angiolini Martinelli, *Linea e ritmo*, fig. 7, p. 32—33.

69 DISH DECORATED WITH A CROSS WITHIN A WREATH, AND FLUTING. 629—641

Silver, niello

The dish, circular in shape, is decorated with turning on the rim. The central design consists of a niello cross with flaring arms, within a circular band of ivy *rinceau*, and three rings. It is surrounded by radiating flutings with rounded terminals. The dish rests on a flat ring foot. The reverse of the bottom has five control stamps of the reign of the Emperor Heraclius.

The Hermitage. Inv. No. ω 824. Diameter 30.9 cm. Weight 1472 gm.
For data on acquisition and provenance, see No. 62.

The dish is chipped and scratched in several places. Some of the niello inlay is lost. The edge is chipped.

For related objects, see Cruikshank Dodd, Nos. 67, 68, and also Nos. 51, 55, 76.

LITERATURE: Бенешевич, *Надписи*, с. 102—104, рис. 2; Бобринский, *Перещепинский клад*, с. 2, табл. III, рис. 3 а—г; Rosenberg, S. 696—697; Maculevič, *Argenterie*, p. 294, N° 6, tabl. XLV, 3; Мацулевич, *Византийский антик и Прикамье*, с. 44; Банк, *Искусство Византии*, с. 122, 125, 128, табл. 60; Cruikshank Dodd, No. 73, p. 208—209.

70 AMPHORA. 6th century

Silver gilt

The amphora has three ornamental bands in *repoussé* work, one under the rim, another round the middle part of the body, and a third round the bottom; the middle band is the broadest of the three. The handles of elaborate form are decorated at the base with dolphins' heads. The reverse of the bottom has a control stamp of the 6th century beneath a layer of gilding.

The Hermitage. Inv. No. ω 828. Height 48.5 cm. Diameter of the base 12.5 cm. Weight 7780 gm.
For data on acquisition and provenance, see No. 62.

The surface of the metal is worn, and scratched in several places. The reverse of the bottom is slightly damaged.

For similar ornamentation, see *The Great Palace of the Byzantine Emperors. First Report*, London, 1947, pl. 40, 43, 49; *Second Report*, Edinburgh, 1958, pl. 48—50.

LITERATURE: Бенешевич, *Надписи*, с. 102, рис. 1; Бобринский, *Перещепинский клад*, с. 3, табл. VIII, рис. 17 а, б; Rosenberg, S. 690—691; Matzulewitsch, S. 7, 80—83, Taf. 17, Abb. 13—14; Cruikshank Dodd, p. 224—225, No. 79; Дьяконова, *Искусство Востока*, № 22, с. 119, 123.

71 DISH WITH A ROSETTE IN A WREATH OF ACANTHUS. 527—565

Silver

The shallow dish, circular in shape, is decorated with turning on the rim. It rests on a ring foot. The central ornament consists of a whirling rosette with fourteen curved petals, within a star-shaped rosette encircled by a double band of turning. This design is surrounded by a band of four acanthus branches forming a garland. The border is plain. The reverse of the bottom shows five control stamps of the reign of the Emperor Justinian.

The Hermitage. Inv. No. ω 351. Diameter 19.8 cm. Diameter of the ring foot 8.7 cm. Weight 240 gm.
Acquisitions 1926. Formerly in the Kungur Museum. Found in the village of Ust-Kishert (Kungur District of the Urals Region) in 1926. Formed part of a treasure comprising objects of local manufacture dating from the 8th—9th centuries.

A crack between the rosette and the garland. Dents in several places.

For similar rosette, see Volbach, *Il tesoro*, tav. LIX, fig. 16.

LITERATURE: Rosenberg, S. 716—717; Matzulewitsch, S. 5, 76, 113—114, Taf. 29, Abb. 27; Мацулевич, *Византийский антик и Прикамье*, с. 145, табл. II, 2; Cruikshank Dodd, p. 82—83, No. 15.

72 DISH WITH VENUS IN THE TENT OF ANCHISES (?). *Circa* 550

Silver gilt

The dish is made of a single sheet of silver; it is shallow, and has a ring foot, and a band of turning on the rim. The scene, lightly chased in low relief, possibly represents Venus in the tent of Anchises (a different interpretation of the subject has also been suggested). The reverse of the bottom is marked with five control stamps of the reign of the Emperor Justinian. There is an inscription in Sogdian, which translates as follows: "Ruler of Bokhara Dazoi". It is datable to the late 6th or early 7th century.

The Hermitage. Inv. No. ω 350. Diameter 26.4 cm. Weight 837 gm.
Acquisitions 1926. Formerly in the Kungur Museum. Found in the neighbourhood of the village of Kopchiki (Kungur District of the Urals Region) in 1926.

Deep dents in several places. Broken through in the right-hand part. Cracks at the sides and in the upper part. Losses of metal. The foot is crushed. Scratches on the surface. Only traces of gilding remain.

LITERATURE: Rosenberg, S. 688—689; Matzulewitsch, S. 3—4, 25—31, Taf. 3—5, Abb. 4, 5; Мацулевич, *Византийский антик и Прикамье*, с. 139—157; Банк, *Искусство Византии*, № 62, с. 122, 125, 128; Cruikshank Dodd, p. 84—85. No. 16; Beckwith, *The Art*, p. 45—46, fig. 56; Volbach, *Silberarbeiten*, S. 31; *L'Art byzantin*, p. 408; В. А. Лившиц, В. Г. Луконин, «Среднеперсидские и согдийские надписи на серебряных сосудах», *ВДИ*, 1964, № 3, с. 165— 167; Angiolini Martinelli, *Linea e ritmo*, fig. 8, p. 33—35; Angiolini Martinelli, *Realtà e fantasia*, p. 55—57.

73—74 DISH WITH A HORSE UNDER A TREE. 527—565

Silver gilt

The dish is round and flat. It bears a lightly chased representation of a horse eating grass under a tree. The broad border is decorated with acanthus leaves and lotus flowers with birds in them. The reverse of the bottom has five control stamps of the reign of the Emperor Justinian.

The Hermitage. Inv. No. ω 280. Diameter 40.5 cm. Diameter of ring foot 16.7 cm. Weight 1623 gm. Acquisitions 1925. Formerly in the collection of S. Stroganov. Found with the treasure of Sludka (a village in the Perm Province) in 1780 (?).

Several large dents. Small losses of metal. Patina. Hardly any gilding remains. In the border, several pictures scratched over the ornament, such as faces, etc. (presumably done by some local people in antiquity).

Akin to our piece in ornamentation is a dish from Lesbos (Σ. Πελεκανίδης, 'Αργυρᾶ πινάκια τοῦ Μουσείου Μπενάκη, 'Αρχαιολογικὴ 'Εφημερίς, 1942—1944, 'Αθῆναι, 1948, εἴκ. 2—3) and also two dishes in the Dumbarton Oaks collection (Ross, *Catalogue*, 1, p. 7—9, pl. VIII, IX).

LITERATURE: Rosenberg, S. 702—703; Matzulewitsch, S. 4, 115—120, Taf. 30, Abb. 28; Банк, *Искусство Византии*, № 52, 53, с. 122, 125, 128; Cruikshank Dodd, p. 66—67, No. 7; Volbach, *Silberarbeiten*, S. 31; Ross, *Catalogue*, p. 8—9; Angiolini Martinelli, *Linea e ritmo*, fig. 9, p. 35—37; Angiolini Martinelli, *Realtà e fantasia*, p. 54—55.

75—77 RELIQUARY. *Circa* 550

Silver

This piece is a casket decorated with busts in circular medallions executed in the *repoussé* technique. On one of the long sides are Christ, Sts Peter and Paul; on the other, the Virgin and two archangels; each of the short sides bears a representation of a young saint (St Sergius and St Bacchus; or, which is less likely, St George and St Demetrius). The lid is decorated with four crosses. The reverse of the bottom and the inside of the lid are marked with four control stamps of the reign of the Emperor Justinian I.

The Hermitage. Inv. No. X 249. Height (with the lid) 11 cm. Length 13 cm. Width 8.5 cm. Weight 350 gm. Acquisitions 1900. Received from the Archaeological Commission. Found at Chersonese in 1897.

Restored from a number of fragments; considerable losses of metal, dents; chipped in several places.

A shrine found in Bulgaria may be compared (Peirce, Tyler, 1, N° 125 b).

LITERATURE: *ОАК за 1897 г.*, 1900, с. 104, 213—214; Н. В. Покровский, *Древняя Софийская ризница в Новгороде*, М., 1913, с. 94—95, табл. XIII; Ch. Diel, «L'Ecole artistique d'Antioche et l'argenterie syrienne,» *Syria*, II, 1921, p. 91; Н. Беляев, «Очерки по византийской археологии. Херсонесская мощехранительница», *SK*, III, 1929, с. 115—131, табл. XVIII—XIX; Rosenberg, S. 704—705; A. Grabar, *Martyrium. Recherches sur le culte des reliques et l'art chrétien antique*, v. 1, Paris, 1946, p. 351—352; A. Grabar, *Martyrium. Recherches sur le culte des reliques et l'art chrétien antique. Album*, Paris, 1943, pl. LXV, 3, 4; Cruikshank Dodd, No. 17, p. 81—87; Banck, *Monuments* (*IV*^e^—*VII*^e^ *s.*), p. 114, fig. 1; А. Л. Якобсон, «Раннесредневековый Херсонес», *МИА*, 63, 1959, с. 200; Buschhausen, Lenzen, *Konstantinisches Silberreliquiar*, S. 158, 166, 200; Buschhausen, *Ein byzantinisches Bronzekreuz*, S. 289; H. Buschhausen, *Die spätrömischen Metallscrinia und frühchristliche Reliquiare*, 1. Teil (*Katalog*), Wien, 1971, B 21, S. 252—254, Taf. 59—60; Angiolini Martinelli, *Linea e ritmo*, fig. 12, p. 39—40; Angiolini Martinelli, *Realtà e fantasia*, p. 59—60; Cruikshank Dodd, *Byzantine Silver Treasures*, p. 48, 50, 54, fig. 39.

78 PATEN WITH ANGELS ON EITHER SIDE OF THE CROSS. 6th century

Silver gilt

The paten rests on a ring foot. It has a raised border and *repoussé* cross with flaring arms. The cross is set with precious stones; on either side of it stands an angle with a staff in his hand, facing the cross (the so-called Glory of the Cross, or *Laus Crucis*). Below the line of the soil are symbolic representations of the four rivers flowing through Paradise.

The Hermitage. Inv. No. ω 209. Diameter 18.6 cm. Weight 576 gm.
Acquisitions 1911. Formerly in the collection of S. Stroganov. Found at Beriozovo, Western Siberia, in 1867.

A round hole in the upper part of the paten; a piece is broken from the foot which is in a very crushed condition; traces of gilding.

Iconographically akin to our piece are some specimens of glyptics and *ampullae* (Г. Филимонов, «Похвала кресту», *Вестник древнерусского искусства*, 1875, IV, с. 58—60; *Early Christian and Byzantine Art Exhibition*, No. 552, pl. LXVII; A. Grabar, *Ampoules de Terre Sainte*, Paris, 1958, pl. XXXII, XXXIII); a consular solidus of Justinian (Manelo Caramessini-Oiconomides, "An Unpublished Consular Solidus of Justinian I", *Museum Notes*, 1966, XII, p. 75—77, pl. XXVII), a silver fibula (W. F. Volbach, «Zwei frühchristliche Goldmedaillons», *Berliner Museen. Berichte aus den Preussischen Kunstsammlungen*, XLIII. Jahrgang, Berlin, 1922, Heft 516, Abb. 69, S. 81).

LITERATURE: Толстой, Кондаков, *Русские древности*, 4, с. 174; Д. А. Хвольсон, Н. В. Покровский, Я. И. Смирнов, «Серебряное сирийское блюдо, найденное в Пермском крае», *МАР*, 22, 1899, с. 8, рис. 3; Айналов, *Эллинистические основы*, с. 202—204; Н. П. Кондаков, *Археологическое путешествие по Сирии и Палестине*, Спб., 1904, с. 22, 286; Muñoz, p. 149—152, fig. 103; O. M. Dalton, *East Christian Art*, Oxford, 1929, p. 325, pl. LIX; J. Villette, *La Résurrection du Christ dans l'art chrétien du II*^e^ *au VII*^e^ *siècle*, Paris, 1957, p. 47, pl. 27; Volbach, *Frühchristliche Kunst*, S. 37, 91, Taf. 245; Банк, *Искусство Византии*, № 61, с. 122, 125, 127; Banck, *Monuments* (*IV*^e^—*VII*^e^ *s.*), p. 115, 118, fig. 2; V. Elbern, «Ein christliches Kultgefäß aus Glas in der Dumbarton Oaks Collection», *Jahrbuch der Berliner Museen*, IV, 1962, S. 26, Abb. 7; Ross, *Catalogue*, 1, p. 98—99; V. Elbern, «Le Calice de verre de la Collection Dumbarton Oaks», *Annales du 2*^e^ *Congrès*

International du verre, Leyde, 1963, p. 60, fig. 13; V. Elbern, «Der eucharistische Kelch im frühem Mittelalter», *Zeitschrift des deutschen Vereins für Kunstwissenschaft*, XVII, 1963, S. 175, Abb. 117; *L'Art byzantin*, p. 497; J. Leroy, *Les Manuscrits syriaques à peintures*, Paris, 1964, p. 52—53; Ch. Walter, "Two Notes on the Deesis", *Revue des études byzantines*, XXVI, 1968, p. 326, fig. 10; Beckwith, *Early Christian and Byzantine Art*, p. 43, fig. 81; Grabar, *L'Art de la fin de l'antiquité*, 3, pl. 89 d; Angiolini Martinelli, *Linea e ritmo*, fig. 13, p. 40—41; Angiolini Martinelli, *Realtà e fantasia*, p. 59; Cruikshank Dodd, *Byzantine Silver Treasures*, p. 28—29.

79 DISH WITH AN ORNAMENTAL ROSETTE. 651—688

Silver

The dish with a scalloped rim rests on a ring foot. In the central roundel, a double octofoil rosette. The fluting which radiates from the central roundel to the rim is executed by chasing from the obverse. The reverse of the bottom bears five stamps of the reign of the Emperor Constant II.

The Hermitage. Inv. No. ω 1218. Diameter 28 cm. Diameter of the ring foot 13.2 cm. Weight 1151 gm. Acquisitions 1967. Formerly in the museum of a local school at the Bolshaya Kocha village, Perm Region. Discovered in the neighbourhood of the village of Martynova (Kocha District, Perm Region) in 1953.

A piece broken off from the edge and subsequently soldered on again. A crack at the rim. Damaged in several places by contact with the plough. Two deep dents at the side of the central roundel.

The work is a sort of a crude copy of the Turushevo dish (cf. No. 80).

LITERATURE: В. Лещенко, «Новое византийское блюдо из Верхнего Прикамья», *СГЭ*, 31, 1970, с. 49—51.

80 DISH WITH AN ORNAMENTAL ROSETTE. 629/30—641

Silver

The shallow dish of a circular shape rests on a ring foot. It has a thick border, with a rim decorated with small *repoussé* facets giving it the appearance of a chain consisting of lozenge-shaped links. The central motif is an octofoil rosette in *repoussé* work within two concentric circles. The reverse of the bottom bears five control stamps of the reign of the Emperor Heraclius.

The Hermitage. Inv. No. ω 389. Diameter 27.5 cm. Diameter of the ring foot 12 cm. Weight 1036.5 gm. Acquisitions 1930. Formerly in the Urals Regional Museum in Sverdlovsk. Found near the village of Turushevo (Omutninsk District of the Viatka Province, the present-day Kirov Region) in 1927.

Slightly dented in several places. A small hole has been made near the edge. The reverse has scratched lines and signs near the rim.

The rosette somewhat resembles that at No. 91.

LITERATURE: Мацулевич, *Византийский антик и Прикамье*, с. 140, рис. 3, табл. I; Cruikshank Dodd, No. 72, p. 206.

81 CENSER (?) WITH CHRIST AND THE APOSTLES. 6th century

Silver

The lower part of the censer is bulbous, and above it the vessel flares outward toward the rim. The foot has the form of a ring. Three loops, with remnants of chains still in them, are attached to the rim. The body is decorated with *repoussé* busts of Christ and the Apostles Peter and Paul in medallions; the spaces between the medallions are decorated with lilies (?). At the base of the neck is a row of beads. The neck is ornamented with floral motifs. The rim is edged with egg-and-tongue ornament.

The Hermitage. Inv. No. X 255. Height 8.8 cm. Maximum diameter 9.7 cm. Weight (with the plaster reinforcement) 226 gm.
Received from the Archaeological Commission in 1908. Found at Chersonese in 1904.

The vessel is restored from fragments and reinforced with plaster on the inside. Cracks and losses of metal.

Stylistically comparable are the reliquary No. 75 and the vase from Homs, Syria (Talbot Rice, *The Art*, pl. 44, 45).

LITERATURE: Banck, *Monuments* (*IV*[e]—*VII*[e] *s*.), p. 1—4, fig. 2; Angiolini Martinelli, *Linea e ritmo*, fig. 10, p. 38—39; Angiolini Martinelli, *Realtà e fantasia*, p. 59—60; Cruikshank Dodd, *Byzantine Silver Treasures*, p. 11, 53, 54, fig. 3.

82 CENSER (?) WITH ANGELS. 613—629/30

Silver

The censer is round, with a vertical rim. The vessel rests on a ring foot. The bowl is chased with half-figures of Christ, Apostles Peter and Paul, and of angels under arches decorated with beading and supported by columns (?) shaped as palm-trees. Under the rim is a band of pounced dots. The reverse of the bottom has a control stamp of the reign of the Emperor Heraclius.

The Hermitage. Inv. No. ω 125. Height 5.7 cm. Diameter 9.1 cm. Weight 344 gm.
Acquisitions 1899. Formerly in the Bock collection.

Considerable losses of metal in the rim. Numerous dents; the metal badly worn.

Columns of a similar type appear in the specimen cited by Cruikshank Dodd, No. 35.

LITERATURE: Rosenberg, S. 724—725; Cruikshank Dodd, p. 203—205, No. 71; Banck, *Monuments (IVᵉ—VIIᵉ s.)*, p. 114—115, fig. 3; K. Kreidl-Papadopoulos, «Bemerkungen zum Justinianischen Templon der Sophienkirche in Konstantinopel», *JÖBG*, XVII, 1968, Abb. 2; Angiolini Martinelli, *Linea e ritmo*, fig. 11, p. 38—39; Angiolini Martinelli, *Realtà e fantasia*, p. 59—60; Cruikshank Dodd, *Byzantine Silver Treasures*, p. 22, fig. 18.

83 DISH WITH MELEAGER AND ATALANTA. 613—629

Silver

The dish is circular in shape, shallow, with a band of turning on the rim. It rests on a ring foot. The inside is decorated with a scene of Meleager and Atalanta resting after a chase. On the left, under a tree, is an attendant with a hare in his hands; on the right is another attendant holding a horse by the bridle. There is a building in the background. The representation is in *repoussé*, finished with engraving. The reverse of the bottom shows five control stamps of the reign of the Emperor Heraclius.

The Hermitage. Inv. No. ω 1. Diameter 27.8 cm. Diameter of the ring foot 12.5 cm. Weight 1523 gm. Acquisitions 1840.

There is a hole in the upper part near the rim. Scratches in several places. Notched on the reverse.

LITERATURE: Rosenberg, S. 662—663; Matzulewitsch, S. 2, 9—17, Abb. 1, 2, Taf. 1; G. de Francovich, «L'Arte siriaca e il suo influsso sulla pittura mediaevale nell'Oriente e nell'Occidente», *Commentari*, II, 1951, p. 15, fig. 11; E. Kitzinger, "Byzantine Art in the Period between Justinian and Iconoclasm", *Berichte zum XI. Internationalen Byzantinischen Kongress*, München, 1958, S. 3—4, Fig. 3, 8; Банк, *Искусство Византии*, № 63, с. 122, 125, 128; Cruikshank Dodd, No. 57, p. 176—177; Beckwith, *The Art*, p. 49, 51, fig. 66; Volbach, *Silberarbeiten*, S. 32; *L'Art byzantin*, p. 408; Weitzmann, *Studies*, p. 134—135, fig. 109; Angiolini Martinelli, *Linea e ritmo*, fig. 16, p. 43—45; Angiolini Martinelli, *Realtà e fantasia*, p. 54—55, 61.

84 DISH WITH SILENUS AND A MAENAD. 613—629/30

Silver gilt

The flat dish rests upon a ring foot. The decoration consists of a band of turning on the rim, and a scene of Silenus and a maenad dancing, executed in *repoussé* work. Below the line of the soil is a grapevine and a leaf (?). The background is gilt. The reverse of the bottom is marked with five control stamps of the reign of the Emperor Heraclius.

The Hermitage. Inv. No. ω 282. Diameter 25.7 cm. Diameter of the ring foot 11.7 cm. Weight 1180 gm. Acquisitions 1925. Formerly in the collection of S. Stroganov. Found in the village of Kalganovka (Solikamsk District of the Perm Province) in 1878.

The surface slightly scratched.

A comparable piece is the fragment of a dish with Silenus (Ross, *Catalogue*, 1, No. 8, p. 9—10, pl. V).

LITERATURE: Rosenberg, S. 664—665; Matzulewitsch, S. 3,18—24, Taf. II, Abb. 3; A. Grabar, *L'Art byzantin*, Paris, 1938, pl. 35; Cruikshank Dodd, No. 70 a, p. 201—202; G. de Francovich, «L'Arte siriaca e il suo influsso sulla pittura mediaevale nell'Oriente e nell'Occidente», *Commentari*, II, 1951, p. 14, fig. 8; Банк, *Искусство Византии*, № 48, 49, с. 122, 125, 128; *Masterpieces*, No. 47, p. 24—25; Talbot Rice, *The Art*, p. 306, pl. 75; Beckwith, *The Art*, p. 49, fig. 62; Ross, *Catalogue*, 1, p. 10; Grabar, *L'Age d'or*, p. 299, pl. 33; *Propyläen Kunstgeschichte*, Taf. 71 a, S. 195; M. Alpatow, «*Die Apokalypse* des Moskauer Kremls», *JÜBG*, XI—XII, 1962—1963, Abb. 13; Angiolini Martinelli, *Linea e ritmo*, fig. 14, p. 41—42; Angiolini Martinelli, *Realtà e fantasia*, p. 59.

85—87 *TRULLA* (CASSEROLE) WITH FISHING SCENES. 641—651

Silver gilt

The casserole has slightly bulbous sides, a flat bottom and a straight handle with an ornamented lunate lip at its juncture with the rim. The rim is decorated with turning. The exterior of the body bears a *repoussé* frieze of fishermen with tridents, spears and nets; of fishes, birds, shells, etc. The handle shows Neptune with one foot resting upon the back of a dolphin. The reverse of the bottom has five control stamps of the reign of the Emperor Constant II.

The Hermitage. Inv. No. ω 292. Maximum diameter 13.5 cm. Height 6.3 cm. Length (with the handle) 26.7 cm. Weight 875 gm.

Acquisitions 1927. Received from the "Antiquariat", Moscow. In the 1870s was in the Obolensky collection. Supposed by Matsulevich to have formed part of the treasure found in the village of Peshnigort (Solikamsk District of the Perm Province) in 1853.

The interior of the *trulla* is damaged in the areas of the crab-fisher and the crab. Most of the gilding has disappeared.

A *trulla* in the Louvre collection may be compared (Cruikshank Dodd, No. 14).

LITERATURE: Rosenberg, S. 720—721; Matzulewitsch, S. 6, 65—71, 75, Taf. 12—15; Maculevič, *Argenterie*, p. 300, tabl. XLIV, 2; Coche de la Ferté, *L'Antiquité*, p. 104; Банк, *Искусство Византии*, № 36—38, с. 121, 124, 127; Cruikshank Dodd, p. 218—219, No. 77; Beckwith, *The Art*, p. 49, fig. 63; Volbach, *Silberarbeiten*, S. 24, Taf. II, 4; Ross, *Catalogue*, 1, p. 18—19; S. Husar, «Antike Grundlagen der frühmittelalterlichen Aesthetik», *Das Altertum*, XV, 1969, H. 2, S. 102; Angiolini Martinelli, *Linea e ritmo*, fig. 15, p. 42—43; Angiolini Martinelli, *Realtà e fantasia*, p. 51.

88—90 EWER WITH THE NEREIDS. 641—651

Silver

The ewer has a flat body, and a neck widening and flaring outward toward the rim, with two loops soldered below the lip for the attachment of a lid. The base is of pyramidal shape. There is a loop for the handle at the side. The base of the neck is ornamented with a moulded collar, centrally ridged. The body of the ewer is worked in *repoussé*. On the front and back, in circular medallions, are nereids riding sea-monsters; on the sides are fishes, birds and shells. The bottom bears five stamps of the reign of the Emperor Constant II.

The Hermitage. Inv. No. ω 256. Height 25.2 cm. Diameter of the front and back 13.5 cm. Weight 1132 gm. Acquisitions 1925. Found, in all probability, in the Perm Province.

The handle and the lid are missing; a dent in one of the sides.

For related representation, see Σ. Πελεκανίδης, 'Αργυρᾶ πινάκια τοῦ Μουσείου Μπενάκη, 'Αρχαιολογικὴ 'Εφημερίς, 1942—1944, 'Αθῆναι, 1948, εἰκ. 2.

LITERATURE: Rosenberg, S. 722—723; Matzulewitsch, S. 5, 89—91, Abb. 19, Taf. 19—21; Мацулевич, *Византийский антик и Прикамье*, с. 150, 154—155, табл. VI; Volbach, *Frühchristliche Kunst*, S. 43, Taf. 253; Банк, *Искусство Византии*, № 40—42, с. 122, 125, 128; Cruikshank Dodd, No. 75 a, b, p. 214—215; Beckwith, *The Art*, p. 49, fig. 64; Volbach, *Silberarbeiten*, S. 32; *L'Art byzantin*, p. 408—409; M. Alpatow, «*Die Apokalypse* des Moskauer Kremls», *JÖBG*, XI—XII, 1962—1963, Abb. 4; Angiolini Martinelli, *Linea e ritmo*, fig. 17, p. 45—46; Angiolini Martinelli, *Realtà e fantasia*, p. 52; Dekan, *Antropomorfné motivy*, s. 63, obr. 1.

91 DISH WITH AN ORNAMENTAL ROSETTE. 527—565

Silver

The dish rests on a ring foot. In the centre, enclosed in a medallion outlined by beading, is a rosette of acanthus leaves. The field is ornamented with curved fluting. The reverse of the bottom bears five control stamps referring, in all probability, to the reign of the Emperor Justinian.

The History Museum, Moscow. Inv. No. 10394. Diameter 38.7 cm. Diameter of the ring foot 16.3 cm. Weight 1600 gm.
Acquisitions 1920s. Formerly in the Shchukin collection. Found in the Novobayazet Region (Armenia).

Several dents and small scratches.

The rosette resembles the leaves of acanthus in No. 73. For similar curved fluting, see Volbach, *Il tesoro*, tav. XLVIII, fig. 2.

LITERATURE: Н. Д. Протасов, «К изучению клейм на византийской серебряной посуде», *Труды отделения археологии Института археологии и искусствознания*, I, 1926, с. 69—74, табл. IX, 3; Matzulewitsch, S. 117—118, Abb. 29, 30; Cruikshank Dodd, No. 6, p. 64—65.

92 TWO SPOONS WITH NARROWING HANDLES. Late 4th—early 5th centuries

Silver

The spoons have bowls widening towards the tip and plain handles narrowing towards the end; one terminates in a kink.

The History Museum, Moscow. Inv. Nos. 42422, 42424. Length from 24 to 28 cm.
Acquisitions 1904. Found in the village of Botoşani (Rumania) with a treasure of silver vessels and coins dating from the beginning of the 5th century.

The spoons are slightly dented.

For related objects, see J. W. Brailsford, *The Middenhall Treasure*, London, 1955, p. 14—15, pl. 8, b, e; A. O. Curle, *The Treasure of Traprain*, Glasgow, 1923, p. 63—64, fig. 41; Ross, *Catalogue*, 1, pl. XVII, and others.

LITERATURE: Мацулевич, *Серебряная чаша*, с. 18, примеч. 1; Matzulewitsch, S. 118.

SPOON WITH A HANDLE OF SPIRAL FLUTING. 7th century

Silver

The bowl of the spoon is oval in shape, narrowing towards the tip opposite the handle; the finial is baluster-shaped. The reverse of the bowl bears two control stamps of the 7th century (Constant ?).

The History Museum, Moscow. Inv. No. 47748. Length 26.8 cm.
Acquisitions 1920s. Formerly in the Shchukin collection. Found in the village of Ordakliu in the Novobayazet Region (Armenia).

The spoons are in a good condition.

LITERATURE: Смирнов, *Восточное серебро*, табл. CXXIII, 51—53; Мацулевич, *Серебряная чаша*, с. 18, примеч. 1; Rosenberg, S. 624—625; Cruikshank Dodd, No. 96, p. 262—263.

THREE SPOONS WITH ROUND HANDLES. 7th century

Silver

The spoons have oval bowls narrowing towards the tip, and round handles with baluster finials. On the reverse of one of them are two stamps of the 7th century.

The History Museum, Moscow. Inv. Nos. 47749—47751. Length about 24 cm.
For data on acquisition and provenance, see Inv. No. 47748

The spoons are in a good condition.

LITERATURE: Смирнов, *Восточное серебро*, табл. CXXIII, 48—50; Мацулевич, *Серебряная чаша*, с. 18, примеч. 1; Rosenberg, S. 622—623; Cruikshank Dodd, No. 97, p. 264—265.

93—94 CHAIN WITH THREE PENDANTS AND A CLASP MADE OF A COIN. 6th century

Gold, onyx

The heavy gold chain is worked in imitation of a cord plaited of gold wire, and is fastened with a clasp made of a gold coin; the clasp is encircled with a border of granulations. The chain supports three pendants in the form of oval medallions set with onyx stones and framed with filigree work and granulations; the reverse of the pendants is decorated with engraved patterns; the central one (which still retains a leaf-shaped pendant), with the monogram IX (Jesus Christ), and the side ones, with crosses having flaring arms, forked, with terminals shaped like those of the cross moline.

The Hermitage. Inv. No. 21341. Length of chain 66 cm. Weight 334.8 gm.
Acquisitions 1893. Received from the Archaeological Commission. Found at Michaelsfeld (the present-day village of Dzhiginskoye) in the area of Anapa (the Kuban Region) in 1892, probably in a burial.

Two pendants are missing. Stones missing from the large and one small medallion. The clasp is detached.

For similar chains, see Артамонов, *История хазар*, с. 77; Кондаков, *Русские клады*, с. 177, 193; W. Dennison, *A Gold Treasure of the Later Roman Period*, London, 1918, No. 9, pl. XXIX, p. 142; А. Т. Сміленко, *Глодоські скарби*, Київ, 1965, табл. I, II.

LITERATURE: *ОАК за 1892 г.*, 1894, с. 93, рис. 55; Кондаков, *Русские клады*, с. 193—195, рис. 104—106; Артамонов, *История хазар*, с. 152.

95 CHAIN WITH A MEDALLION. Late 6th century

Gold

The chain consists of twenty circular plaques stamped with busts of two emperors flanking a cross, and the Greek inscription which reads: ΥΓΙ[ΕΙ]Α (Health); the clasp is in the form of a plain circular plaque with two loops. The chain supports a large medallion showing the Emperor Constantine the Great crowned by two winged figures personifying the sun and the moon; at their feet are stylized representations of two birds drinking from the Fountain of Life. The medallion is decorated with a border of plant scrolls, within an outer band of animals chasing each other.

The Hermitage. Inv. Nos. ω 107, 108. Length of chain 46 cm. Diameter of the medallion 7.9 cm. Weight 39.8 gm.
Acquisitions 1893. Formed part of the treasure found in the neighbourhood of Mersina in the area of Tarsus, Cilicia, in 1889.

From some of the plaques, the loops are missing.

LITERATURE: Кондаков, *Русские клады*, с. 187—192, табл. XVIII; Grabar, *Un Médaillon*, p. 27—49; Банк, *Искусство Византии*, № 66, с. 122, 125, 128; J. Deér, «Der Globus des spätrömischen und des byzantinischen Kaisers: Symbol oder Insigne?», *BZ*, 54, 1961, S. 79, Taf. II, 2; A. Grabar, «Un Reliquaire provenant d'Isaurie», *Cahiers archéologiques*, XIII, 1962, p. 58, fig. 6 (see also: Grabar, *L'Art de la fin de l'antiquité*, 1, p. 195—211; 3, pl. 24—26, 101 c, 108 d); Buschhausen, *Frühchristliches Silberreliquiar*, S. 137, 168, Abb. 11; Buschhausen, Lenzen, *Konstantinisches Silberreliquiar*, S. 192; *Propyläen Kunstgeschichte*, S. 195, Abb. 72.

96 RINGS. 7th century

Gold

a) The ring is massive, with a wire hoop; the bezel flat, of a circular shape; it is engraved with a cruciform monogram evidently giving the name of the owner: Ραβαχάτου.

b) The ring is massive, with a wire hoop; the bezel circular, in the form of two truncated cones with the bases joined together, engraved with a cruciform monogram evidently giving the owner's name: Θελεπχάρου.

The Hermitage. Inv. Nos. ω 1052, 1053. Diameters, 2.7 and 2.6 cm. Weight 26.37 gm. and 21.77 gm.
Acquisitions 1914. Received from the Archaeological Commission. Purchased by B. Khanenko from the villagers of Malaya Pereshchepina in the Poltava Province in 1912; formed part of the Malaya Pereshchepina treasure.

The rings are in a good condition.

For related objects, see *Ars antiqua. Auktion in Luzern, 7. Dezember, 1962 (Antike Kunstwerke)*, S. 46.

LITERATURE: Бобринский, *Перещепинский клад*, с. 6, табл. XVI, рис. 60, 61; Бенешевич, *Надписи*, с. 115—116, рис. 12, 13.

97 EARRINGS. Late 6th century

Gold

The lobes are half-moon shaped, with an openwork design of two confronted birds (peacocks?) with a vase between. Each earring has five beads spaced along the lower margin, a wire hoop and a clasp.

The Hermitage. Inv. No. ω 96. Width of crescent 3.9 cm. Weight 10.7 gm.
For data on acquisition and provenance, see No. 95.

The hoops are slightly out of shape; the metal is worn.

For related objects, see Dalton, *Catalogue*, No. 276, p. 45, pl. V; W. F. Volbach, *Mittelalterliche Bildwerke aus Italien und Byzanz*, Berlin—Leipzig, 1930, S. 132, Nr. 4326; Coche de la Ferté, *Collection*, p. 54—55, pl. VI bis, N° 32 bis; Talbot Rice, *The Art*, p. 302, pl. 65; *L'Art byzantin*, Nos 417—419; Marvin C. Ross, "Jewels of Byzantium", *Art of Virginia*, 1968, No. 1, p. 20; J. Beckwith, "A Byzantine Crystal and a Little Gold", *JÖB*, 1972, 21, p. 14—15, fig. 3.

LITERATURE : Кондаков, *Русские клады*, с. 190, табл. XVIII, 1—2; Банк, *Искусство Византии*, № 67, с. 122, 125, 128; Grabar, *Un Médaillon*, fig. 1, 2.

98 CHAIN WITH A CROSS AND PENDANTS. Late 6th century

Gold, paste, chalcedony

The chain consists of circular links, and supports three tubes with settings for pastes, two pendants and a cross. The clasp is of two round plaques with winged figures holding a cross, and a legend which reads: CONOB. The cross is made of hollow tubes, and has a setting for a jewel (?) in the centre. One of the pendants is pear-shaped and set with a chalcedony, the other is oval, stamped with the figure of an archangel holding a spear in the right hand, and an orb in the left one.

The Hermitage. Inv. No. ω 104. Length of chain 33 cm. Cross 4.9×3.8 cm. Weight 33.9 gm.
For data on acquisition and provenance, see No. 95.

The stone is missing from the setting on the cross.

For similar crosses, see Dalton, *Catalogue*, No. 285, pl. IV; B. Segall, *Katalog der Goldschmiedarbeiten. Museum Benaki*, Athen, 1938, Nr. 273, S. 173, Taf. 52.

LITERATURE: Кондаков, *Русские клады*, с. 187—192, табл. XVIII, 6; Grabar, *Un Médaillon*, fig. 2; Банк, *Искусство Византии*, № 64, с. 122, 125, 128.

99 CHAIN SUPPORTING A CROSS AND PENDANTS. Late 6th century

Gold

The chain is made of links bent and attached to each other so as to form a semblance of a braid; the cross had flaring arms adorned with openwork palmettes at the ends; at the intersection of the cross arms is a cruciform recess for a relic (?). Of the pendants ornamented with an openwork design, two are circular, one shaped as a leaf and one of cylindrical form. The clasp is decorated in openwork.

The Hermitage. Inv. Nos. ω 105, 106. Length of chain 27 cm. Cross 5.7×3.9 cm. Weight 43.8 gm.
For data on acquisition and provenance, see No. 95.

One of the pendants is damaged. The stone from the setting in the cross is lost. Kondakov supposed that originally there was yet another leaf-shaped pendant and another cylinder, both of them now missing.

For related chains with pendants, see Peirce, Tyler, 1, pl. 189 a; Coche de la Ferté, *Collection*, p. 59, pl. V, 44; *L'Art byzantin*, Nos 412, 413, p. 371—372; W. Dennison, *A Gold Treasure of the Later Roman Period*, London, 1918, pl. XXVIII, XXX, XXXIV; Ross, *Catalogue*, 2, No. 4, p. 7.

LITERATURE: Кондаков, *Русские клады*, с. 191—192, табл. XVIII, 12; Grabar, *Un Médaillon*, fig. 12; Банк, *Искусство Византии*, № 65, с. 122, 125, 128; *Propyläen Kunstgeschichte*, S. 195, Taf. 72.

100—101 RING WITH THE SCENE OF A BETROTHAL. 7th century

Gold, jewels, niello

The flat hoop of octagonal shape is engraved with a Greek inscription which reads: Κ . . . Ε ΩC ΟΠΛΩΝ ΕΥΔΟΚΙΑC ΕCΤΕΦΑΝΩCΑCΗΜΑC ("With favour wilt thou compass him as with a shield." *Ps. V, 12*). The flat circular bezel bears the scene of Christ blessing the bride and bridegroom; on the garments of the bridegroom is a garnet, and on those of the bride, an emerald. The robe of Christ and the haloes are filled with niello. Below is a legend which reads: OMONIA (Concord).

The Hermitage. Inv. No. ω 121. Diameter 2.1 cm. Weight 7.9 gm.
Acquisitions 1897. Formerly in the Lobanov-Rostovsky collection.

The ring is in a good condition.

The legend and the scene decorating the bezel are the same as on the ring in the Museum at Palermo *(L'Art byzantin*, p. 375—376, N° 425; Банк, *Два перстня*, с. 36—39, табл. II, 4).

LITERATURE: Банк, *Два перстня*, с. 35—39, табл. II, 1—3.

102 BRACELETS. Late 6th century

Gold

The bracelets are tubular, widening towards the terminals, and have the form of an open circle. The terminals are bordered with thin raised bands.

The Hermitage. Inv. Nos. ω 100, 101. Diameter 6.9 cm and 7 cm. Weight 11.9 gm and 18.86 gm.
For data on acquisition and provenance, see No. 95.

One of the bracelets is restored from three pieces; the other is broken, and has deep dents on the surface.

Comparable to these are the bracelets from Morskoy Chulek, near Taganrog (Артамонов, *История хазар*, с. 77), and many others.

LITERATURE: Кондаков, *Русские клады*, с. 188, табл. XVIII, 7, 8, 10; Grabar, *Un Médaillon*, fig. 7, 8, 10.

103 TWO RINGS WITH FLAT HOOPS. Late 6th century

Gold

The rings have flat hoops with filigree and granular decoration. Both have projecting cone-shaped bezels with a pierced base resembling a six-petalled flower; one is engraved with a scene of Christ blessing a bride and bridegroom; below is an undecipherable legend; the other has a setting for a stone.

The Hermitage. Inv. Nos. ω 97, 98. Diameter 2.1 cm (ω 97); 2.3 cm (ω 98). Weight 8.75 gm and 8.85 gm.
For data on acquisition and provenance, see No. 95.

The stone is missing from No. ω 98.

For similar rings, see P. Metz, *Europäische Bildwerke von der Spätantike bis zum Rokoko*, München, 1957, S. 14, Nr. 12; Банк, *Два перстня*, рис. 1, примеч. 2, 3 на с. 32 и примеч. 1 на с. 33; A. Orlandos, *Collection Hélène Stathatos. Objets antiques et byzantins*, v. 3, Strasbourg, 1963, p. 288, N° 228, pl. XLIV.

LITERATURE: Кондаков, *Русские клады*, с. 190, рис. 99, 100, табл. XVIII, 4—5; Grabar, *Un Médaillon*, fig. 4, 5; Банк, *Два перстня*, с. 31—35.

RING. Late 6th century

Gold

The hoop is round in section; the bezel shaped like a bowl.

The Hermitage. Inv. No. ω 99. Diameter 2.3 cm. Weight 5.07 gm.
For data on acquisition and provenance, see No. 95.

The stone is missing from the setting. The metal is dented.

LITERATURE: Кондаков, *Русские клады*, табл. XVIII, 3; Grabar, *Un Médaillon*, fig. 3.

104 CROSS. Late 6th century

Gold

The cross has flaring arms hexagonal in section, a loop for suspension, and a setting for a stone at the junction of the cross arms.

The Hermitage. Inv. No. ω 95. 5×3 cm. Weight 18.3 gm.
For data on acquisition and provenance, see No. 95.

The gem is missing from the setting.

For related objects, see Dalton, *Byzantine Art*, No. 544, fig. 330; A. Orlandos, *Collection Hélène Stathatos. Objets antiques et byzantins*, v. 3, Strasbourg, 1963, N° 232, pl. XLIV; V. H. Elbern, «Neuerwerbungen Spätantiker und byzantinischer Goldschmiedekunst für die frühchristlich-byzantinische Sammlung», *Berliner Museen*, 1965, N. F., XV, H. 2, Abb. 1; C. Gómez-Moreno, *Medieval Art from Private Collections. A Special Exhibition at the Cloisters. October 30, 1968—January 5, 1969, The Metropolitan Museum of Art*, 1968, No. 130.

LITERATURE: Кондаков, *Русские клады*, с. 190, табл. XIX, 18; Grabar, *Un Médaillon*, p. 544, fig. 18.

AGRAFFE. Late 6th century

Gold, pearls

The agraffe consists of three circular settings for pearls held together by horizontal wire spirals. There is a loop at either end of the agraffe.

The Hermitage. Inv. No. ω 103. 5×1.3 cm. Weight 5.6 gm.
For data on acquisition and provenance, see No. 95.

Two of the stones are missing from the settings. The metal is dented.

LITERATURE: Кондаков, *Русские клады*, табл. XVIII, 11; Grabar, *Un Médaillon*, fig. 11.

105 BUCKLE, TONGUE, AND ORNAMENTAL PLAQUES FROM A BELT. Late 6th century

Gold

The buckle, tongue and seventeen ornamental plaques constitute a set. They are decorated with openwork; many have loops on the reverse. In the centre of the tongue is a Greek inscription reading: ΚΥΡΙΕ ΒΟΗΘΕΙ (O Lord, help [the wearer!]).

The Hermitage. Inv. No. ω 109. 64×2.6 cm (maximum), 2.1×2 cm (minimum). Total weight 96 gm.
For data on acquisition and provenance, see No. 95.

One of the plaques is split in two. Small pieces broken off from different objects of the set.

LITERATURE: Кондаков, *Русские клады*, с. 189—190, табл. XIX, 1—17; Банк, *Искусство Византии*, № 67, с. 122, 125, 128; Grabar, *Un Médaillon*, p. 30, fig. 1—17.

106 CAMEO WITH CHRIST EMMANUEL. 6th century (?)

Three-layered sardonyx, gold

The cameo is oval in shape; the bust of Christ Emmanuel is executed in low relief. The nimbus cruciger is indicated by the extremities of the flaring cross arms; the contour is not outlined. The hairdress of rhythmically repeated strands is done in a higher relief. The garments are rendered summarily; in front is a kind of *loros* adorned with a lozenge-shaped ornament. There are incised letters IC XC (Jesus Christ). The reverse is plain. The mount, also plain, is a later addition.
There are certain stylistic features which make a Western provenance not impossible.

The Hermitage. Inv. No. ω 373. 5.1×4.1 cm (in the mount); 4.3×3.2 cm (without the mount).
Acquired in the second half of the 18th century.

The cameo is in a good condition.

LITERATURE: J. Wirenius-Matzulewitsch, «Quelques camées inédits au Musée de l'Ermitage», *Arethuse*, 20, 1928, p. 100—101, pl. XVIII, 5; Банк, *Искусство Византии*, № 69 a, c. 122, 125, 128; Bank, *Monuments* (*IVe—VIIe s.*), p. 122, fig. 9 a.

107 CAMEO WITH THE ANNUNCIATION. 6th century (?)

Three-layered sardonyx, gold

The figures are executed in low relief. In her left hand Mary holds the yarn which falls into a basket; the angel carries a staff. The reverse is plain. The mount, which is plain too, is a later addition.

The Hermitage. Inv. No. ω 355. 6.1×4.6 cm (in the mount); 5.1×3.6 cm (without the mount).
Acquired in the second half of the 18th century. Formerly in the collection of the Duke of Orleans.

A piece is broken off from the staff of the angel.

For parallels, see No. 108.

Very similar objects are also to be found in the collection of the Bibliothèque Nationale, Paris (E. Babelon, *Catalogue des camées antiques et modernes*, Paris, 1897, Nos 336—338, pl. XXXIX). One of these cameos (N° 338) has been tentatively associated with the name of Anna Comnena. However, the iconography of the Annunciation (in particular, the arrangement of the figures) seems to point to a pre-Iconoclastic date. There are certain features of style which make a Western provenance of the Hermitage cameos not impossible.

LITERATURE: *Catalogue des pierres gravées*, N° 1456, p. 169; Банк, *Искусство Византии*, № 69 б, с. 122, 125, 128; Banck, *Monuments* (*IVe—VIIe s.*), p. 122, fig. 9 b; *L'Art byzantin*, N° 103, p. 194; H. Wentzel, «Die Kamee der Kaiserin Anna. Zur Datierung byzantinisierenden Intaglien», *Festschrift Ulrich Middeldorf*, Berlin, 1968, Abb. 1, 4, S. 11.

108 CAMEO WITH THE ANNUNCIATION. 6th century (?)

Three-layered sardonyx, gold

The cameo is rectangular in shape, with the corners slightly rounded. At the left is the figure of the Virgin, shown from the side; she holds in her left hand a piece of yarn placed in a basket, and her right hand is

stretched forward. At the right is the figure of the angel, also in profile view; he addresses the Virgin, accompanying his words with a gesture of his right hand, while his left is holding a staff. No attempt has been made to realize the artistic potentialities of the natural structure of the stone. To judge by the style, the cameo may have been carved in one of the western provinces of the Empire.
The plain mount is of later work.

The Hermitage. Inv. No. ω 354. 2.7×2.1 cm (with the mount), 2×1.5 (without the mount).

For parallels, see No. 107; see also E. Babelon, *Catalogue des camées antiques et modernes*, Paris, 1897, N°s 336—338, pl. XXXIX; H. Wentzel, «Die Kamee der Kaiserin Anna. Zur Datierung byzantinisierenden Intaglien», *Festschrift Ulrich Middeldorf*, Berlin, 1968, Abb. 1, 4.

LITERATURE: H. Wentzel, «Die Kamee der Kaiserin Anna. Zur Datierung byzantinisierenden Intaglien», *Festschrift Ulrich Middeldorf*, Berlin, 1968, S. 11, Abb. 3.

109 ICON OF THE VIRGIN AND CHILD. 6th century

Encaustic over gesso, wood (larch)

The Virgin is represented half length, with the Child. The haloes bear traces of punched designs. The icon may be a fragment of an *Adoration of the Magi*.
The dating of the icon, and its connection with the Alexandrian school of painting (*КМЗВИ*, *Каталог*, c. 19), cannot be regarded as established beyond doubt.

The Kiev Museum of Western and Eastern Art. Inv. No. 112 жк. Height 36.5 cm. Width 20.5 cm.
Acquisitions 1940. Formerly in the Kiev Central Antireligious Museum. Comes from the collection of Porphyry Uspensky who brought it from Mount Sinai.

The upper corners have been cut away. The icon was restored several times.

LITERATURE: Успенский, *Второе путешествие*, c. 164; Айналов, *Синайские иконы*, c. 343, 361—377, табл. IV; Кондаков, *Памятники*, c. 124, 126, 127, табл. XLVIII; Петров, *Альбом*, c. 4—6, 8—9; Dalton, *Byzantine Art*, p. 316—317; Н. П. Кондаков, *Иконография богоматери*, т. 1, Спб., 1914, c. 153, 159—165, рис. 90, табл. 3; Wulff, Alpatoff, S. 30, 32, 259, Abb. 12; Лазарев, *История*, 1, c. 61; Felicetti-Liebensfels, S. 29—30, Taf. 31 a; *КМЗВИ*, *Каталог*, c. 19, № 1; Lazarev, *Storia*, p. 92—93, tav. 69; *Propyläen Kunstgeschichte*, S. 60; A. Grabar, «Découverte à Rome d'une icône de la Vierge à l'encaustique», in: Grabar, *L'Art de la fin de l'antiquité*, 1, p. 530—531, 533; Weitzmann, *The Icons*, B. 2, p. 15—18, pl. III, XLII.

110—111 ICON OF ST JOHN THE BAPTIST. 6th century

Encaustic over gesso, wood (beech)

St John the Baptist is represented full length, holding in his left hand a scroll with the remnants of the Greek inscription: I . . OA . . . C . . . . . OΥO . . . N . . . A . . . TI . . TOΥ . . . . . ("Behold the Lamb of God, which taketh away the sin of the world." *John, I, 29*). St John wears a long chiton, a himation, and a sheep-skin (the *melote*), fastened round the throat; he has sandals on his feet. On either side of the halo is a small medallion, one bearing the bust of Christ, the other, that of the Virgin. Some of the authorities incline to assign the icon to Alexandria.

The Kiev Museum of Western and Eastern Art. Inv. No. 113 жк. Height 46 cm. Width 25 cm.
For data on acquisition and provenance, see No. 109.

Most of the inscription has perished. Traces of nails along the edges. Losses of paint film in the background and in some areas of the figure.

Iconographically akin to this piece is St John the Baptist on Maximian's Chair at Ravenna (Volbach, *Frühchristliche Kunst*, Taf. 227).

LITERATURE: Успенский, *Второе путешествие*, c. 164; Айналов, *Синайские иконы*, c. 343, 368—377, табл. V; Кондаков, *Памятники*, c. 124—125, 127—128, табл. XLIX; Лихачев, *Материалы*, 1, табл. III, 3; Dalton, *Byzantine Art*, p. 316—317; Петров, *Альбом*, c. 4, 6, 9; Wulff, Alpatoff, S. 18—22, 258, Abb. 9; Лазарев, *История*, 1, c. 61; Felicetti-Liebensfels, S. 26, Taf. 31 a; *КМЗВИ*, *Каталог*, c. 20—21, № 2; Lazarev, *Storia*, p. 92—93, tav. 70; *Propyläen Kunstgeschichte*, S. 60, 179, Taf. XI; Weitzmann, *The Icons*, B. 11, p. 32—35, pl. XIV, LVII.

112—113 ICON OF STS SERGIUS AND BACCHUS. 7th century (?)

Encaustic over gesso, wood (sycamore)

Sts Sergius and Bacchus are represented half length, their heads slightly turned side face towards one another. In the centre above is a medallion with the face of Christ. Each of the martyrs wears a *chlamys* and a chiton with the *clavi* or shoulder-bands; they hold crosses in their hands. Around the neck each has a torque set with three gems. The haloes with punched designs of dots, circles and stars, and also the medallion, are enclosed in a dark border. The assignment of the icon to the Syrian school seems controversial. Highly controversial is also the dating of the icon to the 7th century (*КМЗВИ*, *Каталог*). Ainalov gives convincing proofs in favour of the 6th century.

The Kiev Museum of Western and Eastern Art. Inv. No. 111 жк. Height 28.5 cm. Width 42 cm (with the mount).
For data relative to acquisition and provenance, see No. 109.

The faces have been considerably repainted: and large areas restored in oils. A horizontal crack in the top part of the icon has been filled in and retouched with paint. The inscriptions ΣΕΡΓΙΟΣ and ΒΑΧΟΣ are later additions.

LITERATURE: Успенский, *Второе путешествие*, с. 164; J. Strzygowski, *Orient oder Rom*, Leipzig, 1909, S. 123—124, Abb. 77; Кондаков, *Памятники*, с. 124—125, 128, рис. 52; Айналов, *Синайские иконы*, с. 352—361, 366—367, 376—377, табл. III; Лихачев, *Материалы*, 1, табл. II, 2; Dalton, *Byzantine Art*, p. 316—317; Петров, *Альбом*, с. 5—8; Wulff, Alpatoff, S. 11—13, 257, Abb. 3; Лазарев, *История*, 1, с. 71, 296; Felicetti-Liebensfels, S. 24—25, Taf. 30 a; A. Grabar, *L'Iconoclasme byzantin*, Paris, 1957, p. 81, fig. 71; *КМЗВИ, Каталог*, с. 22—23, № 5; Lazarev, *Storia*, p. 93; *Propyläen Kunstgeschichte*, S. 179, Abb. 42; A. Grabar, «L'Imago clipeata chrétienne», in: Grabar, *L'Art de la fin de l'antiquité*, 1, p. 611; 3, pl. 150 b; Grabar, *L'Age d'or*, p. 186, pl. 201; Weitzmann, *The Icons*, B. 9, p. 28—30, pl. XII, LII—LIII.

114 ICON OF A MALE AND FEMALE MARTYRS. 6th—7th centuries

Encaustic over gesso, wood (sycamore)

The two young martyrs (saints ?), a youth and a girl, are shown half length, holding crosses in their hands. In the space between the figures is a cross illumined by rays from Heaven; it is set with precious stones. The cross, the rays and the haloes of oval shape are slightly raised over the surface of the background. Above are hardly discernible traces of a Greek inscription: . . ΓΙ . . Π . . . Ν.

The question of date has aroused controversy. Ainalov has advanced a series of proofs in support of the conjecture that the icon is datable to the 5th or 6th century.

The Kiev Museum of Western and Eastern Art. Inv. No. 114 жк. Height 54 cm. Width 48.5 cm (with the frame).

For data relative to acquisition and provenance, see No. 109.

The painting has been considerably renovated and restored; the right side of the icon has been repainted and the missing portions of the figure of the female martyr filled in with thin oils. The areas around her eyes and the bridge of the nose are painted over; the eyes, too, are done anew. The gold in the background has flaked off. The inscription and the cross in the centre are considerably abraded.

LITERATURE: Успенский, *Второе путешествие*, с. 164; J. Strzygowski, *Byzantinische Denkmäler*, Wien, 1891, S. 116—117, 118—120, Taf. 8; Кондаков, *Памятники*, с. 124—125; Айналов, *Синайские иконы*, с. 344—352, 375—377, табл. I; Лихачев, *Материалы*, 1, табл. I; Dalton, *Byzantine Art*, p. 316—317; Петров, *Альбом*, с. 4—7; Wulff, Alpatoff, S. 8—10, 257, Abb. 2; Лазарев, *История*, 1, с. 71, 296; Felicetti-Liebensfels, S. 23—24, Taf. 30 b; *КМЗВИ, Каталог*, № 4, с. 22; Lazarev, *Storia*, p. 93; Weitzmann, *The Icons*, B. 15, p. 38—40, pl. XVII, LXI.

115 SEAL WITH NIKE. 6th century

Lead

The seal, roughly oval in shape, bears on the obverse the figure of Nike facing left, with a wreath in her hand, and an inscription reading: NIKA; on the reverse a monogram giving the name of the owner: Θηοδῶρου.

The Hermitage. Inv. No. M 5126. 2.9×2.2 cm.
Acquisitions 1931. Formerly in the Museum of the Russian Archaeological Institute in Constantinople.

Chipped round the edge. The seal is worn.

A seal from the Likhachov collection may be compared (Лихачев, *Некоторые старейшие типы*, рис. 19).

LITERATURE: Панченко, *Каталог моливдовулов*, 9, с. 35, № 74, табл. V, № 15; Лихачев, *Некоторые старейшие типы* с. 8—9, рис. 18.

116 SEAL WITH A GODDESS. 6th century

Lead

The seal, roughly oval in shape, bears on the obverse a bust of a goddess with a cornucopia in her hand, enclosed in a medallion; on the reverse: ΙΩΑΝΝΟΥ.

The Hermitage. Inv. No. M 8263. 2.7×2.3 cm.
Acquisitions 1938. Formerly in the Institute of Books, Documents and Letters, Leningrad. Comes from the Likhachov collection.

Chipped round the edge; the design is worn.

LITERATURE: Лихачев, *Историческое значение*, с. 10—11, табл. V, рис. 6.

117 SEAL WITH THE EMPEROR MAURICIUS-TIBERIUS. 582—602

Lead

The seal roughly circular in shape, bears on the obverse a bust of the Emperor Mauricius-Tiberius; this is surrounded by the inscription *DNMAV... IBPPAVG* (Dominus noster Mauricius Tiberius, perpetuus Augustus). On the reverse is a full-length representation of the Virgin and Child, with crosses on either side.

The Hermitage. Inv. No. M 4463. 2.2×2.2 cm.
Acquisitions 1931. Formerly in the Museum of the Russian Archaeological Institute in Constantinople.

Badly chipped round the edge; the design is worn.

For related objects, see Лихачев, *Некоторые старейшие типы*, рис. 23; Толстой, *Византийские монеты*, V, № 20, 24 and others.

LITERATURE: Лихачев, *Некоторые старейшие типы*, с. 10—11, рис. 22.

118 SEAL WITH EMPEROR PHOCAS. 602—610

Lead

The seal is roughly circular in shape. On the obverse is a bust of the Emperor Phocas, with a pointed beard, surrounded by an inscription which reads: *D*[ominus] *N*[oster] *F*[ocas] *perp*[etuus] *au*[gustus]. On the reverse is a full-length representation of the Virgin and Child in a medallion, flanked by crosses.

The Hermitage. Inv. No. M 4458. 2.6×2.4 cm.
Acquisitions 1931. Formerly in the Museum of the Russian Archaeological Institute in Constantinople.

Chipped round the edge; the design is worn.

Close parallels for the obverse are to be seen on coins of the same emperor (Толстой, *Византийские монеты*, VI, № 2, 3 and others).

LITERATURE: Лихачев, *Некоторые старейшие типы*, рис. 24.

119 SEAL WITH CONSTANS II AND HIS SON. 641—688

Lead

The seal is roughly circular in shape; the obverse bears representations of Constans II Pogonatus and his son Constantine as a boy; the inscription round the edge reads: *D*[omini] *N*[ostri] *Constantinus et Consta* [ntus] (?). On the reverse is a full-length figure of the Virgin flanked by two short crosses.

The Hermitage. Inv. No. M 4561. 2.7×2.6 cm.
Acquisitions 1931. Formerly in the Museum of the Russian Archaeological Institute in Constantinople.

Chipped round the edge; the design is worn.

Close parallels for the obverse appear in coins of the same emperors (Толстой, *Византийские монеты*, VII, № 240, 250 and others).

LITERATURE: Лихачев, *Некоторые старейшие типы*, с. 20—21, рис. 41; *Propyläen Kunstgeschichte*, S. 202, Taf. 101 b.

120 TEXTILE. 7th—8th centuries

Silk

A rectangular piece of silk textile bearing large four-petalled flowers joined together, the points of the petals touching. In the intervening spaces are cocks and vases (?) with flowers (stylized palmettes?), enclosed in ovals.

The Hermitage. Inv. No. КЗ/6330. Height 24 cm. Width 16 cm.
Acquisitions 1923. Formerly in the History Museum, Moscow. Found in the village of Khasaut in the Stavropol area in 1885.

The textile is worn and tends to crack in several places. The colours have faded.

For parallels, see Volbach, *Frühchristliche Kunst*, Taf. 258, S. 94; A. C. Weibel, *Two Thousand Years of Textiles*, New York, 1952, pl. 61.

LITERATURE: *Указатель памятников Имп. Российского исторического музея*, М., 1893, с. 393, № 75; Н. П. Кондаков, *Очерки и заметки по истории средневекового искусства и культуры*, Прага, 1929, с. 339, рис. 100; A. A. Iéroussalimskaia, «Trois soieries byzantines anciennes découvertes au Caucase septentrional», *Bulletin du Centre International d'études des textiles anciens*, Lyon, XXIV, 1966, p. 12—13, 19—26; А. А. Иерусалимская, «О северокавказском шелковом пути в раннем средневековье», *СА*, 2, 1967, с. 69, рис. 10.

121 PLAQUE WITH ST JOHN THE BAPTIST. 11th century (?)

Ivory

The plaque of rectangular shape with a rounded top, is carved with a full-length figure of St John the Baptist in an attitude of prayer, standing under an arch supported by two columns. On the right of the spectator is an incised inscription in Greek: ΥΔΕΟΑΜΝΟC ΤΟΥ ΘΥ Ο ΑΙΡΩΝ ΤΗΝ ΑΜΑΡΤΙΑΝ ΤΟΥ ΚΟC-ΜΟΥ + "Behold the Lamb of God, which taketh away the sin of the world". (Cf. No. 110.)

The Hermitage. Inv. No. 303. Height 12.4 cm. Width 6.7 cm.
Acquisitions 1921. Formerly in the Botkin collection.

Considerable losses in the lower part; the feet and parts of the columns are missing; a number of cracks all over the surface.

For iconographic parallels, see Goldschmidt, Weitzmann, 2, Nr. 52.

LITERATURE: *Каталог собрания М. П. Боткина*, Спб., 1911, табл. 54; Мацулевич, *Византийские резные кости*, с. 51—72; Goldschmidt, Weitzmann, 1, Nr. 225, S. 80, Taf. XXIV; Банк, *Искусство Византии*, № 71, 72, с. 122, 125, 128.

122 PLAQUE WITH CHRIST CROWNING THE EMPEROR CONSTANTINE VII. Mid-10th century

Ivory

The plaque, probably the decoration of a book cover, bears a representation of Christ crowning the Emperor Constantine VII standing before him in an attitude of prayer. Above the head of the Emperor, and in the space between the figures, is an inscription reading: ΚΩΝCΤΑΝΤΙΝΟC ΕΝ ΘΩ ΑΥΤΟΚΡÁΤΩΡ ΒΑCΙΛΕΥC ΡΩΜΑΙΩΗ (Constantine, by the will of God, Autocrat, Emperor of the Romans) and on either side of the figure of Christ, another one: IC XC.

The Pushkin Museum of Fine Arts. Inv. No. П 2 б. 329. Height 18.6 cm. Width 9.5 cm.

Acquisitions 1932. Formerly in the History Museum, Moscow. Comes from the collection of Count Uvarov who acquired it at Echmiadzin.

Considerable pieces are missing from both the sides, and from the lower edge. Down the figure of the Emperor runs a deep crack. A number of minor damages. Two round holes near the canopy.

For parallels, see Goldschmidt, Weitzmann, 2, Taf. XXIX, Nr. 73.

LITERATURE: P. Jurgenson, «Ein neues Denkmal des byzantinischen Porträts», *BZ*, 26, 1926, S. 78—80; Goldschmidt, Weitzmann, 2, Nr. 35, S. 35—36, Taf. XIV, Abb. 13; Beckwith, *Two Exhibitions*, pl. 338, fig. 9; *Masterpieces*, No. 63, p. 33; Talbot Rice, *The Art*, p. 313, pl. 96; Beckwith, *The Art*, pl. 67, fig. 80; Beckwith, *Early Christian and Byzantine Art*, p. 26, fig. 173; Weitzmann, *Studies*, p. 243, fig. 229; E. Kitzinger, "The Gregorian Reform and the Visual Arts. A Problem of Method", *Transactions of the Royal Historical Society*, 22, 1972, 5th series, p. 89, fig. 2; Weitzmann, *Catalogue*, p. 59, 63, pl. XXXVI, fig. 24; Constance Head, "Imperial Partners, Constantine VII and Romanus Lecapenes", *History Today*, XXII, 1972, No. 9, p. 625.

123—127 TRIPTYCH WITH THE FORTY MARTYRS AND WARRIOR SAINTS. Early 11th century

Ivory

The central panel of the triptych is carved with the scene of the martyrdom of the Forty Martyrs of Sebaste. Above is Christ enthroned in a *mandorla* supported by three angels on either side. An inscription in Greek reading: ΟΥ ΑΓΙΟΙ ΤΕCΑΡΑΚΟΝΤΑ (forty saints) is incised on the background. The side panels bear full-length figures of Warrior Saints disposed in two rows, each row containing two figures; on the left-hand leaf, Sts George and Theodore the Tyro (top row), and Sts Demetrius and Mercurius (bottom row); on the right-hand leaf, Sts Eustathios and Eustratios (top row), and Sts Theodore Stratelates and Procopius (bottom row). The name of each of the warrior saints is given in an inscriptions accompanying the figure. The shields of Sts Demetrius and Procopius, and the scabbard of St Theodore Stratelates, are decorated with inscriptions in imitation Arabic. The silver mount and the colouring (gold stars on a blue ground) were added at a later date. The reverse of the side leaves is ornamented with an engraved cross having rosettes at the intersection and at the extremities of the cross arms.
Some of the authorities assign the triptych to the 14th century. But the form of the imitation Arabic lettering points to a date no later than the 11th century.

The Hermitage. Inv. No. ω 299. Height 18.5 cm. Width (when unfolded) 24.2 cm.
Acquisitions 1928. Formerly in the Shuvalov collection.

A crack at the bottom of the right-hand leaf; the swords of Sts Demetrius and Theodore Stratelates, have the points missing.

For parallels, see Goldschmidt, Weitzmann, 2, Nr. 8 and Nr. 6 (from the point of view of style).

LITERATURE: Я. И. Смирнов, «Византийский складень графа П. П. Шувалова», *Художественные сокровища России*, 1902, 2, с. 285—293; K. Mijatev, «Les Quarante Martyrs, fragment de fresque à Vodoča (Macédoine)», *L'Art byzantin chez les Slaves*, I, 1930, p. 104; Goldschmidt, Weitzmann, 2, Nr. 9, S. 27, Taf. III; Банк, *Искусство Византии*, № 77—80, с. 122, 125, 128; O. Demus, "Two Palaeologian Mosaic Icons in the Dumbarton Oaks Collection", *DOP*, 14, 1960, p. 97, 103, fig. 13; D. Talbot Rice, "The Ivory of the Forty Martyrs at Berlin and the Art of the Twelfth Century", *Зборник Радова Византолошког Института*, VIII (*Mélanges G. Ostrogorsky*, 1), Београд, 1963, p. 275—279, fig. 2; *L'Art byzantin*, p. 164; G. C. Miles, "Byzantium and the Arabs: Relations in Crete and the Aegean Area", *DOP*, 18, 1964, p. 27, fig. 57; И. А. Мишакова, «Византийский резной складень в Государственном Эрмитаже», in: *Проблемы всеобщей истории*, М., 1976, с. 325—344.

128 PLAQUE WITH AN ANGEL. 11th century

Ivory

The plaque is rectangular in shape (probably from a casket?), and carved with a full-length figure of an angel (from the *Expulsion of Adam and Eve from Eden*?). The figure stands out in relief against a hollowed background with a margin like a moulded border.

The Hermitage. Inv. No. ω 260. Height 6.8 cm. Width 5.3 cm.
Acquisitions 1925. Formerly in the Stieglitz Museum, Leningrad. Purchased from Bois in Paris in 1883.

A piece is missing from the top part of the plaque to the right of the centre, the damage probably caused by the addition of a lock. There are six round holes for brads.

For related objects, see Goldschmidt, Weitzmann, 1, Nr. 69 c.

LITERATURE: Goldschmidt, Weitzmann, 1, Nr. 71, S. 50, Taf. LI; Банк, *Искусство Византии*, № 75 в, с. 122, 125, 128.

129 PLAQUE WITH THE FOUR SAINTS. 10th century

Ivory

The plaque is a leaf from a triptych. It is carved with four full-length figures disposed in two rows. The figures represent a beardless saint, St John the Baptist with a staff, and two more saints, each holding a book and a stylus (probably Sts Cosmas and Damian). The reverse shows a cross under a concha.

The Hermitage. Inv. No. ω 14. Height 11.4 cm. Width 5 cm.
Acquisitions 1885. Formerly in the Basilewsky collection.

The bottom edge has been glued on to the plaque. Part of the border is missing from the lower edge; there are small losses of ivory in the attributes; some holes; a crack.

For stylistic parallels, see Goldschmidt, Weitzmann, 2, Nr. 127.

LITERATURE: Goldschmidt, Weitzmann, 2, Nr. 128, S. 61, Taf. XLVI; Банк, *Искусство Византии*, № 75 a, c. 122, 125, 128.

130—131 CASKET WITH *PUTTI*, CENTAURS AND ACTORS. 11th—12th centuries

Ivory, wood

The casket has a lid in the shape of a truncated pyramid. The plaques ornamenting the lid are carved with *putti* playing with a panther and a dog; a *putto* standing on his head in a basket; Heracles strangling the lion; two centaurs; two maenads dancing, several figures of musicians, etc. The sides decorated with rosette borders, are inlaid with rectangular plaques (three on long sides, and two on short ones) bearing similar figures. The central panel on the lid is enclosed in an ornamental border; the narrow band between it and the canting sides is also carved with ornamental motifs.

The Hermitage. Inv. No. ω 20. Height 12.0 cm. Length 28.5 cm. Width 19.8 cm.
Acquisitions 1885. Formerly in the Basilewsky collection.

Angle fishplates covered with gilding and hinges are later additions. Part of the narrow ornamental band is missing, as well as a piece from the lid, another from the lower edge of one of the long sides, etc. Cracks in a number of plaques. The wooden framework and the canvas lining inside the casket are modern.

The closest parallel is provided by the casket in the Novgorod Museum Zone (Н. В. Покровский, *Древняя Софийская ризница в Новгороде*, М., 1913, с. 102—108, табл. XV). See also Goldschmidt, Weitzmann, 1, Nr. 47, S. 41, Taf. XXVI.

LITERATURE: Darcel, Basilewsky, p. 13, N° 49, pl. VIII; Goldschmidt, Weitzmann, 1, Nr. 48, S. 41—42, Taf. XXVII, XXVIII; Банк, *Искусство Византии*, № 73, c. 122, 125, 128; Dekan, *Herkunft und Ethnizität*, Abb. 128.

132 CASKET WITH *PUTTI*, MAENADS, AND FIGHTING SOLDIERS. 11th century

Ivory, wood

The casket has a flat sliding lid decorated with *putti* playing with a panther and a dog, a nereid riding a hippocampus, a *putto* standing on his head in a basket, and a maenad dancing. The plaques on the sides show maenads, with various attributes; warriors fighting, characters of antique comedy, musicians, etc. The plaques are enclosed within rosette borders.

The Hermitage. Inv. No. ω 19. Height 11.2 cm. Length 41.2 cm. Width 17 cm.
Acquisitions 1885. Formerly in the Basilewsky collection. Comes from the Castellani collection.

The wooden framework is modern, as well as the lock and the undecorated plaques put in to fill the gaps left by the missing ones; there are cracks.

For related objects, see Goldschmidt, Weitzmann, 1, Nr. 47—49, also 40c, 21a, 31b.

LITERATURE: *Catalogue des objets d'art... Vente à Rome, Palais Castellani*, v. 2, 1884, N° 572; Goldschmidt, Weitzmann, 1, Nr. 51, S. 42—43, Taf. XXXII.

133 CASKET WITH SCENES FROM THE LIFE OF ADAM AND EVE. 11th century

Ivory, wood

The casket has a sliding lid with the Creation of Adam, the Creation of Eve, and the Murder of Abel. The front bears two scenes: the Temptation, or the Fall; and Adam Delving the Soil. On the sides are Plutos, the Sorrow of Adam and Eve; Adam at the Forge, and Eve Blowing the Fire with Bellows. The scenes are decorated with rosette borders. The top edge and the lid are decorated with bands of interlaced ribbons, resembling the guilloche device. The lid is bordered with stylized plant ornament. The scenes have accompanying inscriptions: ΑΔΑΜ ΥΠΝΟCΑC; ΕΥΑ ΕΝΑΞΕΛΘΕΝ ΕΙC ΤΟ ΠΛΕΥΡΑ ΑΥΤΟΥ; Ο ΠΛΟΥΤΟC; ΚΑΗ. ΦΟΝΕΥΗ ΤΟΝ ΑΒΕΛ; IC XC; ΑΔΑΜ.

The plaques bear Greek letters on the back: B on the central one, and Ψ on the front plaque with the representation of Adam.

The Hermitage. Inv. No. ω 17. Height 12.7 cm. Length 46.5 cm. Width 19.3 cm.
Acquisitions 1885. Formerly in the Basilewsky collection. Before 1874 in the Castellani collection.

The missing plaques in the long sides have been replaced by new undecorated ones; some of the ornamental plaques, the ones in a lighter ivory, are also modern. Most of the gilding is gone.

For parallels, see Goldschmidt, Weitzmann, 1, Nr. 67; *L'Art byzantin*, p. 157, N° 43.

LITERATURE: Goldschmidt, Weitzmann, 1, Nr. 68, S. 49—50, Taf. XLVIII, XLIX; Банк, *Искусство Византии*, № 76, с. 122, 125, 128.

134 CASKET WITH RIDERS AND GLADIATORS. 11th—12th centuries

Ivory, wood

The casket has a lid in the shape of a truncated pyramid, and rests on a low base. The central plaque of the lid is decorated with palmettes in medallions; the side plaques, with gladiators and ornamental designs. The body of the casket is inlaid with plaques showing warriors and riders; each side is bordered by an ornamental band consisting of roundels with human heads in profile, alternating with roundels containing rosettes.

The Hermitage. Inv. No. ω 18. Height 19.5 cm. Length 32.5 cm. Width 18.6 cm.
Acquisitions 1885. Formerly in the Basilewsky collection.

Part of the border and a piece from a triangular plaque on the lid are missing, as well as bits of the bottom ornamental band. Some of the plaques are split. Small losses of ivory.

In the opinion of Weitzmann, most of the plaques (e.g., the plaque with two warriors on the front, the riders on the left side, etc.) have been restored in modern times, the surviving details from the original scenes being incorporated in their composition.

LITERATURE: Darcel, Basilewsky, p. 39, N° 50; Goldschmidt, Weitzmann, 1, Nr. 98, S. 56, Taf. LVI, LVII; Банк, *Искусство Византии*, № 74, с. 122, 125, 128; Dekan, *Antropomorfné motivy*, s. 69, obr. 4.

135 CASKET WITH FIGURES OF WARRIORS, ACTORS, ETC. 11th—12th centuries

Ivory, wood

The casket has a flat sliding lid with Heracles strangling the lion, naked warriors, an enthroned deity, and Alexander the Great (?). The front bears some figures of warriors carrying spears and shields, musicians, and a *putto* riding a dolphin. The plaques on the sides show a group of two warriors (right) and part of a fishing scene (left). The bands under the lid are ornamented with vine scrolls.

The Hermitage. Inv. No. ω 21. Height 11.5 cm. Length 37 cm. Width 15 cm.
Acquisitions 1885. Formerly in the Basilewsky collection. Before 1879 in the Castellani collection.

Some plaques from the back have been lost; two ornamental bands and parts of others are missing. The old lock has been replaced by a modern plaque engraved with a representation of the Virgin (17th—18th centuries).
Goldschmidt, Weitzmann, 1, Nr. 43 b, 26 f, 26 a, 31 c, 8 d, 12 d, 41 b, 21 a.

LITERATURE: *Catalogue des objets d'art... Vente à Rome, Palais Castellani*, v. 2, 1884, N° 573; Goldschmidt, Weitzmann, 1, Nr. 44, S. 40, Taf. XXV.

136—139 DIPTYCH WITH THE TWELVE FEASTS OF THE CHURCH. 10th—11th centuries

Ivory

The diptych has a rounded top; the leaves bear twelve scenes of the Feasts of the Church disposed in three rows, four scenes in a row, illustrating the Annunciation, the Visitation, the Nativity, the Presentation of Christ in the Temple, the Baptism of Christ, the Transfiguration, the Entry into Jerusalem, the Crucifixion, the Resurrection, the Incredulity of St Thomas, the Ascension, the Pentecost. The scenes are accompanied by incised inscriptions: Ο ΧΕΡΕΤΙСΜ..; Ο ΑСΠΑСΜ..; Η ΓΕΝΙC.I.C; Η ΥΠΑΠΑΝ..; Η ΒΑΠΤΙC...; Η ΜΕΤΑΜΟΡΦΟCIC; Ο ΒΑΙΟΦΟΡΟC; Η CΤΑΥΡΟCIC; Η ΑΝΑCΤΑCIC; ΤΟΥ ΘΥΡΩΝ ΚΕΚΛΗCΜΕΝ..; Η ΑΝΑ......; Η ΠΕΝΤΗΚΟCΤΗ.

The Hermitage. Inv. No. ω 13. Height 26.4 cm. Width of a leaf 13.3 cm.
Acquisitions 1885. Formerly in the Basilewsky collection.

Traces of hinges which have been replaced by chains. On the top of each leaf is a round hole for suspension. Small pieces are broken from the edges; as well as diverse details in the scenes. Numerous minor cracks.

For iconographic parallels, see G. et M. Sotiriou, *Icônes du Mont Sinaï*, t. 1, Athènes, 1956, pl. 39, 40; Кондаков, *Памятники*, с. 204, рис. 82.

LITERATURE: Darcel, Basilewsky, p. 20—21, N° 60; Schlumberger, *L'Epopée*, 1, p. 617; Goldschmidt, Weitzmann, 2, Nr. 122, S. 60, Taf. XLV; H. Hallensleben, *Die Malerschule des Königs Milutin*, Giessen, 1963, S. 41—42.

140 PLAQUE WITH SIX OF THE TWELVE FEASTS OF THE CHURCH. 10th—11th centuries

Ivory

The plaque, rectangular in shape, bears the Annunciation, the Visitation, the Nativity of Christ, the Presentation in the Temple, the Baptism of Christ, and the Raising of Lazarus. To judge by the absence of any traces of hinges, the plaque must have been one of two companion icons rather than a leaf of a diptych.
The reverse bears an inscription in German and date, 1631; the inscription refers to the plaque being a gift from a husband to his wife.

The Hermitage. Inv. No. ω 25. Height 14.7 cm. Width 10 cm.
Acquisitions 1885. Formerly in the Basilewsky collection.

The bottom left corner broken away and restored. Small losses of ivory; cracks.

For stylistic parallels, see Goldschmidt, Weitzmann, 2, Nr. 127.

LITERATURE: Darcel, Basilewsky, p. 19, N° 57; Goldschmidt, Weitzmann, 2, Nr. 59, S. 43, Taf. XXIII.

141—142 COMB WITH A PEACOCK, AND HERACLES (SAMSON ?) AND THE LION. 11th century

Ivory

The comb is decorated on both sides. On one side is a peacock shown frontally, with the tail spread out, in scrolls of foliage; at his feet are a hare and a dog. On the other side is a tree, with a man carrying a spear and a shield to the left of it; and a group of Heracles, or Samson, and the lion, to the right.

The Hermitage. Inv. No. $\frac{\text{БД 51}}{\text{С 11 1383}}$. Height 12 cm. Width 8.5 cm. Maximum thickness 1.5 cm.

Acquisitions 1952. Found in 1951 during the excavations at Belaya Vezha (Sarkel).

Part of the edge is ornamented with two double interlaced bands; a considerable number of teeth on the thick side are missing. A piece is missing from the background above the lion. The relief is worn.

For related objects, see Peter Lasko, "The Comb of St Cuthbert", in: *The Relics of Saint Cuthbert, Dorham Cathedral*, 1956, pl. XX—XXII; А. В. Банк, «Гребень из Саркела — Белой Вежи», МИА, 75, 1959, с. 333—339, рис. 7—9.

LITERATURE: М. И. Артамонов, «Саркел — Белая Вежа», *МИА*, 62, 1958, с. 74—75, рис. 51, *2*; А. В. Банк, «Гребень из Саркела — Белой Вежи», *МИА*, 75, 1959, с. 333—339; Артамонов, *История хазар*, с. 374; Т. Б. Вирсаладзе, «Фресковая роспись в церкви Архангелов села Земо-Крихи», *Ars Georgica*, 1963, 6, с. 159; В. П. Даркевич, «О некоторых византийских мотивах в древнерусской скульптуре», in: *Славяне и Русь*, М., 1968, с. 413; Даркевич, *Светское искусство Византии*, с. 204—205, 276, ил. 325, 398.

143 PLAQUE WITH THE CRUCIFIXION. 11th century (?)

Ivory

The plaque is rectangular (probably a leaf from a book cover), showing the Crucifixion enclosed within a border of vertical leaves. The scene is of a rather complicated narrative character, with a building in the background, and in the foreground, the figures of Adam and Eve (on the left) and David and Solomon (on the right) rising from their coffins. Above the heads of the angels are traces of an inscription: Η ΣΤΑΥΡΩΣΙΣ. The gilding on the haloes is of later date than the work itself.

The Hermitage. Inv. No. ω 26. Height 19.2 cm. Width 12.8 cm.
Acquisitions 1885. Formerly in the Basilewsky collection.

Some of the details are missing: the spear of Longinus, the hands of the angels, the crook, and others.

The closest parallel is the companion plaque (No. 144). For other parallels, see *Sammlung E. und F. Kofler-Gruninger. Luzern Kunsthaus*, Zürich, 1964, S. 145.

LITERATURE: Goldschmidt, Weitzmann, 2, Nr. 201, S. 74, Taf. LXVI.

144 PLAQUE WITH THE DORMITION. 11th century (?)

Ivory

The plaque is rectangular in shape (in all probability, a leaf from a book cover) showing the Dormition scene enclosed within a border of vertical leaves. There is an architectural background. The figure of Christ is flanked by two objects resembling candlesticks. Two of the mourners wear episcopal robes and omophorions decorated with crosses. In the top corners are two angels, confronted.

The Hermitage. Inv. No. ω 243. Height 19.2 cm. Width 12.8 cm.
Acquisitions 1885. Formerly in the Basilewsky collection.

Small cracks; some of the details missing.

The plaque is a companion piece to No. 143. For parallels, see *Sammlung E. und F. Kofler-Gruninger. Luzern Kunsthaus*, Zürich, 1964, S. 57.

LITERATURE: Goldschmidt, Weitzmann, 2, Nr. 202, S. 74, Taf. LXVI.

145—146 ICON OF ST DEMETRIUS. 11th century (frame, 14th century)

Steatite, silver gilt

The icon carved in steatite is rectangular is shape, with a rounded top. St Demetrius holds a raised sword in his right hand, and the reins of his horse, in his left; there is a round shield strapped behind his left shoulder. On either side of the head is an engraved inscription: Ο ΑΓ . . . ΔΗΜΗΤΡΙΟϹ (probably of later date). The reverse is undecorated.

The *repoussé* frame, mounted on wood, is made up of several parts evidently dating from different periods. Rectangles set against the background of interlaced scrolls bear busts of Christ and the archangels Michael and Gabriel in the upper part; full-length figures of Sts John Chrysostom and Basil, at the sides; and half-figures of Sts Mercurius, Nicetas and Artemius, in the lower portion of the frame. The innermost edge of the frame is decorated with interlaced bands and with bead and reel ornament. The plaques above and below the rectangles in the side margins differ in technique and ornamentation from the rest of the frame.

The Kremlin Armoury. Inv. No. 16625. Height (without the mount) 11.8 cm; width 9.7 cm. Height (in the mount) 31.4 cm; width 26.4 cm.
Acquisitions 1926. Formerly in the Museum of Ceramics and Glass at Kuskovo. Before 1912 in the Moscow Kremlin. According to tradition, the icon was owned by Dmitry Donskoy who received it as a gift from the emperor of Byzantium.

Chipped in the lower part. Corners of the mount damaged. Slight traces of gilding remain.

Somewhat more conventionalized representations of Warrior Saints appear in the steatite icon at the Museo Nazionale, Florence (*Masterpieces*, No. 154, p. 56) and also in the icon which once was at the Museé Archéologique, Angers (Schlumberger, *L'Epopée*, 2, p. 132).

LITERATURE: А. Успенский, *Записные книги и бумаги старинных дворцовых приказов*, М., 1906, с. 3; M. Alpatoff, «Eine Byzantinische Reliefikone des Hl. Demetrios in Moskau», *Belvedere*, 14, 1929, S. 25—36; М. В. Алпатов, *Всеобщая история искусств*, т. 1, М.—Л., 1948, с. 232, рис. 135; *Государственная Оружейная палата*, М., 1958, № 159; *По Кремлю. Краткий путеводитель*, М., 1960, с. 193; H. Wentzel, «Die Kamee mit dem III. Georg im Schloß zu Windsor», *Festschrift Fr. Gerke*, Baden-Baden, 1962, S. 108, Abb. 8; Писарская, *Памятники*, с. 24—25, табл. XLII—XLIII; М. В. Алпатов, «Рельеф Димитрия Солунского в Оружейной палате», in: *Этюды по истории русского искусства*, т. 1, М., 1967, с. 52, ил. 29; *Propyläen Kunstgeschichte*, Abb. 100, S. 202; Bank, *Les Stéatites*, p. 366; Grabar, *Les Revêtements*, N° 46, p. 74, fig. 101; Даркевич, *Светское искусство Византии*, с. 147—148, ил. 209.

147 ICON OF THE DEESIS AND SAINTS. 12th century

Steatite, gilding

The plaque has a rounded top. The panel, divided into three horizontal rows, is hollowed. In the top row is the Deesis, or Christ between the Virgin and St John; in the corners are two cherubs. In the middle row are five saints: Sts Gregory the Theologian, John Chrysostom, Basil, Nicholas and Epiphanius. In the bottom row are Sts Cosmas, Demetrius, George, Theodore and Damian. The figures at either end have scrolls in their hands; those in the middle have crosses. The accompanying inscriptions in Greek give the names of the saints.

The Hermitage. Inv. No. ω 304. Height 18.8 cm. Width 12.2 cm.
Acquisitions 1921. Formerly in the Botkin collection.

The plaque has been restored from a number of fragments. The cherub in the right corner, the top right corner of the middle row, and the face of St Cosmas are missing; the figure of St John the Baptist is almost entirely lost. The haloes of Sts Basil, Nicholas, and Demetrius are cracked. The gilding is badly worn.

The saints in the steatite icon in the Louvre collection shows some features in common with our piece (Coche de la Ferté, *L'Antiquité*, N° 60, p. 60—61, 113).

LITERATURE: N. Izmajlov, «Une Stéatite byzantine du Musée de Chersonèse», *L'Art byzantin chez les Slaves*, II, 1932, p. 47; Banck, *Monuments* (*X*e—*XII*e *s.*), p. 132, fig. 5; Bank, *Quelques problèmes*, p. 238; Bank, *Les Stéatites*, p. 362; Weitzmann, *Catalogue*, p. 97.

148 ICON OF THE CRUCIFIXION AND ENTOMBMENT. 11th—12th centuries

Steatite, gilding

The panel is hollowed leaving a narrow margin. Above is the Crucifixion with two figures on either side facing the cross, and two half-figures of angels in the top corners. Below is the Entombment with the Virgin, Sts John, Nicodemus and Joseph bending over Christ's body; Martha and Mary behind some hills; and in the segment above, four half-figures of angels in the sky. The background is incised with Greek and later Latin inscriptions giving the names of the personages.

The Hermitage. Inv. No. ω 31. Height 24.4 cm. Width 15.5 cm.
Acquisitions 1885. Formerly in the Basilewsky collection.

The panel is broken into five parts. A slanting crack runs the whole length of the icon. Small losses of stone at the lower edge and in the left margin. The Greek inscriptions considerably worn, and the gilding rubbed off.

LITERATURE: Банк, *Искусство Византии*, № 83, с. 122, 123, 125, 128; Banck, *Monuments* (*X*e—*XII*e *s.*), p. 130—132, fig. 4; Bank, *Les Stéatites*, p. 371.

149 ICON OF STS THEODORE, GEORGE AND DEMETRIUS. 12th century

Steatite, gilding

Against a hollowed background bordered by two columns with capitals decorated with figures of birds, under an arch, are full-length figures of the three warriors: St Theodore on the left of the spectator, St George in the centre, and St Demetrius on the right. In the upper corners are busts of archangels in medallions against a background filled with engraved plant scrolls. The haloes of the warriors are adorned with ornamental designs. Above, in a segment of the sky in the centre, is a half-figure of Christ holding martyrs' crowns.

The Chersonese Museum. Inv. No. 84/36445. Height 17.5 cm. Width 13.4 cm.
Acquisitions 1956. Found at Chersonese in the same year.

The icon is restored from a number of fragments; there are losses of stone, mainly in the right part at the lower edge, and also in the middle (part of the figure of St Theodore, etc.). Hardly any gilding remains.

The icon of the Annunciation discovered at Chersonese should be compared (Г. Д. Белов, С. Ф. Стржелецкий, «Кварталы XV и XVI в раскопках в Херсонесе в 1937 г.», *МИА*, 34, 1954, с. 93, рис. 58); also No. 152, the icon of St Pantaleon in the Vatican Museum (Muñoz, p. 120—123, fig. 85) and the icon of Three Warrior Saints in Trnovo (Bank, *Les Stéatites*, p. 367, fig. 3).

LITERATURE: Г. Д. Белов, «Шиферная икона из Херсонеса», *СА*, 1960, 2, с. 257—263; Bank, *Quelques monuments*, p. 16—18, fig. 5; Bank, *Quelques problèmes*, p. 237, pl. 1; Bank, *Les Stéatites*, p. 367—368; Weitzmann, *Catalogue*, p. 95—96, 98; Даркевич, *Светское искусство Византии*, с. 283, ил. 344.

150 ICON OF STS GEORGE AND DEMETRIUS. 11th—12th centuries

Dark schist, gilding

Against a hollowed background enclosed in margins engraved with a continuous ornamental design, are two figures: St Demetrius drawing his sword from the sheath, on the left; and St George on the right. Each wears a long chiton, the so-called *sticharion*, a cloak and armour. Above, in the space between the figures, are inscriptions reading: ΟΑ . . . . ΔΗ . . . ΡΙΟ.; ΟΑ . . . . ΓΕΩΡΓ . . . .

The Hermitage. Inv. No. X 103. Height 19.9 cm. Width 14 cm.
Acquisitions 1895. Found at Chersonese in 1894.

The icon has been restored from a multitude of small fragments. Some pieces are lost, mainly from the background; the frame and the lower portion of the figure of St George have also suffered some damage. Very little gilding remains.

See the image of St Demetrius on a bottom of a serpentine vessel (А. В. Банк, «Два памятника мелкой пластики из Фессалоник», *ВВ*, 34, 1968, с. 265—268, рис. 2; *Il tesoro di San Marco*, 2, N. 74, tav. XII, p. 74).

LITERATURE: *ОАК за 1894 г.*, 1896, с. 55—56, рис. 74; Schlumberger, *L'Epopée*, 1, p. 13; П. Н. Милюков, «Христианские древности Западной Македонии», *ИРАИК*, IV, 1899, примеч. к с. 57, 61, 71—72; Кондаков, *Памятники*, с. 204; H. Gabelentz, *Mittelalterliche Plastik in Venedig*, Leipzig, 1903, S. 142; P. Albert Kuhm, *Allgemeine Kunstgeschichte*, Bd. 2, New York, 1909, S. 298, Fig. 241; С. Гайдин, «Резная шиферная икона св. Димитрия и Георгия», *Сборник Государственного Эрмитажа*, II, 1923, с. 31—42, табл. II; Лихачев, *Материалы*, 1, с. 77, примеч.; Bank, *Quelques monuments*, p. 18; Bank, *Quelques problèmes*, p. 239, pl. 4; А. В. Банк, «Два памятника мелкой пластики из Фессалоник», *ВВ*, 34, 1968, с. 265—268, рис. 1, 3; Bank, *Les Stéatites*, p. 369; Даркевич, *Светское искусство Византии*, с. 280.

151 ICON OF THE ANNUNCIATION. 12th century

Steatite, gilding

The panel is hollowed, leaving a scalloped arch decorated with vertical leaves and supported by twisted columns. Mary holds the distaff and the yarn; the archangel has a staff in his left hand. In the space between the figures is a stylized tree growing in a tub. Under the segment of the sky is the inscription ΧΕΡΕΤΙϹΜΟϹ; on the right, near the column, ΘΥ. The haloes, the throne and the tub are ornamented with engraved designs.

The Chersonese Museum. Inv. No. 3073/37. Height 13.4 cm. Maximum width 10.7 cm.
Acquisitions 1937. Found at Chersonese in the same year.

Restored from several pieces. Considerable damage by fire. The left side missing. The haloes and the *maphorion* of the Virgin bear some slight traces of gilding.

In general design and ornamentation, No. 149 should be compared. The closest parallel is provided by the icon in the Museum of Benaki, Athens (Bank, *Les Stéatites*, p. 373—374, fig. 5).

LITERATURE: Г. Д. Белов, С. Ф. Стржелецкий, «Кварталы XV—XVI в раскопках в Херсонесе в 1937 г.», *МИА*, 34, 1953, с. 93, рис. 58; Bank, *Quelques monuments*, p. 17, fig. 6; Bank, *Les Stéatites*, p. 368, 373—374, fig. 4; Даркевич, *Светское искусство Византии*, с. 282.

152 ICON OF ST DEMETRIUS OR ST GEORGE. 11th century

Steatite

The figure of the young warrior saint is presented against a slightly hollowed background. Over his tunic the saint wears a coat-of-mail. The cuffs and the hem of the tunic are bordered with ornamentation. The absence of an inscription makes precise identification a matter of some difficulty; but the characteristic shape of the ears suggests St Demetrius rather than St George.

The Chersonese Museum. Inv. No. 34 285/32. Maximum height 8 cm. Maximum width 6.1 cm. Acquisitions 1932. Found at Chersonese in the same year.

The lower portion of the figure and of the shield is missing, as well as a considerable part of the left side. Hardly any traces of gilding remain. The background is damaged on the surface.

The icon at Vatopedi on Mount Athos should be compared (А. В. Банк, «Рельеф с изображением Георгия из собрания Эрмитажа», in: *Исследования по истории культуры народов Востока*, М.—Л., 1960, с. 23—24, рис. 2; F. Dölger, *Mönchsland. Athos*, München, 1943, S. 161, Abb. 85).

LITERATURE: Г. Д. Белов, «Раскопки в северной части Херсонеса в 1931—1933 гг.», *МИА*, 4, 1941, с. 246, рис. 79; Bank, *Quelques monuments*, p. 15—16, fig. 4; Даркевич, *Светское искусство Византии*, с. 281.

153 CHALICE. 10th—11th centuries

Agate, gold, rubies. The mounting is modern

The vase, cone-shaped, with a short stem, is mounted in gold. A network formed of curves decorates the sides: the points where the curves converge are marked with sexfoil flowers (rosettes) set with small rubies. Along the rim are the Greek letters: + ΒΒΠΔΚΘΤΞΤΗ. The meaning of the inscription is obscure.

The Hermitage. Inv. No. ω 278. Height 10.7 cm. Diameter 13.5 cm.
Acquisitions 1926. Formerly in the Stroganov collection.

Restored: the missing rosettes replaced (brass instead of the original gold); the empty mounting in the base, which used to contain a garnet, filled with an imitation jewel (of red paste).

In spite of differences in size and decoration, the vases at the Treasury of St Mark's show an affinity with our piece in their general character (*Il Tesoro di San Marco*, 2, N. 40, p. 58—59; N. 41, p. 56—60, tav.; N. 43, 44, p. 61—62, tav. XLV—XLVI; N. 49, p. 63—64, tav. XLVIII, XLIX; N. 51, p. 64—65, tav. I.

LITERATURE: Толстой, Кондаков, *Русские древности*, V, с. 41; Банк, *Искусство Византии*, № 82, с. 122, 125, 128; *Il Tesoro di San Marco*, 2, p. 55, 57, tav. LXXXVIII.

154 CAMEO WITH CHRIST. 10th—11th centuries

Heliotrope

The cameo is rectangular in shape, with a rounded top; it is carved with a full-length figure of Christ in high relief; his right arm at his breast, raised in a gesture of blessing; his left holding a book. His feet rest upon a dais. On either side of the nimbus is the incised inscription IC XC. The mounting, probably a later addition, of non-Byzantine work, is of gold set with emeralds, almandines and agates in cabochon mounts. The reverse is plain. In the lower part of the mounting is an inscription in Russian referring to the weight.

The Kremlin Armoury. Inv. No. 186/Бл. 12×8.2 cm (with the mounting), 8.8×5 cm (without the mounting). Formerly in the Annunciation Cathedral of the Moscow Kremlin.
Slightly chipped.
The cameo from the collection of the Victoria and Albert Museum, London, should be compared (*Masterpieces*, No. 84, p. 38; Beckwith, *The Art*, fig. 102); see also Nos. 159, 167.

LITERATURE: Писарская, *Памятники*, с. 20, табл. XXVIII; Банк, *Покушај класификације*, стр. 5; Даркевич, *Светское искусство Византии*, с. 286.

155—156 CAMEO WITH THE VIRGIN AND CHILD. 11th—12th centuries

Lapis-lazuli, silver gilt

The cameo is rectangular in shape, with a rounded top in the form of a three-lobed arch. It displays an enthroned Virgin in low relief, her head slightly turned towards the Child seated on her left arm. The throne and the garments of Mary are covered with hollowed-out patterns for inlaid decoration. The incised inscription on the throne reads ΜΡ ΘΥ. The silver mounting adorned with pearls and a sapphire is of Russian work, of some later date, and bears an inscription referring to Euphimius, Bishop of Novgorod in the 15th century.

The Kremlin Armoury. Inv. No. 226/Бл. 11.5×7.8 cm (with the mounting), 7×5.5 cm (without the mounting).
Formerly in the Annunciation Cathedral of the Moscow Kremlin.

There is a transverse crack from which bits of stone are missing, in the right-hand part.

LITERATURE: Писарская, *Памятники*, с. 22, табл. XXXII, XXXIII; М. М. Постникова-Лосева, Т. Н. Протасьева, «Лицевое Евангелье Успенского собора как памятник древнерусского искусства первой трети XV века», in: *Древнерусское искусство XV— начала XVI века*, М., 1963, с. 161; Банк, *Покушај класификације*, стр. 9; Даркевич, *Светское искусство Византии*, с. 287.

157—158 CAMEO WITH ST NICHOLAS. 11th century

Two-layered agate, silver

The oval cameo bears a half-figure of St Nicholas in low relief. The saint has a book in his left hand, and his right hand is raised in blessing. To the right and left of the bust runs an incised inscription bearing the name of the saint: ΑΓΙΟ. Η. ΚΟΛ... The silver mounting, shaped like a cross with rounded ends, combined with a square, is set with sapphires, almandines and pearls. The reverse is worked in *repoussé* with a bust of St Spirydon in a roundel; his name is written on either side of his head: Ο ΑΓΙΟC CΠΥΡΙΔΟΝ. The ends of the cross arms and the corners of the square are decorated with plant motifs.

The date of the mounting has not yet been established. In all probability it was manufactured later than the cameo, maybe in the 12th century. A Russian provenance is not unlikely.

The Kremlin Armoury. Inv. No. 19005. 6×4.5 cm (with the mounting), 3×2.5 cm (without the mounting). Acquisitions 1931. Comes from Kostroma.

The cameo is in a good condition.

The representation of St Basil (No. 162) may be compared; see also a cameo with St Nicholas at the Vladimir-Suzdal Museum Zone (Пуцко, *Несколько византийских камей*, с. 129—131, рис. 12).

LITERATURE: *Государственная Оружейная палата*, М., 1958, рис. 131; Marvin C. Ross, "Three Byzantine Cameos", *Greek, Roman and Byzantine Studies*, Cambridge, Mass., 1960, 3, p. 43—45; Banck, «Nouveaux travaux concernant la glyptique byzantine», *BS*, XXIII/I, 1962, p. 58—59; Писарская, *Памятники*, с. 21, табл. XXXI; Пуцко, *Несколько византийских камей*, с. 129—131, рис. 12; Даркевич, *Светское искусство Византии*, с. 290.

159—160 CAMEO WITH CHRIST. 10th—11th centuries

Lapis-lazuli, gold

The cameo rectangular in shape, with a rounded top, is carved in high relief. It bears Christ upon a dais, holding a book in his left hand, and blessing with his right. The limbs in the *nimbus cruciger* and the Gospels cover are inlaid with gold dots. On either side of the nimbus is the incised inscription IC XC. The reverse bears a cross in low relief; the cross arms and the shaft terminate in a trefoil design. On either side of the cross is the inscription IC XC NH KA (Jesus Christ conquers). The gold mounting, of later date, is of Russian work.

The Kremlin Armoury. Inv. No. 187/Бл. 15×7.8 cm (with the mounting), 11.5×7 cm (without the mounting).
Formerly in the Annunciation Cathedral of the Moscow Kremlin.

Losses of stone in the area of the dais and other places. A crack on the reverse.

Comparable is the cameo in the collection of the Victoria and Albert Museum, London (both sides) (*Masterpieces*, No. 84, p. 38; Beckwith, *The Art*, fig. 102). See also the cameo at Nos. 154, 167.

LITERATURE: Писарская, *Памятники*, с. 20—21, табл. XXXIX; Банк, *Покушај класификације*, стр. 5; Даркевич, *Светское искусство Византии*, с. 286—287.

161 CAMEO WITH CHRIST ENTHRONED. Late 11th—early 12th centuries

Heliotrope

The cameo is oval, of a deep green variegated with a considerable quantity of red. Christ is carved in low relief; he is seated on a throne without a back. His right hand is raised in blessing, with his left hand Christ supports an open book which stands upright on his lap. His feet rest on a footstool. On either side of the nimbus is the inscription IC XC. The reverse is plain.

The Hermitage. Inv. No. ω 1208. 3.3×2.7 cm.
Acquisitions 1961. Formerly in a private collection.

Slightly chipped round the edge.

For related objects, see А. Банк, «Византийская камея с изображением Христа на троне», *Зборник Радова Византолошког Института*, XIII (*Mélanges G. Ostrogorsky*, 1), Београд, 1963, стр. 39—42.

LITERATURE: А. Банк, «Византийская камея с изображением Христа на троне», *Зборник Радова Византолошког Института*, VIII (*Mélanges G. Ostrogorsky*, 1), Београд, 1963, стр. 39—42; Банк, *Покушај класификације*, стр. 7.

162 CAMEO WITH ST BASIL. 10th century

Blue chalcedony

The cameo is oval, with a bust of St Basil executed in high relief, a book in his left hand, his right hand raised in blessing. On either side of the bust is an incised inscription indicating the name of the saint: Ο Α . . . C ΒΑCΙΛΕΙΟC. The reverse is plain.

The Hermitage. Inv. No. ω 362. 2.1×1.6 cm.
Acquired in the second half of the 18th century.

Slightly chipped round the edge.

The cameo with Christ in the Ross catalogue (1, No. 120, p. 99—100) shows a distant resemblance with our piece; see also the cameo with St John at Bamberg (H. Wentzel, «Datierte und datierbare byzantinische Kameen», *Festschrift Fr. Winkler*, Berlin, 1959, S. 19, Abb. 9) and the cameo with Christ as a priest at the Novgorod Museum Zone (Пуцко, *Несколько византийских камей*, с. 117—118, рис. 2, 3).

LITERATURE: *Catalogue des pierres gravées*, p. 169, N° 1458; Банк, *Искусство Византии*, № 70 в, с. 122, 128; Банк, *Несколько византийских камей*, с. 213—214, табл. II, 1, 3 а; Banck, *Monuments* (X^e—XIIe *s.*), p. 135, fig. 6; Ross, *Catalogue*, 1, p. 100; Пуцко, *Несколько византийских камей*, с. 118.

163 CAMEO WITH STS GEORGE AND DEMETRIUS. 10th century

Blue chalcedony

The cameo is roughly oval in shape, with full-length figures of Sts George and Demetrius carved in relief, represented frontally, in the type of the martyrs; each saint wears a chiton and a cloak fastened with fibula on the right shoulder, and holds a small cross in his right hand. On either side of each is a lightly incised inscription; one reads ΑΓ. ΟС ΓΕΩΡΓΙΟС, the other, ΑΓ. ΟС ΔΗΜΗ. ΡΙΟС. The figures are done in very high relief, the heads almost in the round. The reverse bears an incised representation of a mounted warrior spearing a dragon (a later addition).

The Hermitage. Inv. No. ω 361. 2.7×2 cm.
Acquired in the second half of the 18th century.

Slightly chipped along the left side.

Closely related to our piece is the cameo in the collection of the London Museum, No. A. 14113 (H. Wentzel, «Die Kamee mit dem Hl. Georg im Schloß zu Windsor», in: *Festschrift Fr. Gerke*, Baden-Baden, 1962, S. 104, Abb. 2). For objects showing a more distant resemblance, see also: Пуцко, *Несколько византийских камей*, с. 131—132, рис. 13; Wentzel, *Die byzantinische Kameen in Kassel*, Abb. 87.

LITERATURE: Банк, *Несколько византийских камей*, с. 214—215, табл. II, 2, 3 б; Банк, *Искусство Византии*, № 70 б, с. 122, 125, 128; Банк, *Геммы — стеатиты — моливдовулы*, с. 46—52; Пуцко, *Несколько византийских камей*, с. 130.

164—165 CAMEO WITH A BUST OF CHRIST. Early 11th century

Heliotrope

The cameo is oval, carved with a bust of Christ Eleimon in relief, holding a book to his breast with the left hand, the right hand open palm outward. On either side of the bust is an inscription reading: ΙС ХС Ο ΕΛΕΗΜΩΗ (Jesus Christ the Merciful). The reverse bears an inscription in five lines which reads: X . . . . Ε Ο ΘΕΟС Ο ΕΙС СΕ ΕΛΠΙΖΩΝ ΟΥΚ, ΑΠΟΤΥΓΧΑΝΕΙ (O Christ of our Lord, he that puts his trust in Thee shall not be disappointed).

The Hermitage. Inv. No. ω 353. 2.8×3 cm.
Acquired in the second half of the 18th century. Formerly in the collection of the Duke of Orleans.

Slightly chipped round the edge.

For related objects, see F. Eichler, E. Kris, *Die Kameen im Kunsthistorischen Museum*, Wien, 1927, Nr. 128, 595, Taf. 20; Банк, *Несколько византийских камей*, с. 210—213.

LITERATURE: *Catalogue des pierres gravées*, N° 1378, p. 158; Банк, *Несколько византийский камей*, с. 210—213, табл. 1, 3, 4; Банк, *Искусство Византии*, № 70 а, с. 122, 125, 128; Банк, *Покушај класификације*, стр. 7.

166 CAMEO WITH THE VIRGIN (companion piece to No. 167). 11th century

Green jasper

The cameo is rectangular in shape, with a rounded top; against a hollowed background is carved in low relief a full-length figure of the Virgin in the Orant attitude, slightly turning left. On either side of the figure is an inscription which reads МР ΘΥ. The reverse is plain.

The Hermitage. Inv. No. ω 358. Height 4.5 cm. Width 3.8 cm.
Acquired in the second half of the 18th century. Formerly in the collection of the Duke of Orleans.

Chipped on the left edge; small losses of stone from the background.

For related objects, see Dalton, *Catalogue*, No. 109, p. 17, pl. III; F. Mely, «Le Trésor de la Sacristie des Patriarches de Moscou», *Monuments Piot*, XII, p. 207—210, pl. XV, 1; Schlumberger, *L'Epopée*, 2, p. 73.

LITERATURE: *Catalogue des pierres gravées*, p. 169, N° 1458; Банк, *Несколько византийских камей*, с. 207—210, табл. I, 1; Банк, *Искусство Византии*, № 81 б, с. 122, 125, 128; Banck, *Monuments* (X^e—XIIe *s.*), p. 135, fig. 8; *L'Art byzantin*, p. 202; Банк, *Покушај класификације*, стр. 8.

167 CAMEO WITH CHRIST (companion piece to No. 166). 11th century

Green jasper

The cameo is rectangular in shape, with a rounded top. Against a hollowed background is carved in low relief a full-length figure of Christ, holding a book in his left hand, his right hand blessing. On either side of the nimbus is the inscription IC XC. The reverse is plain.

The Hermitage. Inv. No. ω 359. Height 4.5 cm. Width 3.8 cm.
Acquired in the second half of the 18th century.

Split in two places in the top part of the left side.

A cameo in the Victoria and Albert Museum, London, should be compared (*Masterpieces*, No. 84, p. 38; Beckwith, *The Art*, fig. 102); see also Nos. 154, 159; Schlumberger, *L'Epopée*, 2, p. 72.

LITERATURE: Банк, *Несколько византийских камей*, с. 207—210, табл. I, 2; Банк, *Искусство Византии*, № 81 а, с. 122, 125, 128; Banck, *Monuments* (X^e—XIIe *s.*), p. 135, fig. 7; Банк, *Покушај класификације*, стр. 5.

168—169 SEAL WITH TWO FIGURES IN IMPERIAL ROBES AND THE ASCENT OF ALEXANDER THE GREAT. 10th century

Lead

The seal bears two figures attired in imperial garments (Constantine and Helen?) and supporting a tall cross with a double traverse; in the other hand the figure on the right—and probably that on the left, too—holds an orb. Traces of Greek inscriptions are discernible. The reverse bears the Ascent of Alexander the Great: he is shown standing in a chariot drawn by two winged griffons, and holding in either hand a bar to which the bait is attached.

The Hermitage. Inv. No. M 4506. Diameter 2.5×2.7 cm.
Acquisitions 1931. Formerly in the Museum of the Russian Archaeological Institute, Constantinople.

Large pieces are missing from the top and the left side; the relief is worn.

The obverse finds parallels on coins of Leo VI and Constantine VII (911—912) (W. Wroth, *Catalogue of the Imperial Byzantine Coins in the British Museum*, v. 2, London, 1908, p. 445, pl. LI, 9) and on a gold ring (Ross, *Catalogue*, 2, No. 122, p. 87—88, pl. LXII).

LITERATURE: А. В. Банк, «Моливдовул с изображением полета Александра Македонского на небо», *ТОВЭ*, III, 1940, c. 181—194; D. Talbot Rice, "New Light on the Alfred Jewel", *The Antiquarium Journal*, XXXVI, p. 215; Coche de la Ferté, *Collection*, p. 35, fig. 26; Ross, *Catalogue*, 2, p. 87; A. Grabar, «Images de l'Ascension d'Alexandre en Italie et en Russie», in: Grabar, *L'Art de la fin de l'antiquité*, 1, p. 295—296; 3, pl. 66 a—b.

170 SEAL WITH THE ANNUNCIATION. 13th—14th centuries (?)

Lead

The Virgin (on the right) is shown standing, with the throne for the background. The inscription reads: ΧΑΙΡΕ . . . ΜΟϹ. The reverse bears an inscription in five lines reading: ΕΠΙϹΦΡΑΓΙ. ΖΟΙϹΗ ΧΑΡΑ ΤΟΝ ΑΓΓΕΛΩΝ ΤΟΥϹ ΑΓΓΕΛΟΥ ΚΑΙϹΑΡΟϹ ΜΙΧΑΗΛ ΛΟΓΟΥϹ (Seal. O Joy of the Angels, the words of the Angel of Caesar Michael). B. Panchenko advanced an opinion that the seal was owned by Michael, son of Andronicus Palaeologus (1282—1328). However, the lettering seems to point to an earlier period.

The Hermitage. Inv. No. M 4685. Diameter 3.7 cm.
Acquisitions 1931. Formerly in the Museum of the Russian Archaeological Institute, Constantinople.

Chipped round the edge.

LITERATURE: Панченко, *Каталог*, 8, с. 212—213, № 18, табл. XXI, 4.

171 SEAL OF THE CATHEDRAL OF HAGIA SOPHIA IN CONSTANTINOPLE. 11th century

Lead

This piece is a seal of the clergy of Hagia Sophia in Constantinople. The obverse bears the Emperor Justinian (left) represented as a Byzantine Emperor of the 11th and 12th centuries, and the Virgin (right), supporting between them a temple shown as a dome surmounted by a tall cross. In the intervening space is a Greek inscription: Η ΑΓΙΑ ϹΟΦΙΑ. The inscription round the edge reads: ΘΚΕΒΟΗΘΕΙ ΟΥϹΤΙΝΙΑΝΟΥ ΔΕϹΠ . . . (O Virgin, help Justinian our Lord). The reverse bears an inscription in six line referring to the ownership of the seal by the "most pious clergy of the Cathedral" (+ ΤΟΙϹΘΕΟ ϹΕΒΕϹΤΑ ΤΟΙ ϹΠΡΕϹ ΒΥΤΕΡΟΙϹ ΚΑΙΕΚΚΛΗ ϹΕΚΔΙΚΟϹ).

The Hermitage. Inv. No. M 8154. Diameter 7 cm.
Acquisitions 1938. Transferred from the Institute of Books, Documents and Letters, Leningrad, with the Likhachov collection. Purchased in Paris from Constantinopolitan antiquaries.

Chipped. The inscription on the obverse is imperfectly executed.

For parallels, see Schlumberger, *L'Epopée*, 1, p. 510; V. Laurent, *Le Corpus des sceaux de l'Empire Byzantin*, t. 5 (*L'Eglise*), Paris, 1963, Nos 113—114, p. 94—95, pl. 17, 18.

LITERATURE: Лихачев, *Моливдовулы*, текст к табл. LXXXI, 1; V. Laurent, «Bulletin de sigillographie byzantine», *Byzantion*, VI, 1931, p. 789 ; V. Laurent, *Le Corpus des sceaux de l'Empire Byzantin*, t. 5 (*L'Eglise*), Paris, 1963, N° 112, p. 90—93 (*Planches*, Paris, 1965, pl. XVI).

172 SEAL WITH THE VIRGIN AND SAINTS. 11th—12th centuries

Lead

The seal is round in shape. The obverse bears half-figures of the Virgin and Child; the inscription reads: ΜΡ ΘΥ. The reverse shows St Eustratios full length, surrounded by four busts of saints in medallions, among them St George (?); the others are not identified. The inscription in Greek reads: Ο ΑΓΙΟϹ ΕΥϹΤΡΑΤΙΟϹ and the one round the edge: . . . ΓΕΝΙΩΜ. ΤΡΟ . . . . . (Belongs to the Metropolitan Eugene).

The Hermitage. Inv. No. M 6202. Diameter 2.4 cm.

Acquisitions 1938. Transferred from the Institute of Books, Documents and Letters, Leningrad, with the Likhachov collection.

Chipped round the edge. Part of the inscription has been cut away.

For parallels, see Schlumberger, *Sigillographie*, p. 24.

LITERATURE: Лихачев, *Моливдовулы*, текст к табл. LVII, 13.

173 SEAL WITH DANIEL IN THE DEN OF LIONS. 11th—12th centuries

Lead

The seal is oval in shape, and bears the prophet Daniel, with two lions at his feet in an attitude of submission. The inscription on either side of the figure reads: Ο ΠΡΟΦΙΤΙC ΔΑΝΙΗΛ. The reverse bears a Greek inscription in seven lines: + CϒΓΚΡΙ. ΗCΚΡΙΤΑΤ. ΚΡΊCΗΓΡΙΓΟΡΙΩCΩ ΔΟϒΛ ΠΑΤΡΙ. ΑΜ. .ΩΗ-ΚΕΧΡΙ. ΜΕΝΩ (Seal of Gregory Doksapator).

The Hermitage. Inv. No. M 8191. 3×2.8 cm.
Acquisitions 1938. Transferred from the Institute of Books, Documents and Letters, Leningrad, with the Likhachov collection.

Chipped round the edge.

LITERATURE: Лихачев, *Моливдовулы*, табл. LXVI, 8; Банк, *Покушај класификације*, стр. 12.

174—175 SEAL OF STAURACIUS. 10th century

Lead

The piece is a circular seal with the bust of a man facing right in full profile; in his left hand is an object which may be a whip; round the edge is the inscription: ΔΟCΚϒ . . Ε ΑΝΟΝΗΝ (Oh Lord, give us the *anon* [food?]). The man wears a headdress with flying streamers behind. The reverse bears an inscription enclosed in a triple circle; the inscription consists of six lines; it reads: ΘΕΟΤΟΚΕ ΒΟΗΘ . . CΤΑϒΡΑ ΚΙΩ Β′Α′ CΠΑΘ . . . ΕΠΗ Τ. ϒΚΙ ΑΚ [ΚΑΙ] ΕΠΗ Τ . . ΒΑΡΒΑ . . . (O Mother of God, help Stauracius, the Imperial Protospatharium, Manager of the Emperor's Private Estate and Head of the Department (?) of the Barbarians).

The Hermitage. Inv. No. 2439. Diameter 2.4 cm.
Acquisitions 1931. Comes from the Museum of the Russian Archaeological Institute, Constantinople.

The inscription on the reverse has been damaged. The seal is chipped round the edge.

In the work by Likhachov (Лихачев, *Моливдовулы*, табл. LXXX, 9—10) are reproduced two related seals from his collection; both are now in the Hermitage (Nos. M 7992 and M 8016). See also Schlumberger, *Sigillographie*, p. 451.

LITERATURE: Лихачев, *Моливдовулы*, текст к табл. LXXX.

176 CROSS WITH THE FOUR EVANGELISTS. 11th century

Gold, *cloisonné* enamels, gems, pearls

The cross has flaring arms terminating in a sort of trefoil, with tubular ribbons for suspension rings at the top and bottom of the shaft. The medallions at the terminals of the cross arms bear busts of the Evangelists executed in *cloisonné* enamel (on the top of the shaft is St Matthew, on the left arm is St Luke, on the right arm, St Mark, and on the bottom of the shaft is St John). At the intersection was probably a bust of Christ in a medallion. The spaces between the medallions, and between the cross arms, are adorned with an ornamental pattern set with gems. The medallions and the settings are enclosed in a filigree border. Between the ends of the cross arms are groups of two pearls. The reverse has a cruciform recess for a relic.

The Pushkin Museum of Fine Arts. Inv. No. АУ 891, П 2б. 328. Height 9 cm. Width 5.8 cm.
Acquisitions 1932 (?). Transferred from the History Museum, Moscow. Formerly in the Uvarov collection. Probably comes from Kiev.

Enamel from the central medallion is missing; so are almost all the stones from the side petals of the trefoils, and a stone near St Mark.

The Martvili cross may be compared; see Amiranachvili, *Les Emaux*, p. 28—31.

LITERATURE: Кондаков, *Византийские эмали*, с. 170—171; *Каталог собрания А. С. Уварова*, М., 1907, отд. VI, с. 182—183, табл. I, № 3; *Masterpieces*, No. 193, p. 65, fig. 7; Frolow, *La Relique*, N° 177, p. 255—256; Frolow, *Les Reliquaires*, p. 218, 227, 247.

177 RELIQUARY WITH THE CRUCIFIXION. 11th century

Gold, *cloisonné* enamels

The reliquary consists of two leaves. One bears Christ on the cross between the Virgin and St John; above is the sun and moon and two figures of flying angels. Under the cross is a skull and bones. The inscription on the cross reads IC XC; and the one at the sides ΙΔΕ Ο ϒ.ΟC CΟϒ (Behold thy son) and ΗΔΟ ϒ ϒ ΜΗΤΗΡ CΟϒ (Behold thy mother).

The other leaf has a cruciform recess in the centre; under the lower traverse are half-figures of Constantine and Helen; there are representations of the sun and the moon in enamel; and inscriptions.

The Kremlin Armoury. Inv. No. 10569. 3×2 cm.
Formerly in the Palace Church at Livadia, Crimea. May have been brought from Georgia.

There are dents and small losses of enamel. The lower edge is uneven.

For parallels, see No. 178.

LITERATURE: Кондаков, *Византийские эмали*, с. 203—204; Frolow, *La Relique*, N° 165, p. 251; Писарская, *Памятники*, с. 19, табл. XXVI; Frolow, *Les Reliquaires*, p. 98, 217, 219, 249.

178 ICON OF THE CRUCIFIXION. 11th—12th centuries

Gold, *cloisonné* enamels, gems, pearls

Christ is shown on the cross, with his eyes closed; on either side of the cross are the Virgin and St John; above are half-figures of flying angels, the sun and the moon. Under the cross is a skull and bones. The inscriptions in Greek read: ΙΔΟΥ Ο ΗΟϹ ϹΟΥ; ΙΔΟΥ Η ΜΡ ϹΟΥ (Behold thy son; behold thy mother). The frame, ornamented with filigree and granular decoration, with twelve settings for precious stones, is of Russian manufacture and dates from 12th—13th centuries.

The Kremlin Armoury. Inv. No. 74. 6×4.5 cm.
Found in 1822 with the Staroriazan treasure.

The stones are missing from the settings, all but three.

For parallels, see No. 177.

LITERATURE: К. Калайдович, *Письма к А. Ф. Малиновскому об археологических исследованиях в Рязанской губернии*, М., 1823, с. 15—29; *Древности Российского Государства*, отд. II, М., 1851, с. 45—47, рис. 33—37; *Опись Московской Оружейной палаты*, ч. 1, М., 1884, с. 43, № 74; Кондаков, *Византийские эмали*, с. 337—338, рис. 105; Кондаков, *Русские клады*, с. 89—91, табл. XVII, 2; Писарская, *Памятники*, с. 19, табл. XXVI; Volbach, *La Stauroteca*, p. 12, tav. X, fig. 28; Даркевич, *Светское искусство Византии*, с. 270.

179 ICON OF THE VIRGIN AND CHILD. 10th century

Gilt bronze, precious stones

The embossed icon presents the Virgin as the Hodegitria, full length, and holding the Child on her right arm; her left hand is placed on her breast. She stands on a *suppedaneum*. Christ has in his right hand a scroll, his left resting on his mother's breast. The Virgin has an ornamented shawl thrown over her left shoulder. Her *maphorion* is edged with a border of small crosses. Her forehead, shoulders and legs over the knees are marked with a cruciform design of incised dots. The contour of her figure is accented by a sequence of precious stones placed at a small distance outside of it.
The work forms part of a large icon in embossed silver, made in Georgia in the 17th century and having in the centre a picture of the Tree of Jesse, of 18th century work.

The Arts Museum of the Georgian SSR, Tbilisi. Inv. No. 6. Height 22 cm.
Acquisitions 1925. Formerly in the monastery at Martvili, Georgia.

Two icons of Georgian work, one of them in gold (from the monastery at Martvili, now in the Arts Museum of the Georgian SSR, Tbilisi) and the other in bronze (from the monastery at Zemo-Krikhi, now in the Kutaisi Museum) may be cited as parallels (Чубинашвили, 1957, табл. 197; Чубинашвили, 1959, ил. 12; Amiranaschwili, *Kunstschätze*, S. 64, Abb. 35; A. Bank, «Les Modèles de Constantinople et les copies locales (d'après les objets d'arts mineurs des Xe—XIIe siècles)», in: *Actes du XXIIe Congrès international d'histoire de l'art. Budapest, 1969*, t. 1, Budapest, 1972, p. 179, ill. 42, *2*, *3*).

LITERATURE: Кондаков, Бакрадзе, с. 75; Чубинашвили, 1957, табл. 197, 198; Amiranaschwili, *Kunstschätze*; S. 92, 94, Abb. 45, 46; A. Bank, «Les Modèles de Constantinople et les copies locales (d'après les objets d'arts mineurs des Xe—XIIe siècles)», in: *Actes du XXIIe Congrès international d'histoire de l'art. Budapest, 1969*, t. 1, Budapest, 1972, p. 179—180, ill. 42, *1*.

180—181 PLAQUES WITH THE APOSTLES JAMES AND BARTHOLOMEW. 10th—11th centuries

Gold, *cloisonné* enamels

The rectangular plaques mounted in the Mstislav Gospels cover (belonging to the copy executed about 1103 for Prince Mstislav Vladimirovich) show the representations of the Apostles James and Bartholomew, each standing on a dais. The accompanying Greek inscriptions give the names of the personages. Each of the apostles has a scroll in his left hand, blessing with his right. The plaques are decorated with pearls.

The History Museum, Moscow. The Synod. Inv. No. 1203 (Manuscript Department). Height of each plaque 3.6 cm. Width 1.6 cm (No. 180); 1.7 cm (No. 181).
Acquisitions 1917. Came from the Patriarchal Vestry in the Moscow Kremlin. Before this the book was in the Archangel Cathedral.

Six nails in the background hold the plaques in their places in the mount. Losses of enamel.

Two companion plaques with representations of apostles in the Khakhuli triptych (Nos. 190—191) may be compared. See also the cover of the Siena Gospels (L. Dami, «L'Evangelario greco della Biblioteca di Siena», *Dedalo*, 1922, III, fasc. IV, p. 228—229).

LITERATURE: Г. Филимонов, *Оклад Мстиславова евангелья*, М., 1861; П. К. Симони, *Мстиславово евангелье. Фототипическое издание*, М., 1910; Успенский, *Патриаршая ризница*, с. 233, 261; М. М. Постникова-Лосева, Н. Г. Платонова, Б. Л. Ульянова, *Каталог русских эмалей на золотых и серебряных изделиях собрания Государственного Исторического музея и его филиалов*, М., 1962, с. 53—54.

182 ICON OF THE DESCENT INTO LIMBO (THE ANASTASIS). 12th century

Cloisonné enamels, gold, silver

The icon is almost square, in a silver mount, with an ornamental border. The background is inscribed with the word Η ΑΝΑCΤΑCΙC. The reverse bears a silver gilt plaque with a Greek inscription in niello, referring to some relic or relics, and a later incised inscription in Russian referring to the weight.

The Kremlin Armoury. Inv. No. 13797. Height 9.5 cm. Width 8.5 cm.
From the Annunciation Cathedral in the Moscow Kremlin.

Chipped in several places; small losses of enamel.

See also the same scene on the cover of the Siena Gospels (L. Dami, «L'Evangelario greco della Biblioteca di Siena», *Dedalo*, 1922, III, fasc. IV, p. 228, 231, colour plate).

LITERATURE: *Государственная Оружейная палата*, М., 1958, рис. 134; Писарская, *Памятники*, с. 20, табл. XXXVII.

183 PLAQUE WITH ST PETER. 12th century

Cloisonné enamels, gold

The rectangular plaque bears a full-length figure of the Apostle Peter facing three-quarters right, with a scroll in his left hand, his right hand blessing. The thick network of cloisons forming a decorative pattern points to a relatively late date. Nevertheless, the opinion of Amiranashvili who assigns the work to the 13th century seems erroneous, for this period was marked by the use of different techniques (see Nos. 190—191).

The Arts Museum of the Georgian SSR, Tbilisi.
Inv. No. 9719 Height 12 cm. Width 5.5 cm.
Came from the Ghelati Monastery as a decoration of the Khakhuli triptych.

Losses of enamel in the left-hand part of the figure and in the area of the neck. Round nail holes along the edges.

The image of St Peter on the *Pala d'oro* has a certain affinity with the plaque (Wessel, *Byzantine Enamels*, p. 146—147; *Il tesoro di San Marco*, 1, tav. XVII).

LITERATURE: Amiranachvili, *Les Emaux*, p. 90—91.

184—185 ICON WITH SCENES OF THE DESCENT INTO LIMBO (THE ANASTASIS), THE ANNUNCIATION, CHRIST AND FIVE SAINTS (inset in a triptych). 10th—11th centuries

Cloisonné enamels, gold, silver, precious stones

The central tier of the icon consists of two scenes, the Descent into Limbo and the Annunciation. The top and bottom tiers comprise three busts each, in panels with heart-shaped ornaments in the corners: above, Christ with a book, flanked by the Apostles Peter and Paul holding scrolls; below, Sts Cosmas, Pantaleon and Damian. The bevel at the left is embellished with an ornamental band of crosses in lozenges.
The two subject scenes with accompanying Greek inscriptions are both archaic in their iconography; thus, in the Annunciation the figure of the Virgin is shown at the left and that of the Archangel, at the right. The enamel plaque forms part of a diptych; it has a silver framing inset with precious stones. The back of the diptych is decorated with a leaved cross within a border of plant ornament.

The inscriptions read as follows: IC XC; NHKA Η ΑΗΑCΤΑCΙC; ΟΑ . . . . ΠΕΤΡΟC; IC XC; ΟΑ . . . . ΠΑΥΛΟC; ΟΑ . . . . ΚΟCΜΑC; ΟΑ . . . . ΠΑΝΤΕΛΕΙ . . . . ; ΟΑ ΔΑΜΙΑΝ.

The Arts Museum of the Georgian SSR, Tbilisi. Inv. No. 664. Height of the triptych 29 cm. Width 14 cm. Size of the enamel 9×9 cm.
Acquisitions 1945. Came from the monastery at Shemokmedi, Georgia.

Several stones missing from the frame. The corners of the silver plate with the cross partly damaged.

A similar scene of the Descent into Limbo, executed in niello, is on the reverse of the Martvili triptych (9th century); a quadrifoil enamel (10th century), also from Martvili, is decorated with the same subject treated in a more laconic manner but close to our specimen as regards iconography (Amiranaschwili, *Kunstschätze*, Abb. 25, 42). The cross within an ornamental border also has some parallels (Банк, *Опыт классификации*, с. 134—135, рис. 4; Банк, *Византийские серебряные изделия*, XIII, рис. 4, 7, с. 217—218).

LITERATURE: Кондаков, Бакрадзе, с. 131—133, рис. 69, 70; Банк, *Византийские серебряные изделия*, XIII, с. 218, рис. 9; Bank, *L'Argenterie*, p. 339; Amiranachvili, *Les Emaux*, p. 87—89.

186 PLAQUE WITH CHRIST ENTHRONED. 11th century

Cloisonné enamels, gold

The rectangular plaque with a rounded top shows Christ seated on a throne with a broad low back. His right hand is raised in blessing, while his left supports a book which rests on his left knee. Christ's feet stand on a *suppedaneum*. The plaque probably formed the central part of a Deesis composition.

The Arts Museum of the Georgian SSR, Tbilisi. Inv. No. 9719. 7×4.5 cm.
Acquisitions 1952. Came from the Ghelati Monastery as a decoration of the Khakhuli triptych.

A similar image is on the Limbourg staurothèque (Talbot Rice, *The Art*, pl. X; Deér, *Die Heilige Krone*, Taf. X, Abb. 16, Taf. XI, Abb. 21).

LITERATURE: Amiranachvili, *Les Emaux*, p. 108; Wessel, *Byzantine Enamels*, No. 34, p. 108; Амиранашвили, *Хахульский триптих*, ил. 15.

187 PLAQUE WITH CHRIST CROWNING THE EMPEROR MICHAEL VII DUCAS AND THE EMPRESS MARIA. 1076—81

Cloisonné enamels, gold

The rectangular plaque shows two figures presented from the front, each standing on a small *suppedaneum*: the Emperor Michael VII Ducas with a *labarum* in his right hand and a scroll in his left, and his wife Maria (daughter of the Georgian King Bagrat IV) with a staff terminating in a leaved cross. Christ appears as a bust in the segment of starry sky above; he crowns the Emperor and the Empress. In the space between the two figures, is a Greek inscription reading: + CTEΦΩ. MIXAHΛ CYN MAPIAM XEPCI MOY (I crown Michael and Maria with mine own hands).
The flat treatment of the figures, and the emphasis on the ornamental in the rendering of the dresses are characteristic of the period.

The Arts Museum of the Georgian SSR, Tbilisi. Inv. No. 9719. 7.2×7 cm.
For accession data, see No. 186.

For the representation of the same emperor, see Deér, *Die Heilige Krone*, Taf. XII, Nr. 22. There seems to be a stronger resemblance between the emperor in our plaque and Michael VII Ducas' co-ruler, Emperor Constantine (Deér, *Die Heilige Krone*, Taf. XII, Nr. 24).

LITERATURE: Кондаков, Бакрадзе, с. 18; Amiranachvili, *Les Emaux*, p. 100—101; Beckwith, *The Art*, p. 110, fig. 136; Wessel, *Byzantine Enamels*, No. 38, p. 115—119; Deér, *Die Heilige Krone*, S. 81—82, Abb. 25; Amiranaschwili, *Kunstschätze*, S. 116, Abb. 71; Амиранашвили, *Хахульский триптих*, ил. 8—9.

188 PLAQUE WITH THE VIRGIN AND CHILD ENTHRONED. 11th century

Cloisonné enamels, gold

The plaque with the Virgin and Child enthroned was once the central element in a set of nine plaques identical in size and execution, six of which showed the apostles (two figures on each plaque, see Nos. 190—191) and two, the archangels Michael and Gabriel.
On either side of the Virgin's head are the letters MP ΘY.

The Arts Museum of the Georgian SSR, Tbilisi. Inv. No. 9719. 5×4 cm.
For accession data, see No. 186.

The set seems to be modelled on the enamels of the Limbourg staurothèque where similar figures of the apostles and archangels are grouped around Christ Enthroned, the throne being identical in form to that on the Khakhuli triptych (Talbot Rice, *The Art*, pl. X).

LITERATURE: Amiranachvili, *Les Emaux*, p. 110—111; Амиранашвили, *Хахульский триптих*, ил. 33.

189 CROSS WITH CONSTANTINE AND HELEN AND THE FOUR PROPHETS. 11th century

Cloisonné enamels, gold

The four-armed cross of quadrifoil type, with disc-like projections at the ends and between each pair of arms, has in the central part full-length figures of Constantine and Helen flanking the Cross with a trefoil on top, and a base below, on which it stands. The end projections are decorated with busts of the prophets: Isaiah at the top, Elijah at the left, Elisha at the right, and Daniel below.

The Arts Museum of the Georgian SSR, Tbilisi. Inv. No. 9719. 7×6 cm.
For accession data, see No. 186.

NOTE. I know of no direct analogies for this work. Amiranashvili's opinion that this enamel is a typically Byzantine art object seems not sufficiently grounded.

LITERATURE: Кондаков, Бакрадзе, с. 8; Frolow, *La Relique*, N° 260, p. 290; Amiranachvili, *Les Emaux*, p. 105; Амиранашвили, *Хахульский триптих*, ил. 16.

190—191 TWO PLAQUES WITH THE APOSTLES. 11th century

Cloisonné enamels, gold

Each of the plaques, rectangular, with a rounded top, shows two figures of the apostles, full length, standing on *suppedanea*. St Peter with a scroll and St John the Evangelist with a book face three-quarter right; and St Paul and St Matthew, each holding a book, face three-quarter left. The plaques probably formed part of a Deesis composition.

The Greek inscriptions indicate the names of the saints: ΟΑ. ΙΩΟ ΘΕ ΟΛΟΓΟϹ; ΟΑ.. ΠΕ ΤΡΟϹ; ΟΑ... ΠΑΥ ΛΟϹ; ΟΑ... ΜΑΤ ΘΕΟϹ.

The Arts Museum of the Georgian SSR, Tbilisi. Inv. No. 9719. 8×5.5 cm (each).
For accession data, see No. 186.

LITERATURE: Кондаков, Бакрадзе, с. 14; Д. Гордеев, «К вопросу о разгруппировании эмалей Хахульского складня», *Мистецтвознавство (Збірник 1-ї Харківської секції науководослідчої катедри мистецтвознавства)*, Харків, 1928, с. 155, Amiranachvili, *Les Emaux*, p. 116—117; Амиранашвили, *Хахульский триптих*, ил. 52—53.

192—195 COMPOSITE ICON WITH THE CRUCIFIXION, CHRIST, SAINTS, AND GOSPEL SCENES. Enamel plaques, 11th and 12th centuries; silver plaques, 11th and 14th centuries

Cloisonné enamels on gold, silver, wood

The icon consists of several separate parts of different date mounted together on a wooden foundation. In the centre are two plaques, one with the Crucifixion, the other with Christ in the Sepulchre, both in *cloisonné* enamel. The inscriptions in Greek read as follows: Η ϹΤΑΥΡΩϹΙϹ (Crucifixion), ΧϹ ΠΡΟΚΕΙΤΑΙ Κ... ϹΗΜΕΖΕΤΑΙ ΘΕ... (Christ did die, and did come as the Lord). The margins are decorated with chased silver gilt plaques of different size. Above the Crucifixion, in the middle, is a scene of the Dormition enclosed in an ornamental border. In the corners are the busts of saints: St Basil in the top left corner, St John Chrysostom in the top right; in the bottom left corner, St Nicholas, in the bottom right, St Athanasius; all but St Basil, in medallions. Between the medallions are St James (left side) and St Gregory the Theologian (right side) executed in *cloisonné* enamel on gold plaques shaped like an egg placed vertically with the big end upwards, and the small end cut away. The Greek inscriptions read: ΟΑΓ. ΙΑΚΩΒΟϹ ΟϹ ΑΔΕΑΦΟ. ΘΕΟ (Saint James the brother of our Lord), ΟΑΓ ΓΡΗ ΓΟΡ. ΟϹ Ο ΘΕ ΟΛ ΟΓ (Saint Gregory the Theologian). In the upper and lower margins are cruciform and rectangular recesses for relics accompanied by Greek inscriptions (St John the Baptist, St John Chrysostom, St Stephen the Younger, St Demetrius, St Theodore). At the sides are three-quarter length representations of Sts Peter and Paul, and the Evangelists John and Matthew (in the inscriptions the names of the personages accompany the wrong figures). In the bottom part is St Theodore on the left, and Christ Bearing the Cross on the right. The intervening spaces between the representations are filled with bands of ornamentation.

The Hermitage. Inv. No. ω 211. Height 34.3 cm. Width 32.5 cm.
Acquisition 1911. Purchased in 1892 by G. Stroganov in Rome; according to the seller, comes from South Italy.

The plaque with Christ in the Sepulchre is split. The representations in the upper corners, a setting in the lower border, and the majority of stones are missing.

Comparable with the central scene is a plaque which was formerly in the Reich Kapelle in Munich, now in a private collection (*L'Art byzantin*, N° 474, p. 403—404; G. Schlumberger, *Un Empereur byzantin du X*[e] *siècle*, Paris, 1890, p. 580; K. Wessel, «Die byzantinische Emailtafel in der Reichen Kapelle der Münchener Residenz», in: *Polychordia. Festschrift Franz Dölger*, III, Amsterdam, 1968, S. 235—245, Taf. XV). Details of the cover of the Siena Gospels should be compared with the enamels in the margins (Лихачев, *Историческое значение*, табл. III; L. Dami, «L'Evangelario greco della Biblioteca di Siena», *Dedalo*, 1922, III, fasc. IV, p. 229, 235, 240).

LITERATURE: Д. В. Айналов, «Икона из собрания графа Г. С. Строганова», *Археологические известия и заметки*, 1893, 9—10, с. 287—297; G. Schlumberger, «Un Tableau reliquaire byzantin inédit», *Mélanges d'archéologie byzantine*, 1895, p. 187—192, pl. XI; Schlumberger, *L'Epopée*, 1, p. 524—525; Кондаков, *Памятники*, с. 261—263; Н. Макаренко, «Несколько предметов из собрания графа Г. С. Строганова», *Старые годы*, 1911, № 10, с. 37—38; O. Wulff, *Altchristliche und byzantinische Kunst*, Bd. 2, Berlin, 1914, S. 601, Abb. 511; Банк, *Искусство Византии*, № 85, с. 123, 126, 128; *L'Art byzantin*, p. 403; Frolow, *Les Reliquaires*, p. 103; Deér, *Die Heilige Krone*, S. 112, Abb. 170—172; Volbach, *La Stauroteca*, p. 12, tav. X, fig. 29; Банк, *Черты палеологовского стиля*, с. 195—198; Grabar, *Les Revêtements*, N° 48, p. 75—76, fig.

196 ICON OF ST THEODORE SPEARING THE DRAGON. 13th century

Cloisonné and *champlevé* enamels on copper, silver, wood

The icon represents the warrior saint Theodore spearing the dragon. There is an inscription in Greek: Ο ΑΓΙΟϹ ΘΕΟΔΟΡΟϹ Ο ΒΑΘΗΡΙΑΚΗϹ. The halo and the shield are richly ornamented. The right and the bottom edge of the icon are bordered by a frame of *repoussé* silver decorated with a full-length figure of St Demetrius, and half-figures of St Pantaleon and an unidentified saint; the intervening spaces are filled with plant ornament. The top edge is bounded by a narrow border of *repoussé* silver. The icon and the frame are mounted on a new wooden panel with edges painted in gold colour.

The Hermitage. Inv. No. ω 28. Height of the panel 24.3 cm. Height of the enamel 19 cm. Width of the panel 21.5 cm. Width of the enamel 16.5 cm.
Acquisitions 1885. Formerly in the Basilewsky collection.

Our piece is probably part of an icon; the break runs down the raised arm of the saint and the trunk of the tree; there are small losses of enamel in this area. Minor damages in the frame.

LITERATURE: Darcel, Basilewsky, p. 26, N° 102, pl. XIV; G. Schlumberger, *Un Empereur byzantin du Xe siècle*, Paris, 1890, p. 561; Кондаков, *Византийские эмали*, с. 154—156; Н. П. Лихачев, *Материалы для истории византийской и русской сфрагистики*, вып. 1, Л., 1928, с. 18, рис. 8; A. Frolov, «Emaux cloisonnés de l'époque postbyzantine», *Cahiers archéologiques*, I, 1945, p. 99, pl. XXIV; Банк, *Искусство Византии*, № 84, с. 123, 125, 128; Дьяконова, *Искусство Востока*, № 24, с. 120, 123; *Эрмитаж*, 1965, № 113; Deér, *Die Heilige Krone*, S. 105, 109, 112—113, Abb. 65; *L'Art byzantin*, p. 396; Ross, *Catalogue*, 2, p. 106.

197—201 TRIPTYCH WITH THE DEESIS. 11th century

Silver, *cloisonné* enamels on gold

The triptych has a loop at the top. The representations in *cloisonné* enamel have survived on two of the panels: on the central panel bearing Christ Enthroned, and on the right-hand leaf showing a full-length figure of St John the Baptist in an attitude of prayer. The left-hand leaf bears a highly schematic representation of the Virgin in *repoussé* silver, which seems to have replaced the original enamel. The back of the triptych is decorated with a bust of the Virgin and Child executed in the same manner. When folded, the triptych shows on the outside a cross with settings for the stones (?); between cross arms are eight-petalled rosettes enclosing small crosses. The panels are bordered with bands of openwork squares, in some of which glass and pastes have been preserved. At the corners, along the edges, and in some other areas are small wire loops probably intended for the attachment of stringed pearls.

The Hermitage. Inv. No. ω 1192. Height 8.3 cm. Width when unfolded 16 cm; when folded 8 cm. Acquisitions 1956. Formerly in the Alexander Palace at Pushkin (near Leningrad). Comes from the Saidanaya Monastery in the neighbourhood of Damascus, where it was at the beginning of the 20th century.

Pieces of gold leaf missing from the areas right of the throne and left of the head of St John the Baptist. Considerable losses of enamel in the right-hand leaf. Almost all the stones and pastes are missing from the settings in the borders; also loops and hinges. There are breaks.
The plaques on the left-hand leaf and on the reverse are of later date but evidently of medieval work.

In its general decorative scheme the piece resembles the so-called Martvili triptych, and two triptychs in the collection of Pierpont Morgan, New York (Amiranachvili, *Les Emaux*, p. 25—27; *Early Christian and Byzantine Art Exhibition*, Nos. 530, 531, pl. LXX, LXXI). The lid of the Limbourg staurothèque may be considered a prototype for the enamels (Talbot Rice, *The Art*, pl. X); some details of the mount of the Khakhuli Mother of God should also be compared (Amiranachvili, *Les Emaux*, p. 102—103). See also: *Mostra dell'arte in Puglia dal tardo Antico al Rococo. Pinacoteca provinciale di Bari. Catalogo*, 1964, N. 4, p. 5—6, tav. 1; Volbach, *La Stauroteca*.

LITERATURE: Ф. И. Успенский, «Археологические памятники Сирии», *ИРАИК*, VII, София, 1902, с. 103—106, табл. 4; Н. П. Кондаков, *Иконография богоматери*, т. 2, Пг., 1915, с. 251—253, рис. 134, 135; Банк, *Выставка византийских материалов*, с. 344; Bank, *Quelques problèmes*, p. 239, pl. 5; А. В. Банк, «Византийский складень с перегородчатыми эмалями из Синайского монастыря», *Палестинский сборник*, 19 (82), 1969, с. 239—245.

202 RELIQUARY (the so-called PHILOTHEUS' STAUROTHÈQUE). 12th century

Silver, wood

The staurothèque (container for a cross) is rectangular in shape; it has the form of a box with the traces of a sliding lid (now missing), and a cruciform recess. The decoration consists of *repoussé* silver panels mounted on wood; on either side of the cruciform recess, under the lower traverse, are full-length figures: St Cosmas on the left, and St Damian on the right. Above are two busts in medallions; the one on the left, of St Cyrus; the one on the right, of St Pantaleon. The background is filled with ornamental designs. Along the margins framing the missing lid is an inscription in Greek: + ΖΟΗΦΟΡΟΝ ΠΕΦΥΚΕ ΤΟΥ CΤ[ΑΥ]ΡΟΥ ΞΥΛ[Ο]Ν ΕΝ ΩΠΕΡ ΑΥΤΟC ΠΡΟCΠΑΓΕΙC Χ[ΡΙCΤΟ]C ΘΕΛΩΝ ΑΠΑCΙΝ ΕΒΡΑΒΕΥCΕ ΤΗΝ C[ΩΤΗ]ΡΙΑΝ ΘΗΚΗΝ ΙΩ[ΑΝΝΗC] ΔΕ ΤΕΥΧΕΙ ΝΥΝ ΠΟΘΩ (Vivifying was the wood of the cross on which Christ, choosing of his own free will to be crucified, secured salvation for all. And John lovingly fashions of it a reliquary). The sides are decorated with vertical palmettes in circles. There is a loop at the top and fragments of clasps at the edges.

The Kremlin Armoury. Inv. No. 1. Height 20.5 cm. Width 17 cm.
Tradition names the Patriarch Philotheus as the owner of the reliquary. It is said to have been brought from Constantinople by the Metropolitan Alexius in 1354.

The sliding top is missing.

For related objects, see No. 207; Банк, *Византийские серебряные изделия*, XIV, с. 234—242.

LITERATURE: A. Weltmann, *Le Trésor de Moscou* (*Oroujeinaia Palata*), Moscou, 1861, p. 20; *Опись Московской Оружейной палаты*, т. 1, М., 1884, с. 5—7; Банк, *Византийские серебряные изделия*, XIV, с. 237, 240—241, рис. 7; Frolow, *La Relique*, p. 512—513, N° 729; Писарская, *Памятники*, с. 16—17, табл. XII, XIII; Frolow, *Les Reliquaires*, p. 97, 101, 126, 218, 222, fig. 43; Volbach, *La Stauroteca*, p. 7, tav. III, fig. 7; Grabar, *Les Revêtements*, p. 77—78, fig. 103.

203—204 RELIQUARY WITH A LEAVED CROSS. 11th century

Silver gilt, paste

The reliquary has the form of a rectangular triptych of massive sheet silver, with a sliding lid. Under the lid is a cruciform recess for a relic flanked by roundels in the upper part and by oblongs in the lower. Over the central panel is another recess for a relic (?) with a setting for a jewel in the left corner. The leaves, both on the outside and inside, and the sliding lid are decorated with roundels, encircled by bands of openwork squares, which must originally have contained enamels; on the sliding lid are four small medallions and a large one within a lozenge; each of the side leaves has two medallions on the outside, and ten medallions decorating the inside. The lower part of the reliquary is bordered with a band of lozenges. The squares forming the openwork frames were filled with coloured glass; and the intervening spaces between the medallions, with paste. The reliquary has a loop at the top; the sliding lid is fitted with a ring. The reverse of the reliquary bears a *repoussé* representation of a leaved cross with arms terminating in rosettes, set against a background filled with ornamental designs, and enclosed in a border of floral scrolls. On either side of the cross is an inscription in Greek which reads: IC XC.

The Hermitage. Inv. No. ω 264. Height when folded 26.3 cm. Width 21.5 cm. Thickness 2.3 cm.
Acquisitions 1925. Formerly in the Museum of the Stieglitz School of Art and Design, Leningrad. Purchased in Paris, from Bois, in 1883.

Enamels have been lost from the medallions, as well as paste and glass in the frames; of these hardly anything has survived. The openwork bands on either side of the cruciform recess are considerably damaged, and in part missing. The corners have been broken away. Losses of metal from the corners and edges on the back lid.

Comparable is the reliquary in the Marienstern Monastery in Saxony (Johann Georg, «Eine Staurothek im Kloster Marienstern», *Monatshefte für Kunstwissenschaft*, 1914, VIII, S. 249—250, Taf. 49—50) and the one at S. Giovanni in Laterano (C. Cecchelli, «Il Tesoro del Laterano», *Dedalo*, 1926, VII, p. 231—236; see also Банк, *Византийские серебряные изделия*, XIII, с. 214—218; XIV, с. 241—242.

NOTE. The dating of A. Frolov who assigns the reliquary to the 12th century, does not seem convincing.

LITERATURE: Банк, *Византийские серебряные изделия*, XIII, с. 211—221; Банк, *Искусство Византии*, № 86, с. 123, 126, 128; Frolow, *La Relique*, N° 430, p. 374; Banck, *Monuments* (*X*[e]*—XII*[e] *s.*), p. 126—127, fig. 1; Frolow, *Les Reliquaires*, p. 58, 61, 126, 159, 178, fig. 14; Volbach, *La Stauroteca*, p. 8, 13, tav. III, fig. 8, tav. XII, fig. 34; Даркевич, *Светское искусство Византии*, с. 218, ил. 359.

205—206 RELIQUARY IN THE FORM OF A TEMPLE. 1059—67

Silver

The reliquary in the form of a temple of octagonal shape is a model of the sanctuary of St Demetrius at Thessalonica. The four narrow walls are ornamented with embossed vine motif; over the walls are chalices under arches. One of the broad walls bears the scene of Christ crowning the Emperor Constantine Ducas and his wife Eudocia and the inscription: ΚΩΝCΤΑΝΤΙ[ΝΟC] ΕΝ Χ[ΡΙCΤ]Ω ΤΩ ... ΠΙCΤΟC ΒΑCΙ[ΛΕΥC] ΡΩΜΕΩΝ ΔΟΥΚΑC; + ΕΥΔΟΚΙΑ ΕΝ Χ[ΡΙCΤ]Ω ΤΩ Θ[Ε]Ω ... ΒΑCΙ[ΛΗCCΑ] ΡΩΜΕΩΝ (Constantine Ducas, by the grace of God Autocrat and Emperor of the Romans. Eudocia, by the grace of God Empress of the Romans); another has a folding door with the figures of Sts Nestor and Louppos on the leaves. The saints' names are written beside the heads. The remaining two walls have the following inscription on them: ΣΑΦΗC ΠΕΦΥΚΑ ΤΟΥ ΚΙΒΩΡΙΟΥ ΤΥΠΟC ΤΟΥ ΛΟΓΧΟΝΥΚΤΟΥ ΜΑΡΤΥΡΟC ΔΗΜΗΤΡΙΟΥ ΕΧΩΔΕ ΧΡΙCΤΟΝ ΕΚΤΟC ΕCΤΗΛΩΜΕΝΟΝ CΤΕΦΟΝΤΑ ΧΕΡCΙ ΤΗΝΚΑΛΗΝΞΥΝΩΡΙΔΑ Ο Δ'ΑΥΜΕ ΤΕΥΞΑC ΙΩΑΝΝΗC ΕΚ ΓΕΝΟΥC ΑΥΤΟΡΕΙΑΝΩΝ ΤΗΝ ΤΥΧΗΝ ΜΥCΤΟΓΡΑΦΟC (I am a true image of the sanctuary of the martyr Demetrius pierced by a lance. On the outside I have a sculpted Christ who with his hands is crowning a fair couple. And he that has carved me is John of the house of Autorianes (?), a mystograph by his trade).
The corners are decorated with columns, and in the spaces between the arches are winged palmettes. The ornaments and inscriptions are executed by chasing. Inside the reliquary is a silver box. Grabar regards the reliquary as a receptacle for the pyx with the blood of St. Demetrius (in the monastery of St Athanasius of Mount Athos), which he believes to have originally been kept inside the silver box.

The Kremlin Armoury. Inv. No. 15279. Height 16 cm. Width 11.5 cm.
Came from the Patriarchal Vestry in the Moscow Kremlin.

The top of the roof is missing. Dents on the columns and along the lower edge. Small cracks and losses of silver, mostly near the edges.

The object is unique as regards its shape, though reliquaries claimed to contain the relics of St Demetrius are numerous, and there are many parallels for the ornamental motifs (Банк, *Опыт классификации*, с. 136—137, рис. 8; Bank, *L'Argenterie*, p. 355).

LITERATURE: И. И. Срезневский, «Древний византийский ковчежец», *Христианские древности*, т. VIII, 1862—1863; Писарская, *Памятники*, с. 15—16, табл. X, XI; A. Grabar, «Quelques reliquaires de Saint Démétrius et le martyrium du Saint à Salonique», *DOP*, V, 1950, p. 1—28 (Grabar, *L'Art de la fin de l'antiquité*, 1, p. 446—453, pl. 118—119); R. Rüchert, «Zur Form der byzantinischen Reliquiare», *Münchener Jahrbuch für bildende Kunst*, VII, 1957, S. 32, Abb. 20; Rudt de Collenberg, *Le «Thorakion»*, p. 355, note 2; Bank, *Quelques problèmes*, p. 239, pl. 6; Bank, *L'Argenterie*, p. 343—344; Банк, *Опыт классификации*, с. 137—138, рис. 11.

207—208 STAUROTHÈQUE. Late 11th—early 12th centuries

Silver gilt, wood

The staurothèque (container for a cross) is a wooden box with a recess shaped as a two-armed cross; it has a sliding lid, and two loops, one fitted to the top, the other to the lid. The planks composing the box and the lid are covered on all sides with plates of silver gilt chased with different representations and ornamental designs. On the obverse of the lid is the Crucifixion. Above the heads of the Virgin and St John standing on either side of the cross is an inscription in Greek: IΔE O ϒOC COϒ; IΔOϒHM[HT]HP COϒ (Behold thy son; behold thy mother). In the margins are busts of saints in medallions set against the background of plant ornament. In the upper border are the archangels Michael and Raphael on either side of the *Hetimasia*, Uriel and the now missing Gabriel; in the left margin (counting from the top downwards) Sts Peter, John the Theologian, Luke, Andrew, Simon, Thomas, Nicholas, Theodore. In the right margin are Sts Paul, Matthew, Mark, Bartholomew, James, Philip, John Chrysostom and yet another John. On the bottom of the lid are Sts Cosmas, Pantaleon and Damian. The back of the lid is decorated with a two-armed Calvary cross, probably a later addition, flanked by trees and accompanied by an inscription IC XC; NI KA. Inside the staurothèque, on either side of the cruciform recess, are Constantine and Helen; above are half-figures of angels; along the border, acanthus leaves. The sides and the top of the box are decorated with vine scrolls, cinquefoils and semi-palmettes. The back bears a leaved cross with the letters IC XC in medallions at the sides (probably the work of a different master).

The Hermitage. Inv. No. ω 839. Height 29 cm. Width 20.5 cm. Thickness 4.2 cm.
Acquisitions 1930. Formerly in the Russian Museum.

A medallion in the top right-hand corner, and the bust of St Damian from the medallion in the lower margin, are missing; the medallions at the top and bottom of the left side are damaged. Losses of metal along the lower edge and in the back.

For related objects, see No. 202; *Masterpieces*, No. 126, fig. 11; Банк, *Византийские серебряные изделия*, XIV, с. 236—241.

LITERATURE: А. П. Смирнов, *Памятники византийской живописи*, Л., 1928, с. 11, 27; Банк, *Византийские серебряные изделия*, XIV, с. 234—241; Банк, *Искусство Византии*, № 87, с. 123, 126, 129; Frolow, *La Relique*, N° 408, p. 363—364; Frolow, *Les Reliquaires*, p. 98, 166, fig. 44; *Propyläen Kunstgeschichte*, S. 197, Taf. 77; Rudt de Collenberg, *Le «Thorakion»*, p. 316, fig. 55 (détail).

209 ICON OF CHRIST ENTHRONED. 12th century

Bronze

The icon is embossed and finished in the technique of *repoussé* work; it has a rounded top and a border of beading between two thin raised bands crudely ornamented with nicks. Christ is represented seated on the throne holding a book in his left hand, his right hand raised in blessing. On either side of his nimbus are the letters: IC XC. The throne, the cushion and the book are decorated with ornamental designs. The top is pierced with three holes for attachment to a wooden backing.

The Hermitage. Inv. No. X 872. Height 12 cm. Width 9 cm.
Acquisitions 1955. Found, together with a bronze lamp, in a small temple tomb at Chersonese in the same year.

The bottom left corner and most of the left border are missing. There are dents on the surface. Small losses of metal in the face and shoulders of Christ.

LITERATURE: Г. Д. Белов, «Отчет о раскопках в Херсонесе в 1955 г.», *СГЭ*, 10, 1956, с. 57; Г. Д. Белов, «Отчет о раскопках в Херсонесе в 1955 г.», *ХС*, V, 1959, с. 67, рис. 53.

210 ICON OF CHRIST ENTHRONED AND SAINTS. 12th—13th centuries

Bronze

The icon is rectangular in shape, with the edges slightly raised; the representation is stamped and finished in *repoussé*. The central panel enclosed in a wavy border, bears the figure of Christ seated upon a low-backed throne. Above is the inscription: IC XC. The margins are ornamented with quatrefoils and dots in the intervening spaces. This ornament is interrupted by small panels with the figures of the Virgin (accompanied by the letters MP Θϒ, St John the Baptist and busts of saints, on a plain ground; of the busts, only two have survived: that of St Pantaleon in the middle of the lower margin, and that of St Damian in the bottom right corner. The icon must originally have been mounted on wood.

The Hermitage. Inv. No. X 1038. Height 24.3 cm. Width 18 cm.
Acquisitions 1955. Found at Chersonese in the same year.

The icon is in a highly damaged condition: all the representations of saints in the upper margin have been lost; of the rest, only that of St Pantaleon escaped damage. The face of Christ is missing. A number of small losses and cracks in the areas of the throne, the background, and the ornamental bands.

LITERATURE: Г. Д. Белов, «Отчет о раскопках в Херсонесе в 1955 г.», *ХС*, V, 1959, с. 53—55, рис. 38; Ross, *Catalogue*, 1, p. 74.

211 CROSS WITH CHRIST, SAINTS AND ANGELS. Late 11th century

Copper

The cross arms have the edges bent back, at right angle to the front face (or strips of metal soldered on along the edges perpendicular to the front); from the back, the cross is hollow. At either end the shaft terminates in a small protuberance. The inside is plain. The decoration is executed by undercutting the surface as in damascening (?); at the intersection is Christ Blessing (with a book?); on either side of him is a group of six apostles. Above, in the upper part of the shaft, is a full-length figure of St Theodore; below, in the bottom part, is St George. The inscriptions in Greek read: IC XC; ϒ ΑΓΗϒ. ΑΠΟCΤΟΑ; Ο ΑΓΙΟC ΘΕΟ-ΔΟΡΟC. Each of the side faces of the traverse is decorated with a figure of an archangel wearing the *loros*. The upper faces of the traverse bear three busts of angels; the side faces of the shaft are ornamented with four busts in the part above the traverse, and two in the portion below.

The Kievo-Pechersky Museum of the History of Culture. Inv. No. 3221 кпл. Height 23.33 cm. Width 14.8 cm. Thickness 2.77 cm.
According to tradition, the cross was owned by a monk of the Kievo-Pecherskaya Lavra, one Mark, nicknamed the Grave-Digger (it was his duty to make graves for the deceased brethren) whose name is mentioned about the year 1090. The cross is in the Kievo-Pecherskaya Lavra.

Of the figure of St George and some of the busts of angels, only traces remain. Losses of metal in different parts.
Errors in the inscriptions, as well as certain peculiarities of technique and style, suggest that the cross may be the work of a Russian master.

Similar in composition and style are the crosses reproduced by N. Kondakov (Н. П. Кондаков, *Иконография Богоматери*, т. 2, Пг., 1915, рис. 60); also see M. Rosenberg, *Geschichte der Goldschmiedekunst: Niello*, Frankfurt am Main, 1924, Abb. 47—49.

LITERATURE: И. Фундуклей, *Обозрение Киева в отношении к древностям*, Киев, 1847, с. 171—172; Н. Сементовский, *Киев, его святыни, древности, достопамятности и сведения, необходимые для его почитателей и путешественников*, Киев, 1864, с. 162; Н. Закревский, *Описание Киева*, т. 2, М., 1868, с. 633—634, табл. X; В. Прохоров, *Христианские древности*, Спб., 1875, табл. XI; Frolow, *La Relique*, p. 295.

212—214 BOWL WITH ST THEODORE, BIRDS, ANIMALS AND FISHES. 11th century

Silver

The vessel has the form of a shallow bowl with an almost vertical rim slightly flaring outward which bears an incised inscription in Greek on the outside. The inscription reads: + Κ[ϒΡΙ]Ε ΒΟΗΘΗ ΤΟΝ ΔΟϒΛΟΝ COϒ ΘΕΟΔΟΡΟΝ ΤΟϒΡΚΕΛΗΝ (O Lord, help thy slave Theodore Tourkelus). The sides are chased on the exterior with representations of real and fantastic creatures: birds, sphinxes, animals, snakes and fishes, devouring human beings and each other (probably a scene from the Day of Judgement). In the centre of the interior, in a roundel, is a bust of St Theodore holding a spear in his right hand and with his left grasping his sword below the handle. On either side is an inscription reading: ΟΑ . . ΘΕ ΟΔΟΡΟC. The reverse of the bottom shows traces of a foot; on the rim there are traces of the junction of the handle to the body of the vessel. The bowl may have been manufactured in the Balkan Peninsula.

The Hermitage. Inv. No. ω 1207. Height 5.2 cm. Diameter 14 cm.
Acquisitions 1950. Formerly in the Solikamsk Museum. Found in 1949 near the village of Penyakhino (Solikamsk District of the Perm Region).

The foot and the handle are missing.

The representation is close to that in the Leznic Church (Rumania) (Vasile Dragut, *Pictura murala din Transilvania (sec. XIV—XV)*, București, 1970, il. 45. Some of the figures find parallels in Bulgarian woodcarving and in Serbian stone-carving (Н. П. Кондаков, *Македония*, Спб., 1906, табл. III; L. Bréhier, *La Sculpture et les arts mineurs byzantins*, Paris, 1936, p. 81, pl. XLIII; А. Дероко, *Монументална и декоративна архитектура у средневековној Србији*, Београд, 1953, сл. 63, 69, 72).

LITERATURE: О. И. Бадер, «Камская археологическая экспедиция», *КСИИМК*, XXXIX, 1951, с. 89, 95; О. И. Бадер, «О восточном серебре и его использовании в древнем Прикамье», in: *На Западном Урале. Сборник статей Пермского краеведческого музея за 1951 г.*, Пермь, 1952, с. 190—191; Банк, *Выставка византийских материалов*, с. 344, 347; Дьяконова, *Искусство Востока*, № 23, с. 119, 123; A. Grabar, «L'Art profane en Russie», in: Grabar, *L'Art de la fin de l'antiquité*, 1, p. 333; Даркевич, *Светское искусство Византии*, с. 262—263, ил. 310, 375а—в.

215—217 BOWL OF THE *BRATINA* TYPE WITH SCALE DECORATION. 12th century

Silver gilt

The deep bowl with rounded walls and a vertical rim rests on a low foot. It is made of a double sheet of silver and decorated on the outside with seven rows of embossed scale-like shapes with various designs. The scales of the upper row bear the figures of a queen, attendants, musicians, dancers, acrobats; the second row shows figures of fantastic creatures and birds; the third, animals; the fourth, birds, and lions' heads; the fifth, human and animal heads, and the sixth and seventh, three- and five-petalled flowers. The foot is ornamented with *Sirin* birds, animals, and birds. In the roundel on the inside of the bottom is St George mounted, and an inscription which reads: ΟΑ . . C ΓΕΩΡΓΙΟC. Along the rim on the outside are running animals, separated by stylized trees. On the reverse of the bottom, a scratched inscription in Russian, referring to the weight. Scholars disagree about the provenance of this work. Some regard it as Byzantine, others as Russian (the latter opinion is not, however, sufficiently well grounded).

The Hermitage. Inv. No. 3. Height 11.7 cm. Diameter of the rim 18.5 cm. Weight 985 gm.
Acquisitions 1877. Discovered near the town of Beriozovo, Tobolsk Province.

Dents with losses of silver. The inner wall is pushed inside at the roundel; two cracks. Edge of the foot crushed. In places, traces of minor damages by mechanical factors.

Bowl No. 218 has a similar frieze of animals alternating with trees. The lid from a vessel, found in the Nenets National Area, shows trees of a like description but more strongly stylized (cf. No. 220).

LITERATURE: А. Спицын, «Из коллекций императорского Эрмитажа», *Записки отделения русской и славянской археологии*, VI, вып. I, Спб., 1897; А. В. Банк, «Серебряная братина XII—XIII веков», in: *Памятники эпохи Руставели*, Л., 1938; А. Грабар, «Светское изобразительное искусство в домонгольской Руси и „Слово о полку Игореве"», *Труды отделения древнерусской литературы Института литературы АН СССР*, XVIII, 1962, с. 265; Б. А. Шелковников, *Русское художественное стекло*, Л., 1968, с. 33—34, рис. 11; А. Н. Свирин, *Ювелирное искусство Древней Руси XI—XII веков*, М., 1972, с. 74—77, ил. 31, 32; Даркевич, *Светское искусство Византии*, с. 78—99, 156—186, ил. 104—159.

218—219 BOWL WITH SCENES UNDER ARCHES. 12th century

Silver

The deep bowl with rounded sides and a vertical rim is embossed with twelve scenes arranged under arches: the Ascent of Alexander, Samson (or Heracles) Rending the Lion, King (Alexander?) Riding on a Bird, a musician, two figures of riders with a spear and a bow, a dancing girl, two figures of warriors. Below are traces of another frieze which has not survived. The rim is decorated with animals running, separated by trees. On the inside of the bottom are engraved two griffins in a roundel.

The Hermitage. Inv. No. ω 72. Height 9 cm. Diameter of the rim 13.8 cm. Weight 465.5 gm.
Acquisitions 1885. Formerly in the Basilewsky collection.

The foot and the greater part of the lower frieze are missing, as is the figure left of the Ascent of Alexander, and the lower portion of the subject left of this, and of three to the right. On the opposite side of the bowl, three human heads and one head of a bird have been preserved from the lower frieze. The surface is dented in places. Cracks on the outside, and on the inside of the bottom.

LITERATURE: Даркевич, *Светское искусство Византии*, с. 63—77, 150—158, ил. 83—103.

220—224 LID FROM A VESSEL, WITH MUSICIANS, DANCERS AND ACROBATS. 12th century

Silver

The lid is tall and slightly bulbous in shape, with a plain vertical rim. The exterior is covered with medallions formed of interlacing bands and containing engraved figures against a dotted background; in the broader frieze are ten figures: six musicians playing the lute, the zourna, and the cymbals; two acrobats; and two dancers. In the narrower frieze are eight running animals: hares, hounds, a stag, and a panther, or an ounce; and two peacocks, one shown frontally, the other from the side. The intervening spaces are filled with birds and cinquefoils. In the centre are traces of a knob by which the lid was raised.

The Hermitage. Inv. No. ω 1193. Diameter at the rim 13.5 cm. Maximum diameter 16 cm. Height 9 cm.
Acquisitions 1957. Found in the area of the river Sredniaya Khodosta, in the Taz Peninsula (Nenets National Area).

There are dents in several places; and a long crack with a small hole on either side of it. Similar in form is the lid of the vessel No. 225.

NOTE. The categorical statement of B. Shelkovnikov (Шелковников, *Русское стекло*, с. 218, 220—221, рис. 7) concerning the Russian provenance of the vessel, is not supported by sufficient proof.

LITERATURE: А. В. Банк, «Крышка серебряного сосуда из Ненецкого округа», *СГЭ*, 15, 1959, с. 49—52; A. Banck, «Byzance et l'Orient d'après quelques données de l'art appliqué du XIe et du XIIe siècles», *Труды XXV Международного конгресса востоковедов*, 1962, с. 555—561; А. В. Банк, «Серебряный сосуд из так называемого Тартуского клада», *Древние могильники и клады (Археологический сборник, II)*, Таллин, 1962, с. 275—286; Шелковников, *Русское стекло*, с. 218, 220—221, рис. 7; Э. А. Лапковская, «Серебряная с чернью чаша XII века», *ТГЭ*, VIII, 1965, с. 131; Б. А. Шелковников, *Русское художественное стекло*, Л., 1968, с. 35—36; Даркевич, *Светское искусство Византии*, с. 100—117. 165—173, ил. 163—179, 251 а, б.

225—226 VESSEL WITH A LID, DECORATED WITH HUNTERS AMONG ORNAMENT, AND BIRDS. 12th century

Silver

The vessel consists of two separate parts, a bowl with an almost vertical border and a lid with the rim fitting into it. The reverse of the bottom shows traces of a foot, and the lid, those of a knob. The exterior of the vessel is covered with interlacing devices formed by broad bands between double contour lines. Within the cartouche-shaped designs are figures of warriors (or hunters), with legs bent in the knee, holding a shield in front, and the sword raised as if to strike. The engraved design is emphasized by a niello inlay on a hollow ground. Around the rim are stylized vine scrolls. There are traces of gilding. The interior decoration has for its central motif a medallion of concentric circles in which are two birds back to a back, with heads turned towards a stylized plant between them.

The Hermitage. Inv. No. ω 1217. Total height 11 cm. Maximum diameter of the bowl 12.2 cm. Diameter at the rim 10.6 cm. Maximum diameter of the lid 11.8 cm.
Acquisitions 1915. Found on the outskirts of the town of Yuryev (now called Tartu) with a hoard of silver objects.

Both parts are badly damaged, showing dents, breaks, cracks, scratches, and small holes.

Similar in form is the lid from the Nenets National Area. See No. 220.

NOTE. B. Shelkovnikov's opinion that the vessel is of Russian origin (Шелковников, *Русское стекло*, с. 221) seems erroneous.

LITERATURE: А. В. Банк, «Серебряный сосуд из так называемого Тартуского клада», *Древние могильники и клады (Археологический сборник, II)*, Таллин, 1962, с. 275—286; A. Banck, «Byzance et l'Orient d'après quelques données de l'art appliqué du XIe et du XIIe siècle», *Труды XXV Международного конгресса востоковедов*, 1962, с. 555—561; Шелковников, *Русское стекло*, с. 221; Даркевич, *Светское искусство Византии*, с. 118—126, ил. 180—187.

227 DISH WITH A BIRD. 12th century

Glazed pottery

The dish is made of red clay; it has vertical sides and a border flaring outward, and rests on a cone-shaped hollow foot. Engraved through slip is a bird facing right, with a spiral-like design (probably a snake?) in front, and a leaf back of the figure. The border is decorated with a band of incised hatches. The dish is coated with a transparent yellow glaze (on the exterior, only in the upper part).

The Hermitage. Inv. No. X 298. Height 10 cm. Diameter 22 cm. Diameter of the foot 7.8 cm.
Acquisitions 1898. Received from the Archaeological Commission. Found at Chersonese.

Restored from a number of fragments; considerable losses of glaze.

For related objects, see Ch. H. Morgan, *The Byzantine Pottery (Corinth, XI)*, Cambridge, Mass., 1942, No. 1011, p. 120, fig. 97; Якобсон, *Средневековый Херсонес*, с. 195, № 99, табл. XXXVI.

LITERATURE: *ОАК за 1896 г.*, 1898, с. 166; Банк, *Искусство Византии*, № 89, с. 123.

228 DISH WITH A FANTASTIC CREATURE FIGHTING A SERPENT. 12th century

Glazed pottery

The dish is made of red clay; it is flat, with a rounded border and a cone-shaped ring foot. The interior decoration consists of a fantastic creature and a serpent in fight, engraved through slip. The border is ornamented with triangles, palmettes and rosettes in ovals, and stained with brown. The dish is covered on both sides with a transparent yellow glaze. There are incised circles on the exterior.

The Hermitage. Inv. No. X 282. Height 5 cm. Diameter 35 cm. Diameter of the foot 11 cm.
Acquisitions 1895. Found at Chersonese.

Restored from a number of fragments; the lacunae filled with plaster. Pieces of glaze are missing. The exterior bears traces of fire.

The dish is almost identical in form and design with another Chersonese dish in the Hermitage collection (Bock, *Poteries*, p. 24—26, N° 11; Якобсон, *Средневековый Херсонес*, с. 195—196, № 99, 103).

LITERATURE: Кондаков, *Русские клады*, с. 39, рис. 14; Bock, *Poteries*, N° 12, p. 26—27; Толстой, Кондаков, *Русские древности*, с. 28—29, рис. 18.

229 DISH WITH A FANTASTIC ANIMAL. 12th—13th centuries

Glazed pottery

The dish is made of white clay; it has a ring foot, and a raised edge slightly turned inwards; the interior is painted with a design in green and violet under a transparent glaze. The design shows a fantastic animal making a leap to the right, its head turned in the opposite direction. The rim is coloured violet.

The Hermitage. Inv. No. X 276. Diameter 15 cm. Height 6.8 cm.
Acquisitions 1895. Found at Chersonese.

A piece is broken from the rim; a considerable part of the foot is missing. There is a hole in the foot.

LITERATURE: Bock, *Poteries*, p. 40—41, N° 26; Якобсон, *Средневековый Херсонес*, с. 220, табл. XXVI, 14; Банк, *Искусство Византии*, № 91, с. 123, 126, 129.

230 DISH WITH A FANTASTIC ANIMAL. 12th century

Glazed pottery

The dish is made of red clay. It has a raised border with a flat rim, and rests on a ring foot. The interior shows a fantastic animal engraved through slip; there are brown stains on slip. The border is ornamented with double lines crossing, and circles of different size. The dish is coated with a transparent yellow glaze. The reverse has stripes.

The Hermitage. Inv. No. X 727. Diameter 34.5 cm. Diameter of the foot 10 cm.
Acquisitions 1955. Found at Chersonese in the same year.

Restored from a number of fragments; considerable losses of glaze.

LITERATURE: Г. Д. Белов, «Два поливных блюда из Херсонеса», *СГЭ*, 11, 1959, с. 48—49; Г. Д. Белов, «Отчет о раскопках в Херсонесе в 1955 г.», *ХС*, V, 1959, с. 42—43, рис. 28; Банк, *Искусство Византии*, № 90, с. 123, 126, 129; Megaw, *Zeuxippus Ware*, p. 80, 82, pl. 17 b.

231 DISH WITH A HERO KILLING A FANTASTIC BEAST. 12th century

Glazed pottery

The dish is made of red clay. It is flat, with a slightly raised edge, and coated with a transparent glaze of a light colour, with yellow and brown stains. The decoration consists of a scene of a man fighting a fantastic animal (Dighenes Akrites?). The border is ornamented with a band of triangles and hatched lines. The reverse bears concentric circles. The foot is cone-shaped and hollow.

The Hermitage. Inv. No. X 728. Diameter 31.8 cm. Diameter of the foot 10.1 cm.
Acquisitions 1955. Found at Chersonese in the same year.

Restored from a number of fragments; the gaps filled with plaster.

LITERATURE: Г. Д. Белов, «Два поливных блюда из Херсонеса», *СГЭ*, 11, 1957, с. 48—49; Г. Д. Белов, «Отчет о раскопках в Херсонесе в 1955 г.», *ХС*, V, 1959, с. 42—43, рис. 27; Банк, *Искусство Византии*, № 88, с. 123, 126, 129; *Propyläen Kunstgeschichte*, Taf. 84 b; A. H. S. Megaw, "Byzantine Pottery (4th—14th century)", in: *World Ceramic. An Illustrated History*, London, 1968, p. 105, fig. 316; Megaw, *Zeuxippus Ware*, p. 80—81, pl. 20 a; Даркевич, *Светское искусство Византии*, с. 153, ил. 222.

232 BOWL WITH A BIRD. 13th century

Glazed pottery

The bowl is made of red clay. The interior and the upper part of the outside are covered with a green glaze. The rim is vertical, broad, slightly flaring outward. The cup rests on a ring foot. The interior bears a bird facing left, with an ornamental crest and tail, within concentric circles; it is engraved through slip. The rim is also decorated with concentric circles.

The Hermitage. Inv. No. X 317. Diameter 16 cm. Height 7.8 cm.
Acquisitions 1896. Received from the Archaeological Commission. Found at Chersonese.

Restored from a number of small fragments. A large piece is broken from the foot, and several small bits from the rim. In the lower portion losses of glaze in several places.

For related objects, see Ch. H. Morgan, *The Byzantine Pottery (Corinth, XI)*, Cambridge, Mass., 1942, No. 1309, p. 300, fig. 206.

LITERATURE: *ОАК за 1895 г.*, 1897, с. 92, рис. 237.

233 ICON OF THE ARCHDEACON STEPHEN. 11th century

Egg tempera over gesso, wood

The panel is hollowed. Archdeacon Stephen is shown full length, with an incense burner in his right hand, and a red kerchief in his left one.

The Hermitage. Inv. No. I 5. Height 32 cm. Width 18.5 cm. Thickness 2 cm.
Acquisitions 1930. Formerly in the Russian Museum. Came with the Likhachov collection.

There is a distant resemblance between this piece and the image on silk reproduced by Talbot Rice (*The Art*, p. XVI).

LITERATURE: Лихачев, *Материалы*, 1, табл. XVIII, 35; Кондаков, *Русская икона*, 3, с. 99, рис. 12; Лазарев, *История*, 1, с. 325; Lazarev, *Storia*, p. 259.

234 ICON OF ST PANTALEON. 10th—11th centuries (?)

Egg tempera over gesso, wood

The panel is hollowed. The icon shows a half-figure of St Pantaleon with a casket in his left hand, and a stylus in his right one. He wears a chiton with an ornamental band round the collar, and a cloak. The halo is rendered by a dotted contour. The facial type is distantly reminiscent of the Faiyum portraits. Above is an inscription indicating the name of the saint: ОАГІОС ПАNТЕΛЕНМОN.

The Pushkin Museum of Fine Arts. Inv. No. 2864. Height 52 cm. Width 34 cm.
Acquired in 1933. Formerly in the Tretyakov Gallery. Comes from the Ostroukhov collection.

The face and garments of the saint are damaged. Part of the panel at the bottom has been cut away. There are losses, mainly in the lower part; and traces of nails.

The icon of St Pantaleon which was formerly in the Kievo-Pecherskaya Lavra should be compared (Петров, *Альбом*, табл. 6; Wulff, Alpatoff, S. 48—52, 260).

NOTE. A thorough study of the specimen was made in the process of restoration. The supposition that it is executed in the technique of encaustic was refuted as erroneous, and the dating to a period as early as the 10th century was found to be highly questionable.

LITERATURE: А. Стрелков, *Фаюмский портрет*, М.—Л., 1936, с. 82, 89—90; Лазарев, *История*, 1, с. 95, 307; Felicetti-Liebensfels, S. 44, Taf. 37 b; V. Poutsko, «Saint Pantéléimon, icône à l'encaustique», *Byzantion*, XLIII (1973), 1974, p. 181—194, pl. I.

235—236 ICON OF THE VIRGIN AND CHILD (OUR LADY OF VLADIMIR). First half of the 12th century

Egg tempera over gesso, wood

The panel is hollowed. The icon shows a half-figure of the Virgin of the Eleusa type, holding the Child on her right arm. All that remains of the original Byzantine work, are the faces; the Virgin's with darker olive-green flesh tones; and the Child's painted in lighter tints. A layer of a dark red colour adds warmth to the cheeks.

The Tretyakov Gallery. Inv. No. 14 243. Height 104 cm. Width 69 cm.
Acquisitions 1930. Formerly in the History Museum, Moscow. The icon was brought from Constantinople. It was first at Vyshgorod (near Kiev), in 1155 it went to Vladimir, and in 1395 to Moscow where it was placed in the Assumption Cathedral in the Kremlin.

The icon was repeatedly repainted and enlarged in Russia in the 13th, late 14th, early 16th, and lastly in the 19th centuries. In the early 15th century the reverse was painted with the *Hetimasia*. The icon was cleaned at the order of the All-Russia Restoration Committee in 1918.

The icon served as a model for a great number of later versions of the Our Lady of Vladimir iconographic type.

LITERATURE: M. Alpatov, V. Lasareff, «Ein byzantinisches Tafelwerk aus der Komnenenepoche», *Jahrbuch der Preussischen Kunstsammlungen*, 1925, S. 140—155; Felicetti-Liebensfels, S. 51—52, Taf. 47; Talbot Rice, *The Art*, p. 330, pl. 171; А. Н. Свирин, *Древнерусская живопись в собрании Государственной Третьяковской галереи*, М., 1958, рис. 3, 4; Антонова, Мнева, *Каталог*, 1, № 5, с. 58—64; табл. 7—10; Lazarev, *Storia*, p. 204, fig. 325—326; Delvoye, *L'Art byzantin*, p. 266, ill. 135; Beckwith, *Early Christian and Byzantine Art*, p. 131, fig. 240; *Propyläen Kunstgeschichte*, S. 178, 180, Taf. XII; Talbot Rice, *The Byzantine Painting*, p. 11, pl. I.

237—238 ICON OF ST GREGORY THE THAUMATURGUS. 12th century

Egg tempera over gesso, wood

The panel is hollowed, leaving broad margins. It bears a half-figure of St Gregory the Thaumaturgus holding a book in his left hand, his right raised in blessing. The crosses and ornamental bands round the wrists are decorated with an elaborate design executed with great delicacy; there is a dark blue band round the collar. He holds a book which has gold fastenings and a red cover bearing a cross and corner ornaments, and adorned with pearls. On either side of the figure is the Greek inscription indicating the name of the saint: Ο ΑΓΙΟϹ ΓΡΗΓΟΡΙΟϹ Ο ΘΑΥΜΑΤΟΥΡΓΟϹ.

The Hermitage. Inv. No. I 4. Height 81 cm. Width 53 cm. Thickness 3.3 cm.
Acquisitions 1935. Formerly in the Russian Museum.

The panel is split vertically; it is reinforced from the back (approximately in the middle), and the split is stopped and painted over on the surface. There are cracks in the areas of the right hand, the left shoulder, the book, and the background. The losses in the margins, and the cracks are filled in.

LITERATURE: Wulff, Alpatoff, S. 66—69, 262—263, Taf. 24; Кондаков, *Русская икона*, 3, с. 89, 100, рис. 14; Лазарев, *История*, 1, с. 125—126, 324; 2, табл. 199; А. Банк, «Икона Григория Чудотворца», in: *Сокровища Эрмитажа*, Л., 1948, с. 135—138; Felicetti-Liebensfels, S. 45, Taf. 38 a; Банк, *Искусство Византии*, № 94, 95, с. 123, 126, 129; *Эрмитаж*, Л., 1964, № 46; Lazarev, *Storia*, p. 204, tav. 327; О. С. Попова, «Галицко-волынские миниатюры раннего XIII века», in: *Древнерусское искусство. Художественная культура домонгольской Руси*, М., 1972, с. 314.

239—241 ICON OF THE APOSTLE PHILIP AND STS THEODORE AND DEMETRIUS. Late 11th—early 12th centuries

Egg tempera over gesso, wood

The Apostle Philip holding a scroll, St Theodore with a spear and a sword, and St Demetrius with a spear and a shield are shown full length against a hollowed background, under carved ornamental arches resting upon columns of elaborate shape. Each figure is accompanied by an inscription giving the name of the personage: Ο ΑΓ . . . ΦΗΛΙΠΠΟϹ; Ο ΑΓ . . . ΘΕΟΔΩΡΟϹ; ΟΑ . . . ΤΡΙ . . . The clothing of the saints is decorated with dots of white paint, intended to imitate embroidery in river pearls.

The Hermitage. Inv. No. I 186. Height 41 cm. Width 50 cm. Thickness 5.5 cm.
Acquisitions 1935. Formerly in the Russian Museum.

The panel has been cut at the side and at the lower edge. Considerable losses in the lower part and the right side filled in and repainted. The panel is riddled with worm holes at the top and still more in the bottom part. The corners are broken away.

The icon, in all likelihood, formed part of a frieze.

LITERATURE: А. П. Смирнов, *Памятники византийской живописи*, Л., 1928, с. 10, рис. 2; Кондаков, *Русская икона*, 3, с. 101; Лазарев, *История*, 1, с. 126, 324; 2, табл. 201; Банк, *Искусство Византии*, № 97, 98, с. 123, 126, 129; *Masterpieces*, No. 207, p. 66; Lasareff, *Trois fragments*, p. 118—119, pl. 31, *1*; Lasarev, *Storia*, p. 205, tav. 338; A. Orlandos, *L'Architecture et les fresques byzantines du monastère St. Jean à Patmos*, Athènes, 1970, p. 263; Лазарев, *Три фрагмента*, с. 111.

242 ICON OF STS GEORGE, THEODORE AND DEMETRIUS. 12th century

Egg tempera over gesso, wood

The panel is hollowed, leaving a margin. The full-length figures of the warrior saints are painted in front view. At the left is St George supporting a spear with his right hand, his left resting on a shield; in the centre, St Theodore with a spear in his right hand and a shield in his left; and at the right, St Demetrius with a raised sword in his right hand, his left placed on the sheath. Each figure is accompanied by an inscription giving the name of the saint: Ο ΑΓΙΟC ΓΕΩΡΓΙΟC; Ο ΑΓΙΟC ΘΕΟΔΩΡΟC; Ο ΑΓΙΟC ΔΗΜΗΤ-ΡΙΟC.

The Hermitage. Inv. No. I 183. Height 28.5 cm. Width 36 cm. Thickness 2.3 cm.
Acquisitions 1930. Formerly in the Russian Museum.

The bottom left corner cut away; the corners all damaged. A deep wide crack runs along the lower margin, from the left edge to the centre. The panel split in several places, with the losses filled in. The light blue background of later date has been removed during restoration.

Lazarev compares the icon with the warrior saints in the Church of Our Saviour at Nereditsa (В. К. Мясоедов, *Фреска Спаса Нередицы*, Л., 1925, табл. LI, LIV), but his idea of the degree of similarity existing between them is somewhat exaggerated.

LITERATURE: Н. П. Сычев, «Древлехранилище памятников русской иконописи и церковной старины», *Старые годы*, 1916, январь — февраль, с. 8; А. П. Смирнов, *Памятники византийской живописи*, Л., 1928, с. 27; Кондаков, *Русская икона*, 3, с. 101; Лазарев, *История*, 1, с. 126; 2, табл. 204; Lazarev, *Storia*, p. 205, 258.

243 ICON OF THE DESCENT INTO LIMBO (THE ANASTASIS). 12th century

Egg tempera over gesso, wood

The Descent into Limbo is enclosed in a frame of carved wood, shaped as an arch with a cornice, supported by two columns. In the centre is Christ standing above the gates of hell; he wears a golden chiton and a white *himation*; on the left are Adam (kneeling in his sepulchre), and Eve; on the right, David, Solomon, and St John the Baptist. The sepulchres are coloured in imitation of marble. The background shows a rocky landscape. Above is the inscription: Η ΑΝΑCΤΑCΗC. Characteristic of the period is the laconic manner of treating the subject and the conventional rendering of the landscape and of isolated details, such as the figure of Christ over the abyss, suspended in space.

The Hermitage. Inv. No. I 8. Height 31.5 cm. Width 18 cm. Thickness 3 cm.
Acquisitions 1930. Transferred from the Russian Museum.

The right-hand column has been sawn into two pieces down the side. The lower edge has been broken and trimmed in an uneven line. The reverse of the upper edge is bevelled, and riddled with worm holes. Losses of gesso along the sides, mainly, in the area of the carved border. Losses of paint film in the area of the breast of Christ.

This icon, together with No. 244, may have formed part of a larger composition, probably a frieze with the Twelve Feasts. See also Chatzidakis, N[os] 88, 91.

LITERATURE: Лихачев, *Материалы*, 1, табл. X, 16; Кондаков, *Русская икона*, 3, с. 101—102; Wulff, Alpatoff, S.74, 76, 263, Abb. 28; Лазарев, *История*, 1, 126, 325; 2, табл. 200; *Masterpieces*, No. 206, p. 66; *Α. Ξυγγόπουλος, Ὁ ὑμνολογικός ἐικονογραφικός τύπος τῆς ἐις τοῦ ᾿Αθην καθόδου τοῦ ᾿Ιησου. ᾿Επετηρὶς τῆς ῾Εταιρείας βυζαντινῶν σπουδῶν, ΙΖ*, 1941, *σελ.* 114—116, *πίν.* 2; Chatzidakis, p. 397—398, N° 89; V. Lazareff, *Trois fragments*, p. 119, pl. 32, 4; Лазарев, *Три фрагмента*, с. 111—112.

244 ICON OF THE PENTECOST. 12th century

Egg tempera over gesso, wood

The Pentecost is shown in an arched frame of carved wood; the arch is corniced, and supported by columns. On either side of a building is a group of six apostles; the figure of St Peter terminates the group on the left; and that of St Paul, the group on the right. Above the apostles is a segment of the sky radiating twelve rays. There are traces of an inscription in Greek. The reverse is plain, showing traces of paint.

The Hermitage. Inv. No. I 6. Height 32 cm. Width 18.5 cm. Thickness 3 cm.
Acquisitions 1930. Formerly in the Russian Museum.

Both the columns have been sawn into two down the middle. The lower edge is cut in an uneven line; and the upper slopes on the reverse. Losses in the lower part—among them, the figure of the apostle in the middle of one of the rows,—are stopped with mastic and retouched with colour. A piece of wood has been inserted in the bottom left part. There are worm holes.

For parallels, see No. 243. See also Chatzidakis, N[os] 88, 91.

LITERATURE: Wulff, Alpatoff, S. 74, 77, 264; Кондаков, *Русская икона*, 3, с. 101—102; Лазарев, *История*, 1, с. 126, 325; Lasareff, *Trois fragments*, p. 119, pl. 33, *5*; Chatzidakis, p. 397, N° 90; Лазарев, *Три фрагмента*, с. 111, 113.

245 ICON OF THE TRANSFIGURATION. 12th century

Egg tempera over gesso, wood

Christ blessing, with a scroll in his hand, is shown in a *mandorla*; his *nimbus cruciger* is adorned with pearls and gems in each limb. Elijah and Moses stand on mountain tops. The Apostles Peter and John are below. The background is red. The inscription in Greek reads: Η ΜΕΤΑΜΟΡΦΟCIC. The reverse is plain, and has traces of white paint. The upper edge is cut in an uneven slanting line.

The Hermitage. Inv. No. I 7. Height 23.2 cm. Width 23.7 cm. Thickness 2.5 cm.
Acquisitions 1930. Transferred from the Russian Museum.

The edges of the icon have been cut away; parts of figures and the entire figure of the apostle on the right (both the paint layer and gesso) are missing from the lower portion of the panel; parts of the haloes of Christ and Moses are also missing.

For comparable icons, see *L'Art byzantin*, N° 180, p. 244—245; М. Хадзидакис, «Иконы в Греции», in: *Иконы на Балканах*, с. XXIV, XXXIX, № 37.

LITERATURE: Wulff, Alpatoff, S. 72—74, 263—264, Abb. 27; Кондаков, *Русская икона*, 3, с. 96—98, рис. 11; Лазарев, *История*, 1, с. 126, 324; 2, табл. 203; Chatzidakis, p. 398—399, N° 87b; Lazarev, *Storia*, p. 205, tav. 330.

246 ICON OF ST NICHOLAS. Late 13th—early 14th centuries

Miniature mosaic, wood. Silver mount (14th century)

The icon bears a half-figure of St Nicholas the Wonder Worker, with a book in his left hand, his right hand raised in blessing. The chasuble is decorated with gold. The background is silver, showing traces of gold lettering. The mount is adorned with alternating circles and lozenges in filigree work.

The Kiev Museum of Western and Eastern Art. Inv. No. 139 брк. Height of the mount 19 cm. Width 15 cm. Height without the mount 10 cm. Width 8 cm.
Formerly in the Khanenko collection. Comes from the Episcopal Museum of Art and Archaeology in the town of Vich, near Barcelona.

The tesserae are loose in some places; a few are missing.

St Nicholas from the collection of Porphyry Uspensky should be compared (Лихачев, *Материалы*, 1, табл. III, 4).

NOTE. During a cleaning and restoration in 1964—65, some new data have emerged suggesting a possibility of a later date.

LITERATURE: Кондаков, *Памятники*, с. 107—109, рис. 50; Muñoz, p. 139, 170—171; Н. Макаренко, «Выставка церковной старины в музее бар. Штиглица», *Старые годы*, 1915, июнь—август, с. 65—70, 81; Лазарев, *История*, 1, с. 124; *КМЗВИ*, *Каталог*, с. 21, № 3; В. В. Филатов, «Портативная икона „Св. Николай" Киевского музея», *BB*, 33, 1968, с. 220—238, рис. 1, 2; В. В. Филатов, «Реставрация портативной иконы „Св. Николай"», *Сообщения ВЦНИЛКР*, 21, 1969, с. 76—87; Grabar, *Les Revêtements*, N° 34, p. 63, fig. 73.

247—248 RELIEFS WITH THE APOSTLES PETER AND PAUL. 12th century

Marble

The full-length figures of the Apostles Peter and Paul are executed in low relief; each of the apostles is shown standing under an arch supported by twisted columns, Peter with a scroll and the keys in his left hand, Paul with a book, the right hand blessing. The engraved inscriptions in Greek on either side of the figures indicate the names of the saints. The inscription below the figure of St. Paul reads . . . ΛΕΝΗΠΑΡΕΡΧΧΟΥ . . ICEI. The reverse is plain in both cases.

The Hermitage. Inv. Nos. ω 833, ω 834. Thickness 7 cm. Height 66 cm. Width 34.2 cm (No. ω 833). Height 83 cm. Width 54 cm (No. ω 834).
Acquisitions 1930. Formerly in the Museum of the Russian Archaeological Society, Petrograd. Found in the Chepina fortress in Bulgaria during the excavation works conducted by P. Syrku in 1879.

The lower part of No. ω 833 is missing; it is broken in a slanting line at the level of the left knee of the figure. The face is damaged. Several pieces missing from the upper edge. No. ω 834 shows considerable losses in the lower part of the slab. The face has been cut away.

NOTE. In all probability, the reliefs are the work of local Bulgarian masters, executed during the period of Byzantine domination and fully reflecting the traditions of contemporary Byzantine sculpture.

LITERATURE: П. Сырку, «Старинная Чепинская крепость у с. Доркова и два византийских рельефа из Чепины», *BB*, V, 1898, с. 603—617, 841—842, табл. III; Н. Шмиргела, *Скулптурата по нашите земи*, София, 1961, стр. 112, обр. 181; Т. Силяновска-Новикова, «Нови данни за развитието на скулптурата в България през епохата на феодализма (XII—XIV в.)», *Известия на института за изобразителни изкуства*, 1963, VI, стр. 80—82, обр. 16; Соня Георгиева, «Църква в родопската крепост Цепина», *Археология*, 1963, 3, стр. 48—53; J. Maksimović, «La Sculpture byzantine au XIIIe siècle», in: *L'Art byzantin du XIIIe siècle. Symposium de Sopocani*, Beograd, 1967, p. 28, fig. 15; A. Orlandos, *L'Architecture et les fresques byzantines du monastère de St. Jean à Patmos*, Athènes, 1970, p. 124.

249 SEAL WITH CHRIST AND THE EMPRESS EUPHROSENE. 1195—1203

Lead

The seal bears a full-length figure of Christ, with a Gospels book in his left hand; on either side is an inscription in Greek which reads: IC XC; Ο ΧΑΛΚΗΤΗ (Jesus Christ the Chalkites). The epithet derives from the icon of Christ over the Chalke gate in Constantinople. The reverse shows the Empress Euphrosene (wife of the Emperor Alexius III Angelus Comnenus who reigned from 1195 to 1203). She holds a sceptre in her right hand. On either side of the figure is the inscription: ΕΥΦΡΟϹΥΝΙ. ΕΥϹΕΒΕϹΤΑΤΗ ΑΥΓΟΥϹΤΗ ΔΟΥΚΑΙΝΑ (The Most Pious Euphrosene of the House of Ducas).

The Hermitage. Inv. No. M 8213. Diameter 4.3 cm.
Acquisitions 1938. Received from the Institute of Books, Documents and Letters, Leningrad, with the Likhachov collection. Purchased in Paris from Constantinopolitan antiquaries.

The surface is chipped.

LITERATURE: Лихачев, *Моливдовулы*, текст к табл. XXIX, 2; Панченко, *Каталог*, 8, с. 49.

250—251 SEAL WITH THE EMPEROR (?) DAVID. 13th or 15th century

Lead

The seal bears on the obverse a representation of the Emperor (or the Biblical King and Prophet) David seated upon a throne; he holds a sceptre in his right hand, and a scroll (?) in his left one; there is an inscription reading: ΔΑΔ ΒΑϹΙ ΛΕΥ Ϲ, and another on the right, of which the letters, very imperfectly executed, are discerned with difficulty. As to the reading of the inscription in six lines occupying the reverse, there is a considerable divergence of view: . . . ΒΑϹΙΛΕΥ . . ΦΑΛΕϹ ΓΡΑΦΩ . . ΥΡΟϹ: — ΔΑΔ Κ.-ΜΝΗΝΟΥ ΒΑϹΙΛΕΓΓΟ ΝΟΥΓ . ΙΝΟΥ ([may] the decrees of David Comnen, descended from the royal line, ever stand inviolate). Depending upon its construction (the summary of the suggested readings see in Лихачев, *Моливдовулы*, — note to pl. XXXI, 2—3), the figure on the obverse is identified either as the portrait of the last Emperor of Trebizond (1458—62) whose name was David, or—the opinion favoured by Likhachov—as a representation of the Prophet David. In the latter case the seal is likely to have been owned by the brother of the first emperor of Trebizond, Alexius I (1204—22).

The Hermitage. Inv. No. M 4555. 4.4×4.6 cm.
Transferred from the Museum of the Russian Archaeological Institute in Constantinople.

Losses of metal from the surface of the obverse, right side; and several places on the reverse.

For related objects, see Schlumberger, *Sigillographie*, p. 424—425.

LITERATURE: Г. П. Беглери, «Печать трапезундского императора Давида», *ИРАИРК*, VIII, София, 1902—1903, с. 247—248; *Κωνσταντόπουλος, Τὸ λεγόμενον μολυβδόβουλλον τοῦ αὐτοκράτορος Τραπεζοῦντος, Δαβτδ, Journal International d'archéologie numismatique*, VIII, 1905, p. 121—130 (see also: *Journal International d'archéologie numismatique*, IX, 1906, p. 237—249, 293—322; X, 1907, p. 113—156).

252 EWER WITH FANTASTIC BIRDS WITH THE HEAD AND BREAST OF A WOMAN. 13th century

Glazed pottery

The ewer is made of red clay; the body is spherical, the neck short, slightly widening toward the rim; the handle flat; it rests on a ring foot. The exterior is decorated with two fantastic birds with the head and breast of a woman, engraved through slip; the neck and handle have an ornament of interlaced bands (?). The painting is executed in green and brown under a transparent yellow glaze. The interior has yellow glaze on slip.

The Hermitage. Inv. No. X 352. Height 22.4 cm. Diameter of the ring foot 7.6 cm.
Acquisitions 1915. Found at Chersonese.

The ewer is restored from a number of fragments. Considerable portions of the body and the neck are missing; the gaps are filled in with plaster.

For representations of similar subjects, see Якобсон, *Средневековый Херсонес*, с. 208—209, № 135, 137, табл. XXXIII, and D. Talbot Rice, *Byzantine Glazed Pottery*, Oxford, 1930, p. 114, pl. XV b.

LITERATURE: Якобсон, *Средневековый Херсонес*, с. 209, № 136, табл. XXXIII.

253—255 HELMET WITH THE DEESIS AND SAINTS. 13th century

Iron, silver and gold damascening

The helmet has a broad vertical crown and a pointed top, hexagonal in the lower part and cone-shaped above; its form resembles that of a cap. It is hammered from a single sheet of iron, and ornamented all over with silver and gold damascening. The horizontal brim is decorated with ornamental designs in silver damascening, and octofoil rosettes in gold damascening. The crown bears half-figures of Christ, the Virgin and St John the Baptist; and those of the Archangels Michael and Gabriel, two seraphs, St Nicholas and two apostles; all executed in silver inlay against an ornamented background. The conical top is adorned with designs in silver and gold.

The Kremlin Armoury. Inv. No. ОП. 4416. Height 38.5 cm. Diameter 22 cm.
Comes from the basic collection of the Kremlin Armoury.

Numerous minor damages round the edge of the brim. The crown has holes several places, damaging some of the figures.

LITERATURE: *Древности Российского государства*, отд. III, M., 1853, с. 21, табл. 19; А. Бельтман, *Московская Оружейная палата*, M., 1860, табл. 20; *Опись Московской Оружейной палаты*, M., 1884, с. 32—33; *Художественные сокровища России*, II, 1902, с. 255, табл. 108; Ф. Я. Мишуков, *Золотая насечка и инкрустация на древнем вооружении. Государственная Оружейная палата Московского Кремля*, M., 1954, с. 126—129, рис. 1; *Художественные памятники Московского Кремля*, M., 1956, с. 85, рис. 5; *Государственная Оружейная палата Московского Кремля*, M., 1958, № 3; B. Rybakov, K. Neubert, *Der Moskauer Kreml. Die Rüstkammer*, Prag, 1962, S. 12, Taf. 7, 8; Писарская, *Памятники*, с. 17, табл. XIV—XVII.

256—258 ICON OF THE VIRGIN AND CHILD. 13th—14th centuries

Egg tempera over gesso, wood. Silver framing

The panel is hollowed. The icon shows the half-figure of the Virgin of the Hodegetria type, with two busts of angels in the top corners. The silver framing of *repoussé* work fills the background, and includes the haloes. It is adorned with interlacing scrolls of plant ornament, palmettes, and rosettes. In the margins are rectangular plaques with representations: of the *Hetimasia*, with busts of St Peter (?) and St Paul on either side, in the middle of the top margin; Sts John, Luke and Cosmas in the left margin; Sts Matthew, Mark and Damian on the right; St Pantaleon in the centre of the bottom margin. The two bottom corners show full-length figures of Constantine Acropolitus (left) and Maria Comnena, his wife (right). The accompanying inscriptions read: [Δ] ΟΥΛΟϹ ΤΟΥ ΧΥ ΚΩΝϹΤ ΑΝΤΙ ΝΟϹ Ο ΑΚΡΟ ΠΟΛΙ ΤΗϹ; ΜΑΡΙΑ ΚΟΜΝΗ ΝΗ ΤΟΡ ΝΙΚΙ ΝΑ Η ΑΚΡΟ ΠΟΛΙ ΤΙ ϹϹΑ (Christ's slave Constantine Acropolitus; Maria Comnena Tornikina Acropolitissa).

The Tretyakov Gallery. Inv. No. 27222. Height 40 cm. Width 32 cm.
Acquisitions 1930. Formerly in St Sergius's Monastery of the Holy Trinity at Zagorsk.

Repainted in Russia (all but the figures of angels) in the 15th—17th centuries. The plaque with St Peter is missing.

NOTE. Constantine Acropolitus, son of the historian George Acropolitus (1220—1282), was, as well as his father, the Grand Logothete; his wife, daughter of the Prefect of Peloponnesus and Theodora of the house of Tornikes (or, according to Ducange, of the house of Tarchaneiotes), bore the name of Paleologina in her mother's right.

LITERATURE: Лихачев, *Материалы*, 1, табл. VIII, № 12; Н. П. Кондаков, *Изображение русской княжеской семьи*, Спб., 1906, с. 80—84; Лихачев, *Историческое значение*, с. 110, рис. 246; Н. П. Кондаков, *Иконография богоматери*, т. 2, Пг., 1915, с. 201, 203, рис. 93; Антонова, Мнева, *Каталог*, 1, с. 262—263, табл. 172; Donald M. Nicol, "Constantine Acropolites", *DOP*, XIX, 1965, p. 249—265, fig. 1, 2; K. Onasch, *Die Ikonenmalerei*, Leipzig, 1968, Taf. 29; Beckwith, *Early Christian and Byzantine Art*, p. 152; Belting, *Das illuminierte Buch*, S. 72; Банк, *Черты палеологовского стиля*, с. 157, 159; Grabar, *Les Revêtements*, N° 18, p. 45—46, fig, 43, 44.

259—260 ICON OF THE VIRGIN AND CHILD. 13th century

Gold, jewels, wood

The top of the icon is fitted with a hinged loop; the wooden core is faced on all sides with gold plates worked in *repoussé*, both the obverse and the reverse being decorated. The central portion of the obverse shows, against a hollowed background, the Virgin enthroned, of the Eleusa type, under an arch resting upon two slender twisted columns. In the right corner is an inscription: ΜΡ ΘΥ. The corners over the arch are filled with trefoils. The margins are decorated with plant motifs; four oval settings with stones in them, of Russian fifteenth century work, mounted over the old painted representations (of the *Hetimasia* and St George) are disposed in the middle of each margin, on the top of the ornament; the corners of the side margin are occupied with busts in medallions; above are angels, below, warrior saints, and in either margin, two prophets. The reverse bears a leaved cross, Greek letters IC XC, NI KA and an inscription, the meaning of which is obscure and requires further study. The loop in the form of a faceted bead is adorned with a stone in an ornamental setting, probably also of Russian work.

The Hermitage. Inv. No. ω 840. Height 8.3 cm. Width 6.6 cm.
Acquisitions 1930. Formerly in the Russian Museum.

Two new nails and two holes from old ones; the icon is dented, and in places put out of shape. A piece is missing from the hinge. The loop is detached. Bits are broken from two of the stones.

For iconographic parallels, see V. Lasareff, "Studies in the Iconography of the Virgin", *Art Bulletin*, XX, 1938, fig. 10, 12—15. For the method of mounting the stones, see Ю. Д. Аксентон, «Способы оформления вставок из драгоценных камней по памятникам ювелирного искусства Древней Руси», in: *Сборник трудов Всесоюзного научно-исследовательского и проектно-конструкторского института ювелирной промышленности*, вып. 3, Л., 1973, с. 128—129, рис. 9, 12.

NOTE. Likhachov, and Lazarev after him, erroneously describe the icon as a silver one.

LITERATURE: Лихачев, *Историческое значение*, с. 153, рис. 359; V. Lasareff, "Studies in the Iconography of the Virgin", *Art Bulletin*, XX, 1938, p. 38, fig. 11; Банк, *Искусство Византии*, № 101, с. 123, 126, 129; В. Н. Лазарев, «Этюды по иконографии Богоматери», in: *Византийская живопись*, M., 1971, с. 284, 287; Банк, *Черты палеологовского стиля*, с. 265—266.

261 ICON OF THE PROPHET SAMUEL. Late 13th century

Miniature mosaic

The mosaic icon shows a full-length figure of the Prophet Samuel facing right, his arms raised; in the top right corner is a segment of the sky, with a *manus Dei*. The background in the lower portion of the icon is decorated with lozenges and crosses. There is a double border consisting of an inner band of small orna-

mental designs, and an outer one (modern) of white cross-shaped devices against a gold ground. Traces of a Greek inscription remain.
The Hermitage. Inv. No. ω 30. Height 21.7 cm. Width 13.5 cm.
Acquisitions 1885. Formerly in the Basilewsky collection.

The icon has a modern slate backing and a bronze frame. The tesserae forming the background in the upper part are almost all missing; so are those of the halo and the robe. Hardly any tesserae have survived in the outer border; it is painted instead.

LITERATURE: Darcel, Basilewsky, N° 47, p. 25; Dalton, *Byzantine Art*, p. 433; Лазарев, *История*, 1, с. 163, 343; 2, табл. 263 а; Банк, *Искусство Византии*, № 100, с. 123, 126, 129; Банк, *Мозаичная икона*, с. 192; *Эрмитаж*, Л., 1964, № 53; Lazarev, *Storia*, p. 284, tav. 421; Е. С. Овчинникова, «Миниатюрная мозаика из собрания Государственного Исторического музея», *ВВ*, 28, 1968, с. 213—214, 219, 223; Попова, *Новгородская миниатюра*, с. 128—129.

262 ICON OF CHRIST EMMANUEL. Late 13th century

Miniature mosaic, wood, coloured glass

The icon shows, against a hollowed background, a half-figure of Christ Emmanuel, with a scroll in his left hand, his right hand blessing. The broad margins are decorated with gilding over gesso, and coloured stones inset in the board. The nimbus of Christ has traces of ornamental rosettes. The bevel is decorated. The original background was of silver (?). The face is modelled by fine gradations of colour. The reverse retains traces of plant scrolls painted over gesso. The mosaic consists mainly of natural stones and plates of gold and silver.

The History Museum, Moscow. Inv. No. 53066/6. Height 18 cm. Width 13 cm. Thickness 2.6 cm. Height of the mosaic panel 9.5 cm. Width 7 cm.
Acquisitions 1922. Formerly in the Rumiantsev Museum, Moscow, where it came from the Sevastyanov collection.

Losses in the background over the head of Christ. Vertical cracks running the entire length of the icon. A horizontal crack in the middle. Five of the stones missing from their settings, as well as most of the gilding and gesso in the margins.

The image of Christ Child in the early 14th century icon in the Banjani Church (Skopje area) has a certain stylistic affinity with our specimen (P. Miljković-Pepek, «Deux icônes nouvellement découvertes en Macédoine», *JÖB*, 21, 1972, p. 205—208, fig. 4).

LITERATURE: *Отчет по Московскому публичному музею за 1864 г.*, CXXII, отд. II, с. 98, 130; Е. С. Овчинникова, «Миниатюрная мозаика из собрания Государственного исторического музея», *ВВ*, 28, 1968, с. 207—224; Lazarev, *Storia*, p. 285, tav. 429.

263 ICON OF THE FOUR SAINTS. 14th century

Miniature mosaic, wood

The icon shows busts of the four saints: Sts John Chrysostom and Basil in the top row, the former on the left, and the latter on the right; and Sts Nicholas (left) and Gregory the Theologian (right), in the bottom row. The figures are separated by thin bands of lozenges and triangles. The books inlaid with metal plaques are modern.

The Hermitage. Inv. No. ω 1125. Height 16 cm. Width 11.5 cm.
Acquisitions 1938. Received from the Institute of Books, Documents and Letters, Leningrad, with the Likhachov collection.

The icon has survived in a fragmentary condition; the background, haloes and books are missing; the lower portions of the figures have suffered heavy damage; here the gaps are filled with mastic coloured to imitate tesserae. The mosaic icon was mounted on a new panel in the 19th century. The new mount, consisting of a frame with recesses containing relics of saints, and incorporating parts of a 14th century icon sawn into small squares, with silver plaques with Russian inscriptions covering the background, has been removed in accordance with a decision of the Hermitage Restoration Commission, and is preserved separately.

A very close parallel for the representation of St John Chrysostom appears in an icon of this saint from the Nelidov collection now at Dumbarton Oaks (Ross, *Catalogue*, 1, No. 125, p. 104).

LITERATURE: Банк, *Мозаичная икона*, с. 185—193.

264 ICON OF ST THEODORE. Early 14th century

Miniature mosaic, wood

The icon shows a half-figure of St Theodore with a spear in his right hand and a triangular shield in his left. His chiton is embellished with crosses. The halo and the shield are richly ornamented. Within two large and two small rectangles, inscriptions indicating the name of the saint: ΟΑΓ ΘΕ ΟΔΩ ΡΟϹ Ο ϹΤΡΑ ΤΗ ΛΑ ΤΗϹ.
The Hermitage. Inv. No. ω 29. Height 9 cm. Width 7.4 cm.
Acquisitions 1885. Formerly in the Basilewsky collection.

Tesserae are missing from the lower portion of the icon; the shield has suffered heavy damage. A few of the tesserae have been lost and restored in the areas of the halo and the left shoulder.

The haloes and the inscriptions in the icon of the Annunciation in Talbot Rice, *The Art*, pl. XXXVIII are to be compared.

LITERATURE: Darcel, Basilewsky, N° 18, p. 25; Schlumberger, *L'Epopée*, 1, p. 309; Lasareff, *Byzantine Icons*, p. 250; Лазарев, *История*, 1, с. 221, 361; 2, табл. 289 г; Банк, *Мозаичная икона*, с. 192; Банк, *Искусство Византии*, № 99, с. 123, 126, 129; Beckwith, *The Art*, p. 137, fig. 182; *Эрмитаж*, Л., 1964, № 53; Lazarev, *Storia*, p. 368, tav. 470; Лазарев, *Византийские иконы*, с. 331.

265 RELIEF WITH ST LUKE THE EVANGELIST. Late 13th century

Marble

The relief, probably part of an ambo, shows, against a sunk background, the figure of St Luke, turning one-quarter right. He holds with both hands a book in a decorated cover. The inscription indicates the name of the saint: ΟΑΓ Λ Ο Υ ΚΑС. The slab is slightly curved in shape.

The Hermitage. Inv. No. ω 1165. Height 104 cm. Width 53 cm. Thickness 8 cm.

Acquisitions 1930. Formerly in the Russian Museum where it came from the Museum of Old Russian Art, Academy of Arts.

The edges chipped, especially at the left border. Small losses of marble in the area of the book.

For an iconographically close image, see R. Lange, *Die byzantinische Reliefikone*, Recklinghausen, 1964, Nr. 16, 8, 68. For general features of style, see *Ibid*., Nr. 22, S. 78—79.

LITERATURE: В. Прохоров, *Каталог музея древнерусского искусства*, Спб., 1879, с. 53, № 104; A. Bank. «Relief en marble à l'image de saint Luc l'évangéliste», *JÖB*, 21, 1972, S. 7—11, Abb. 1.

266—268 ICON OF ST GEORGE WITH SCENES FROM HIS LIFE. Late 12th—13th centuries

Wood, carved and painted over gesso

The icon is carved with a full-length figure of St George, shown frontally. His right hand supports a spear, his left rests on a shield. The figure is flanked by a vertical band, divided by rows of ornamental patterns into six panels carved with scenes from the saint's life. On the left, St George before the Emperor Diocletian; St George Taken to Prison; The Stoning of St George; St George Broken on a Wheel; St George in a Lime-pit. On the right, The Clubbing of St George; St George Raises a Man from the Dead; St George Cures the Ox of Glycerius; St George Throws Down the Idols; The Beheading of St George. The two scenes at the bottom are almost entirely spoiled. There are traces of inscriptions in Greek lettering. Each of the scenes shows vestiges of painting over a gesso coating. The icon is set in a wooden case.

The Museum of Ukrainian Art, Kiev. Inv. No. CK 285. Height 107 cm. Width 82 cm.
Acquisitions 1968. Formerly in the Mariupol Museum of Local Studies. Brought from the Crimea in 1778.

The icon was badly damaged. Restored by Pertsev in the Russian Museum, Leningrad. Traces of considerable damage by fire in the area of the face and the upper portion of the figure; also in the subject scenes. Pieces of wood missing from the background, St George's right shoulder and his left foot. Serious damage by wood-boring beetle. Losses in the paint layer and gesso coating.

Two icons in carved wood, from Kastoria, are related to our specimen. One of them shows St George standing three-quarters right, with painted scenes of his life; the other represents the saint frontally (R. Lange, *Die byzantinische Reliefikone*, Recklinghausen, 1964, Nr. 49—50, S. 121—126). See also Р. Шмерлинг, «Мраморная скульптура из Вани», *Сообщения АН Грузинской ССР*, 17, 1956, с. 185—191. For parallels for the subject scenes, see Г. Н. Чубинашвили, «Один из памятников первостепенного значения грузинской чеканки в Сванетии», *Ars Georgica*, 3, 1950, с. 95—118, табл. 33—40.

LITERATURE: А. Л. Бертье-Делагард, «К истории христианства в Крыму», *Записки Одесского общества истории и археологии*, XXVIII, 1910, с. 1—71, приложения, с. 72—108; В. Пуцко, «Мариупольский рельеф св. Георгия», *Зборник Радова Византолошког института*, Београд, 13, 1971, стр. 313—331, рис. 1—6; *Государственный музей украинского искусства УССР*, Киев, 1972, № 1.

269 ICON OF CHRIST PANTOCRATOR. 13th century

Egg tempera over gesso, wood

Christ Pantocrator is shown full length, with a closed book in his left hand, his right hand blessing. The panel is hollowed and slatted on the reverse. Noteworthy are the markedly elongated proportions of the figure, and the modelling of the face achieved by the use of white lights laid on in fine lines.

The Hermitage. Inv. No. I 2. Height 47.5 cm. Width 30 cm. Thickness 1.8 cm.
Acquisitions 1930. Formerly in the Russian Museum. Came with the Likhachov collection.

The top right corner has been cut away; the slatting is modern. Partial losses in the gesso ground. The gold background is considerably crackled and partly flaked off. The wood at the edges is riddled with worm holes.

LITERATURE: V. N. Lasarev, "Duccio and Thirteenth Century Greek Ikons", *BM*, LXI, 1931, p. 154; Лазарев, *История*, 1, с. 169, 201; 2, табл. 265 б; Lazarev, *Storia*, p. 285, tav. 429; Попова, *Новгородская миниатюра*, с. 120, 123.

270 ICON OF THE ASSEMBLY OF THE APOSTLES. Early 14th century

Egg tempera over gesso, wood

The panel is hollowed. The icon shows the Assembly of the Apostles; the two on the right in the front row hold books (one has it half open, the other closed); the two others and one in the back row hold scrolls. Below is indicated the ground on which the figures stand. Above is an inscription consisting of three lines; the top line reads: Η CΥΝΑΞΙC ΤΩΝ ΔΩΔΕΚΑ ..... ΑΠΟCΤΟΛΩΝ (The Assembly of the Twelve Holy Apostles); their names follow. The diversity of attitudes, the individualized treatment of the faces, and the pictorial manner of execution are typical of the period.

The Pushkin Museum of Fine Arts. Inv. No. 2851. Height 38 cm. Width 34 cm.
Acquisitions 1932. Transferred from the History Museum, Moscow. Formerly in the picture gallery of the Rumiantsev Museum where it came as a gift from A. Muravyov. Comes from the Sevastyanov collection.

The upper margin, the right one and part of the lower one, have been covered with gesso anew. The reverse of the icon has been covered with gesso, and coloured with oil paint.

LITERATURE: Айналов, *Византийская живопись*, с. 121—144; Wulff, Alpatoff, S. 114—116, 270; Lazareff, *Byzantine Ikons*, p. 250; Лазарев, *История*, 1, с. 221, 361, табл. XLVI; 2, табл. 305; Felicetti-Liebensfels, S. 85—86, Taf. 104 b; Talbot Rice, *The Art*, p. 336, pl. XXXV; Beckwith, *The Art*, p. 142—143, fig. 191; Lazarev, *Storia*, p. 368, 414, tav. 495, 496; O. Demus, *Byzantine Art and the West*, New York, 1970, p. 237, pl. V; Лазарев, *Византийские иконы*, с. 331—333; Weitzmann, *Studies*, p. 332.

271 ICON OF THE PROPHET ELIJAH IN THE WILDERNESS. 14th century

Egg tempera over gesso, wood

The panel is hollowed. The Prophet Elijah is shown against a rocky landscape seated on the ground three quarters left, his right elbow resting on his knee, his head supported on his right hand. His gaze is directed upwards. On the hill to the right is a raven holding an orange-coloured loaf. At the foot of the rocks are some flowers. The background bears an inscription which indicates the saint's name: Ο ΠΡΟΦΗΤΗC ΗΛΙΑC. The letters of the inscription, painted in vermilion, are ligatured. Noteworthy is the powerful figure of the prophet, his comparatively small head, and the pictorial manner of execution.

The Hermitage. Inv. No. I 187. Height 35.5 cm. Width 28 cm. Thickness 3 cm.
Acquisitions 1930. Formerly in the Russian Museum.

The panel is curved and riddled with worm holes. All the corners are broken away, and the margins badly damaged. There are numerous cracks filled with stopping, and losses in the paint layer.

For iconographic parallels of later date, see Talbot Rice, *The Byzantine Painting*, pl. 163.

LITERATURE: Кондаков, *Русская икона*, 2, табл. 132; 3, с. 152; Банк, *Искусство Византии*, № 102, с. 123, 126, 129; Felicetti-Liebensfels, S. 83—84, Taf. 100 b; Lazarev, *Storia*, tav. 501; Д. Тасић, «Споменици цариградског сликарства у последњем веку самосталности», in: *Моравска школа и њено доба*, Београд, 1972, стр. 15.

272—273 ICON OF THE ANNUNCIATION. First half of the 14th century

Egg tempera over gesso; canvas on wood

The panel is hollowed; the figures of the Virgin and the Archangel appear against an elaborate architectural background represented with an illusion of space. In the middle ground is the figure of a servant girl standing by the side of a column, with her arm round the shaft. There is a magnificent gold throne with a red cushion. The inscription in vermilion reads: Ο ΕΥΑΓΓΕΛΙCΜΟC.

The Pushkin Museum of Fine Arts. Inv. No. 2860. Height 55 cm. Width 43 cm.
Acquisitions 1933. Formerly in the History Museum, Moscow.

A piece is missing from the left side of the panel, badly riddled with worm holes. In the lower part of the icon, losses of paint film and gesso (down to the canvas); both the figures are damaged.

LITERATURE: Lasareff, *Byzantine Ikons*, p. 250—255; Лазарев, *История*, 1, с. 221—222, 361; 2, табл. 308; *Masterpieces* No. 231, p. 72; Beckwith, *The Art*, p. 144—145, fig. 193; Lazarev, *Storia*, p. 368—369, 405, tav. 499; Лазарев, *Византийские иконы*, с. 332, 336, 338.

274—275 ICON OF THE DORMITION. First half of the 14th century

Egg tempera over gesso; wood

The panel is hollowed. In the foreground is the couch of the Virgin, over which groups of apostles and angels are stooping. The elaborate composition crowded with figures is characteristic of the time. In the top left part appear traces of an inscription in red: Η ΚΟΙΜΗCΙC ΤΟΥ ΘΕΟΤΟΚΟΥ.
Above the head of Christ are the letters IC XC, above the Virgin—ΜΡ ΘΥ.

The Pushkin Museum of Fine Arts. Inv. No. 2861. Height 45 cm. Width 34 cm.
Acquisitions 1933. Formerly in the History Museum, Moscow. Comes from the Sevastyanov collection.

The panel is badly tunnelled by worms; all the corners have been broken away. Losses of the paint film and gesso at the edges; pieces broken from the edges in several places. Numerous losses in paint layer and gesso ground.

The icon depicting the same subject, now at the Hermitage (Wulff, Alpatoff, S. 116—118, Taf. 44), shows some features in common with this piece.

LITERATURE: Wulff, Alpatoff, S. 116—117, 271; Lasareff, *Byzantine Ikons*, p. 250; Лазарев, История, 1, с. 221, 361; 2, табл. 306; Felicetti-Liebensfels, S. 71, Taf. 85 b; *Masterpieces*, No. 233, p. 73, fig. 15; Beckwith, *The Art*, p. 144—145, fig. 144; Lazarev, *Storia*, p. 368, 414—415, tav. 498; Talbot Rice, *The Byzantine Painting*, p. 157, pl. XXIV; Лазарев, *Византийские иконы*, с. 332, 334, 338.

276 ICON OF THE VIRGIN AND CHILD, WITH SAINTS. 14th century

Egg tempera over gesso; wood

The panel is slightly hollowed, the Virgin of the Eleusa type is shown half-length. Her robes are of a deep brown colour, edged with gold and fringed. Beneath the Virgin's *maphorion* is a veil which accentuates the shape of her face. The Child's cheek is pressed against his mother's. There are traces of an inscription in vermilion. In the margins are figures of saints facing toward the centre, holding books, sometimes half open; the top and the bottom margins bear four such figures each and the side ones, three. The faces, executed with delicacy and precision of touch, display certain traits of a graphic manner.

The Hermitage. Inv. No. I 181. Height 33.1 cm. Width 26.8 cm. Thickness 1.7 cm.
Acquisitions 1930. Formerly in the Russian Museum.

The panel is warped; the losses in the corners, along the right side of the bottom edge, and partly in the upper edge, are filled with wax. The lower parts of the figures of the saints in the bottom margin have not survived. Losses filled in the left part of the figure of the Virgin. The paint layer is abraded (especially in the faces).

LITERATURE: Н. П. Кондаков, *Иконография Богоматери. Связи греческой и русской иконописи с итальянской живописью раннего Возрождения*, Спб., 1911, с. 50; Н. П. Кондаков, *Иконография Богоматери*, т. 2, Спб., 1915, с. 264; Wulff, Alpatoff, S. 120—122, 272—273; Кондаков, *Русская икона*, 2, табл. 123; 4, с. 217; Lasareff, *Byzantine Ikons*, p. 256; Лазарев, *История*, 1, с. 228, 366; 2, табл. 320; Lasarev, *Storia*, p. 375, 418, tav. 528; Лазарев, *Византийские иконы*, с. 340, 342.

277 ICON OF ST JOHN THE BAPTIST. 14th century

Egg tempera over gesso, wood

The icon is hollowed, leaving a margin. St John the Baptist is shown half-length, three quarters left, in an attitude of prayer. The work may be a leaf from a triptych with the Deesis. The hair of the saint falls down to his shoulders in broad long locks. The face is rendered by plastic modelling. There are traces of an inscription: ΟΑ С . ΙΩ Α . . .

The Hermitage. Inv. No. I 241. Height 20.8 cm. Width 17 cm. Thickness 1.7 cm.
Acquisitions 1930. Formerly in the Russian Museum where it came with the Likhachov collection.

Losses of the paint film and gesso at the edges, more extensive in the area of the bottom right corner. A vertical crack at top left. Traces of hinges along the left edge.

The work shows some features in common with the icon in the monastery on Mount Sinai (K. Weitzmann, "Mount Sinai's Holy Treasures", *National Geographic*, January, 1964, p. 117).

LITERATURE: Лихачев, *Материалы*, 1, табл. X, № 475; А. П. Смирнов, *Памятники византийской живописи*, Л., 1928, с. 28.

278 ICON WITH SIX OF THE TWELVE FEASTS OF THE CHURCH. 14th century

Egg tempera over gesso, wood

The panel is hollowed. The scenes are separated by plain bands of background between two ruled lines. In the top row are the Entry into Jerusalem and the Crucifixion; in the middle row, the Descent into Limbo (the Anastasis), and the Ascension; in the bottom row, the Pentecost and the Dormition. Below are busts of six saints. The scenes and the busts of saints are accompanied by Greek inscriptions ΒΑΙΟΦΟΡΟϹ; Η ϹΤΑΥΡΩϹΙϹ; Η ΑΝΑϹΤΑϹΙϹ; Η ΑΝΑΛΗΨΙϹ; Η ΠΕΝΤ . . . ; Η ΚΟΙΜ . . . ; ΟΑ . . . ΓΕΩΡΓΙΟϹ; ΟΑ . . . ΘΕΟΔΩΡ . . ; ΟΑ . . . ΦΕΟ . . ΡΟϹ Ο ϹΤΡΑΤΙΛΑΤΗϹ; ΟΑ . . . ; ΟΑ . . .
The icon is executed in miniature technique, which is characteristic of the period.

The Hermitage. Inv. No. I 182. Height 31 cm. Width 20 cm. Thickness 1.8 cm.
Acquisitions 1930. Formerly in the Russian Museum.

The panel is warped and riddled with worm holes, especially along the sides and the lower edge. The corners are missing. The lower portion of the scene of the Pentecost is damaged. The paint layer is considerably worn.

The mosaic diptych at the Museo dell'Opera del Duomo in Florence can be compared (Talbot Rice, *The Art*, pl. XXXVI, XXXVII); the icons in the British Museum (Лазарев, *История*, 2, табл. 310; *L'Art byzantin*,

N° 172, p. 240—241) and those in the monastery of Mount Sinai (G. et M. Sotiriou, *Icônes du Mont Sinaï*, v. 1, Athènes, 1956, fig. 208—212; v. 2, 1958, p. 190—191) show a more distant resemblance.

LITERATURE: Lasareff, *Byzantine Ikons*, p. 255; Лазарев, *История*, 1, с. 222, 362; 2. табл. 309; *L'Art byzantin*, p. 141; М. В. Алпатов, «Икона времени Андрея Рублева», in: *Этюды по истории русского искусства*, т. 1, М., 1967, с. 99, ил. 66; Lazarev, *Storia*, p. 369, 415, tav. 502; Лазарев, *Византийские иконы*, с. 338.

279 ICON OF ST JOHN THE BAPTIST. 14th century

Egg tempera over gesso, wood

The panel is hollowed, leaving a raised margin. It bears St John the Baptist shown half-length, facing left, in the Deesis attitude. The contrasting combination of the almost black *himation*, the bright red of the robe, and the gold ground is unusual. The manner in which the face is executed—divided, as it were, into parts— reminds one of some Serbian paintings.

The Hermitage. Inv. No. I 457. Height 87.5 cm. Width 66 cm.
Acquisitions 1935. Formerly in the Russian Museum.

The panel is warped; the three planks composing it, are held together by modern slats. There are cracks along the junction. Considerable losses of paint, together with gesso, in the corners and the right side. Losses in the right shoulder are filled in. The ground is almost entirely missing.
For parallels, see S. Radojčič, *Iconi di Serbia e Macedonia*, Beograd, 1961, tav. 4, 5, 40, 41; П. Милковић-Пепек, «О сликарима митрополиту Јовану и јеромонаху Макарију», in: *Моравска школа и њено доба*, Београд, 1972, с. 11.

LITERATURE: Кондаков, *Русская икона*, 2, табл. 76, с. 340; Банк, *Искусство Византии*, № 103, с. 123, 125, 129; Lazarev, *Storia*, p. 378, 419, tav. 538; *8th Annual Exhibition of Icons. 4th June—27th July 1968. London Temple Gallery*, No. 1 (note 5); Лазарев, *Византийские иконы*, с. 354, 356.

280 ICON WITH THE RAISING OF LAZARUS. 14th century

Egg tempera over gesso, wood

The scene is shown against the background of two mountains with a building emerging beyond. The figures form several groups arranged in different planes: some are in the foreground, others in the middle ground or in the background. The figure of Christ is given prominence by the use of colour. On either side of the head are the letters IC XC.
Characteristic of the later Byzantine painting are the figures of the youths in the right foreground, carrying away the coffin lid. One of them is shown in profile view, the other from the back.

The Russian Museum. Inv. No. ДРЖ 1407. Height 53.5 cm. Width 44 cm. Thickness 4.5 cm.
Transferred from the Museum Reserve in the late 1920s.

Additions in the upper and lower margins. Considerable losses in the paint layer and ground. The reverse of the panel badly tunnelled by the wood-boring beetle. The bottom left corner is broken off.

The icon in the Ashmolean Museum, Oxford, is of somewhat later date (*L'Art byzantin*, N° 181, p. 245). See also the *Raising of Lazarus* in the Pantanassa Church at Mistra (G. Millet, *Les Monuments byzantins de Mistra*, Paris, 1910, pl. 140, *3*).

LITERATURE: Лазарев, *Византийские иконы*, с. 355—356.

281—284 ICON OF CHRIST PANTOCRATOR. 1363

Egg tempera over gesso, wood

The panel is hollowed, leaving a margin. Christ is shown half-length; his right hand is raised in blessing, in his left one is a book fastened with clasps, with a gem-studded cover. He wears a chiton with the clavus, and a himation. In the lower portion of the margins are portraits of donors; of the figure in the left margin, only traces of a headdress, part of the contour outlining the head, and the inscription . . . HCIC TOϒ ΔOϒ-ΛOϒ ΘEOϒ AΛEΞIOϒ TOϒ MEΓAΛOϒ CTPATOΠEΔAPXOϒ (Prayer of the God's slave, the Grand Stratopedarch Alexius) have survived. The donor in the right margin wears a tall headdress, and garments made of a fabric with a double eagle pattern; he is shown in an attitude of prayer, facing towards the centre; above his head is the inscription + ΔEHCIC TOϒ ΔOϒΛOϒ ΘEOϒ IΩ[ANNOϒ] TOϒ MEΓAΛOϒ ΠPIMIKϒPIOϒ (Prayer of the God's slave, the Grand Primicerion John). These two persons are described in the written sources of the period as founders of the church of Christ Pantocrator; the foundation of the church refers to 1363. A milder expression of Christ and the modelling of the face by means of fine white lines are characteristic of the art of the period.

The Hermitage. Inv. No. I 515. Height 106 cm. Width 79 cm.
Acquisitions 1930. Formerly in the Russian Museum.

The panel is slightly warped; there are numerous worm holes; the upper edge and the corners have been broken away, the panel is split down the middle and has been reinforced on the reverse; the missing piece in the lower part has been replaced. The losses along the split, in the areas of the face and the robes, have been filled in, as well as those in damaged places all over the surface. The figure of the donor in the left margin is almost entirely missing; that of the donor in the right margin, damaged in the lower part.

The authors of the catalogue *L'Art byzantin* compare N°s 200—202, p. 254—255; but they probably exaggerate the resemblance.

LITERATURE: А. П. Смирнов, *Памятники византийской живописи*, Л., 1928, с. 15, рис. 3; Кондаков, *Русская икона*, 2, табл. 121; 3, с. 104; P. Lemerle, «Sur la date d'une icône byzantine», *Cahiers archéologiques*, Paris, II, 1947, p. 129—132; А. В. Банк, «Письмо в редакцию», *BB*, 7, 1953, с. 317—318; Лазарев, *История*, 1, с. 228, 365; 2, табл. 318; Банк, *Искусство Византии*, № 104, 105, с. 123, 126, 129; *L'Art byzantin*, p. 255; Beckwith, *Early Christian and Byzantine Art*, p. 152, pl. 288; Lazarev, *Storia*, p. 375, 417, tav. 526; Talbot Rice, *The Byzantine Painting*, p. 113, pl. 103; Belting, *Das illuminierte Buch*, S. 72.

285 ICON OF ST ANASTASIA. 14th century

Egg tempera over gesso, wood

The icon is hollowed, leaving a margin. It shows a half-figure of St Anastasia, with a leaved six-arm cross on a long shaft in her right hand and a decorated pharmacy jar on her left hand, covered over by the end of her *maphorion*. On the reverse, there is a leaved cross painted in brown over gesso.

The Hermitage. Inv. No. I 471. Height 99 cm. Width 65.5 cm. Thickness 3 cm.
Acquisitions 1931. Formerly in the Museum of the Russian Archaeological Institute in Constantinople.

The panel is broken at the right edge. Badly riddled with worm holes, especially at the bottom edge, and chipped in the lower portion. A vertical split runs from the top edge down to the middle. Small indentations and cracks over the surface. The background, once probably silver coloured, has rubbed off.

Iconographically, the work resembles the icon of St Marina (15th century) in the Byzantine Museum in Athens (*Иконы на Балканах*, табл. 83, с. LXXXVIII; *Frühe Ikonen*, Wien—München, 1965, Taf. 83, S. XXXV).

LITERATURE: M. Alpatov, «Byzantinisches Erbe in der altrussischen Malerei», in: *Actes du XXIIe Congrès international d'histoire de l'art, Budapest, 1969*, t. 1, Budapest, 1972.

286 BASE FOR A CROSS. 14th century (?)

Wood

The base for a cross is four-sided, with a round border at the top, and hollow inside. The four faces bear Gospels scenes carved in relief, each enclosed in a three-lobed arch. The scenes show the Annunciation, the Baptism, the Nativity and the Descent into Limbo. Above the arches are figures of flying angels. Below the scenes are inscriptions in Greek containing lines from psalms of appropriate contents. The corners are decorated with vertical protuberances carved with a trailing vine, birds and animals. Traces of colouring appear in places.

The Hermitage. Inv. No. ω 220. Height 18 cm. Diameter 8.5 cm. 9×8 cm (at the foot).
Acquisitions 1914. Formerly in a private collection.

Two of the corner ornaments are missing. There are worm holes. Pieces are broken from the lower part. Cracks and minor losses of wood.

For related ornamental motifs, see No. 287, and also *Каталог собрания древностей гр. А. С. Уварова*, отд. VIII—IX, табл. X; А. П. Смирнов, «Греческий деревянный поставец под крест из собрания Гос. Академии истории материальной культуры», *SK*, 1927, 1, p. 147--156.

287 FRAGMENT OF A TRIPTYCH (?) WITH GOSPEL SCENES. 14th century (?)

Wood

The piece is carved in high relief, with two Gospel scenes, the Raising of Lazarus and the Dormition. Under each scene is an inscription in three lines containing bits from psalms chosen to suit the subjects represented. Over the three-lobed arch are two flying angels. The scenes are framed within an arch decorated with plant motifs and supported by columns carved with a trailing vine and figures of animals (a two-headed basilisk, snakes, goats, monkeys, and two birds with necks interlaced); the cubiform bases and capitals of the columns are decorated with representations of the prophets Jonah and David, Sts Nicholas, Elizabeth, Gregory the Theologian and an unidentified prophet. The piece is tentatively defined as a fragment of a triptych. There is a short foot (?) under the column.

The Hermitage. Inv. No. ω 265. Height 24 cm. Width 7.5 cm.
Acquisitions 1918. Formerly in the Kondakov collection. Comes from Mount Athos.

The left side is broken away.

Another fragment of the object is in the Walters Art Gallery, U.S.A. For parallels also see No. 286.

LITERATURE: Кондаков, *Памятники*, с. 202—203, табл. XLVII; Schlumberger, *L'Epopée*, 3, p. 665; G. Sotiriou, «La Sculpture sur bois dans l'art byzantin», *Mélanges Charles Diehl*, II, 1390, p. 172.

288 ICON OF THE VIRGIN AND CHILD (KNOWN AS OUR LADY OF PIMEN). Second half of the 14th century

Egg tempera over gesso, wood

The panel is hollowed, leaving a margin. The Virgin, in the Hodegetria position, is shown half-length; she wears a chiton, and a white veil under her maphorion; the Child has a yellow-brown, gold-woven chiton; he holds a rolled red scroll in his hand. Remains of the gold ground in the area of the heads. The faces show a greenish carnation. The panel is slatted on the reverse.

The Tretyakov Gallery. Inv. No. 28 638. Height 67 cm. Width 48 cm.
Acquisitions 1930. Formerly in the History Museum, Moscow; came in 1918 from the Chrismal Chamber of the Patriarch's Palace in the Moscow Kremlin. Before 1918 in the Annunciation Cathedral of the Kremlin. According to tradition the icon was brought from Constantinople by the Metropolitan Pimen in 1381 or 1388.

The gold ground is almost entirely missing. There is a vertical crack down the middle, running almost the whole length of the panel; losses in the background and some small pieces in the area of the Virgin's maphorion are stopped and painted over. The reverse is painted with the Annunciation in the 18th century.

LITERATURE: Лазарев, *История*, 1, с. 229, 366; 2, табл. 322; *Masterpieces*, No. 223, p. 337; Talbot Rice, *The Art*, p. 193, pl. XLIV; Beckwith, *Two Exhibitions*, p. 371, fig. 2; Антонова, Мнева, *Каталог*, № 327, с. 373; Talbot Rice, *The Byzantine Painting*, p. 158, pl. 126; Лазарев, *Византийские иконы*, с. 340—341, 344.

289 ICON OF THE APOSTLE PETER. Late 14th century

Egg tempera over gesso; canvas on wood

The icon is one of the Vysotsky tier to which Nos. 290 and 291 also belong. The panel is hollowed. The Apostle Peter is represented in half-length, in an attitude of prayer, facing three quarters right. He holds an open book in his left hand, his right hand blessing. The apostle wears a blue chiton and a yellow himation. In the top corners are traces of an inscription in Greek (?).

The Tretyakov Gallery. Inv. No. 12728. Height 148 cm. Width 96.5 cm.
Acquisitions 1930. Formerly in the Central Restoration Workshops, Moscow, where it came from the Church of Our Lady in the Vysotsky Monastery at Serpukhov. Arrived from Constantinople in the late 14th century being sent by Athanasius Vysotsky to Athanasius Junior, Father Superior of the monastery.

The book, the inscription on the book and the inscription above were repainted in the 16th century by a Russian master.

For related objects, see No. 290, and also other icons of the same tier which is one of the few known Byzantine tiers (there exist but seven icons).

LITERATURE: В. Н. Лазарев, «Новые памятники византийской живописи XIV века (Высоцкий чин)», *BB*, 4, 1951, с. 122, 131, рис. 6 (*Византийская живопись*, М., 1971, с. 364); Антонова, Мнева, *Каталог*, № 329, с. 375—376, табл. 246; Talbot Rice, *The Byzantine Painting*, p. 157, pl. 122; Д. Тасић, «Споменици цариградског сликарства у последнем веку самостоятности», in: *Моравска школа и њено доhа*, Београд, 1972, с. 13—14.

290 ICON OF THE ARCHANGEL GABRIEL. Late 14th century

Egg tempera over gesso; canvas on wood

The icon belongs to the Vysotsky tier. The panel is hollowed. The Archangel Gabriel is represented in half-length, in an attitude of prayer, facing three quarters left; he has a staff in his right hand, and wears a chiton of golden brown, and a dark green *himation*. The icon is executed in a dry graphic manner. There are traces of a red inscription above.

The Tretyakov Gallery. Inv. No. 12729. Height 146 cm. Width 106 cm.
For data on acquisition and provenance, see No. 289.

A number of cracks; the longest one, in the right-hand part, runs the whole length of the icon in the vertical direction.

The icon of Archangel Gabriel in the monastery on Mount Sinai shows certain features in common with this piece (G. et M. Sotiriou, *Icônes du Mont Sinaï*, v. 1, Athènes, 1956, fig. 237). See also No. 289.

LITERATURE: В. Н. Лазарев, «Новые памятники живописи XIV века (Высоцкий чин)», *BB*, 4, 1951, с. 129—141, табл. 5 (*Византийская живопись*, М., 1971, с. 363); Антонова, Мнева, *Каталог*, № 239, с. 375—376, табл. 245.

291 ICON OF THE APOSTLE PAUL. Late 14th century

Egg tempera over gesso; canvas on wood

The icon is one of the Vysotsky tier. The panel is hollowed. The Apostle Paul is represented in half-length, facing three quarters left; he holds a closed book with both hands. The apostle wears a blue chiton and a *himation* of a deep cherry colour. Above are traces of an inscription in Greek.

The Tretyakov Gallery. Inv. No. 12 752. Height 149 cm. Width 98.4 cm.
For data on acquisition and provenance, see No. 289.

The inscriptions are of a later date than the icon, and written in Russian.

For parallels, see other icons of the same tier.

LITERATURE: В. Н. Лазарев, «Новые памятники византийской живописи XIV века (Высоцкий чин)», *BB*, 4, 1951, с. 122, 141, рис. 7 (*Византийская живопись*, М., 1971, с. 365); Антонова, Мнева, *Каталог*, № 329, с. 375—376, табл. 247; Lazarev, *Storia*, p. 376, 419, tav. 537.

292—293 ICON OF ABRAHAM ENTERTAINING THE THREE ANGELS. 15th century

Egg tempera over gesso; canvas on wood

The oblong panel is hollowed. It shows three angels seated at a rectangular table on which are different vessels. Abraham and Sarah wait at table. There is an architectural background; on the left is the Oak of Mamre. In the background above are traces of an inscription descerned with great difficulty. The restrained colouring of great beauty, and the pictorial manner of execution which is still in evidence in this piece, though side by side with the budding elements of the graphic manner, intimate a date in the late 14th, or the earliest part of the 15th century. D. Charalambus-Muriki in a work recently published assigns the icon to the late 15th century; but the author had no opportunity to study the original. The icon is slatted on the reverse.

The Hermitage. Inv. No. I 1. Height 36 cm. Width 54.2 cm. Thickness 2.7 cm.
Acquisitions 1930. Formerly in the Russian Museum, where it came with the Likhachov collection.

Losses of paint film and gesso along the top edge and in the lower part. A horizontal crack running the whole width of the icon. A minor crack in the bottom right part. In the face of the angel in the middle the high lights are rubbed off. The gilding is lost in places. The inscription has almost disappeared.

There is a number of icons akin to our piece in iconography and colouring, but differing from it in point of style; see the icons in the Narbonne Museum, France, in the Byzantine Museum and the Museum of Benaki, Athens; and others discussed in the article by D. Charalambus-Muriki.

LITERATURE: Н. Пунин, «Заметки об иконах в собрании Н. П. Лихачева», *Русская икона*, 1914, 1, с. 7, 31; Айналов, *Византийская живопись*, с. 90—91; Н. В. Малицкий, «К истории композиции ветхозаветной Троицы», *SK*, II, 1928, с. 40; Lasareff, *Byzantine Ikons*, p. 256; Лазарев, *История*, 1, с. 229, 366; 2, табл. 323; Felicetti-Liebensfels, S. 103, Taf. 136 a; Банк, *Искусство Византии*, № 106, 107, с. 123, 126, 129; *Ντ. Χαραλάμπους-Μουρίκη*, *'Η παράσταση τῆς φιλοξενίας τοῦ 'Αβραάμ σε μία εἰκόνα τοῦ Βυζαντινοῦ Μουσεὶου*, *Δελτίον τῆς Χριστιανικῆς 'Αρχαιολογικῆς 'Εταιρείας, περ. Δ, τ. Γ, 'Αθῆναι*, 1963, *σελ*. 87—114, *πίν*. 34; В. Д. Лихачева, «Художественная функция бытовых предметов в иконе „Троица“ Государственного Эрмитажа», *BB*, 26, 1965, с. 239—247; Lazarev, *Storia*, p. 376, 418, tav. 531; Лазарев, *Византийские иконы*, с. 349.

294—295 *SAKKOS* OF THE METROPOLITAN PETER. 1322

Satin, embroidery

The *sakkos* belonged to the first Metropolitan of Moscow, who bore the name of Peter (1308—1326). The satin bears on an azure ground a pattern of roundels containing gold crosses, in continual vertical bands separated by vertical stripes. Around the neck and sleeves there run orphreys of silver and gold adorned with pearls; they are Russian work of different date; among the persons whose representations are embroidered in the orphreys are the Metropolitans Peter and Alexius (1354—77). In front are buttons of diverse shapes.

The Kremlin Armoury. Inv. No. 12 041. Length 145 cm. Width 142 cm. Transferred from the Treasury of the Patriarchs of Moscow. There is an entry in an old inventory to the effect that "in the year 6830 (1322) was finished this *sakkos* of Peter the Miracle Maker".

The *sakkos* was repeatedly renovated.

NOTE. The *sakkos* was originally an imperial garment; later it became a vestment of the patriarch. It consists of rectangular pieces of textile sewn together at the shoulders; and buttons down the sides. There are short wide shoulder pieces which do duty for sleeves.

LITERATURE: Савва, *Указатель*, с. 17; Успенский, *Патриаршая ризница*, с. 240; Левинсон-Нечаева, *Одежда и ткани*, с. 330; *Художественные памятники Московского Кремля*, М., 1956, с. 111, ил. 14; *Государственная Оружейная палата Московского Кремля*, М., 1958, № 255; B. Rybakov, K. Neubert, *Der Moskauer Kreml. Die Rüstkammer*, Prag, 1962, S. 125, Taf. 85; Писарская, *Памятники*, с. 27, табл. LII.

296—299 *EPITRACHELION* OF THE METROPOLITAN PHOTIUS. 15th century

Satin, embroidery

The *epitrachelion* is embroidered with different coloured silks and gold and silver thread. In the centre (i.e. the part worn on the neck) is a bust of Christ. Nearer to the shoulders are full-length figures of the Virgin and St John the Baptist. The ends are embroidered with 88 medallions adorned with pearls, containing half-length figures of the apostles, the prophets, the saints, disposed in rows, four in a row; they are accompanied by Greek inscriptions. In the spaces between the medallions are cherubs. The ground is embroidered with plant motifs. The buttons are of gold, done in openwork and filigree. The fringe is of later date.

The Kremlin Armoury. Inv. No. 12106. Length 150 cm. Width 34.5 cm.

Transferred from the Patriarchal Vestry in the Moscow Kremlin. Brought from Constantinople in 1408 together with other vestments, when Photius was appointed to the Moscow metropolitan see.

LITERATURE: Савва, *Указатель*, с. 17; Успенский, *Патриаршая ризница*, с. 218, 249; А. Н. Свирин, *Древнерусское шитье*, М., 1963, с. 52, рис. на с. 58; Л. И. Якунина, *Русское шитье жемчугом*, М., 1955, с. 29; Писарская, *Памятники*, с. 27—28, табл. LIII—LV.

300—304 "MAJOR" *SAKKOS* OF THE METROPOLITAN PHOTIUS. First half of the 15th century

Satin, embroidery

The *sakkos* is embroidered with gold and silver thread, and coloured silks; the central part bears the Crucifixion (above) and the Descent into Limbo (below) enclosed within crosses, on the front; and the Ascension and the Dormition, on the back. The central scenes are surrounded by other Feasts of the Church and busts of saints in medallions. The central parts of the *sakkos* are enclosed in a band filled with a Greek inscription containing the text of the Nicene Creed. On either side are full-length figures of saints under arches, two in each of the four upper rows, and one in each of the rows below. Beside the latter representations are Abraham's Sacrifice, and Jacob's Ladder. The rectangles at the hem show the Grand Prince of Moscow Vasily Dmitrievich and his wife Sophia Vitovtovna, with accompanying inscriptions in Russian (right); and the Emperor John Palaeologus and his wife Anna Vasilyevna, with accompanying inscription in Greek (left). The contours are outlined in seed pearls. By the side of John is a representation of the Archbishop Photius, with an accompanying Greek inscription reading: Ο ΠΑΝΙΕΡΩΤΑΤΟϹ ΜΗΤΡΟΠΟΛΙΤΗϹ ΚΥΕΒΑ ΚΑΙ ΠΑϹΗϹ ΡΩϹΙΑϹ ΦΩΤΙΟϹ (Metropolitan of Kiev and All Russia, Photius).

The Kremlin Armoury. No. 12 002. Length 135 cm. Width at the hem 123 cm.
Transferred from the Patriarchal Vestry in the Moscow Kremlin.

The ornamentation in pearls is of Russian work (?).

A close parallel to this piece is No. 305, and also the so-called Dalmatic of Charlemagne at the treasury of St Peter's Cathedral, Vatican (Talbot Rice, *The Art*, pl. 195; Айналов, *Византийская живопись*, табл. V—VII).

LITERATURE: Савва, *Указатель*, с. 18; Успенский, *Патриаршая ризница*, с. 201—205, 240—241; Левинсон-Нечаева, *Одежда и ткани*, с. 331; В. Н. Лазарев, «Московская живопись, шитье и скульптура первой половины XV века», in: *История русского искусства*, т. 3, М., 1955, с. 192; *Художественные памятники Московского Кремля*, М., 1956, с. 111, рис. 78; *Государственная Оружейная палата Московского Кремля*, М., 1958, рис. 257; А. С. Верховская, *Западноевропейская вышивка XII—XIX веков в Эрмитаже*, Л., 1961, с. 8—9; Писарская, *Памятники*, с. 28—29, табл. LVI—LXI; *Оружейная палата*, М., 1964, с. 184, 186.

305—307 "MINOR" *SAKKOS* OF THE METROPOLITAN PHOTIUS. 14th—15th centuries

Satin, embroidery

The *sakkos* is embroidered with gold and silver thread and silks of different colours; it bears scenes of the Feasts of the Church, representations of different saints, and the text of the Nicene Creed. The centre of the front is decorated with scenes of the Crucifixion and the Descent into Limbo enclosed within crosses; the centre of the back with the Transfiguration and the Ascension. The crosses are flanked by full-length figures of the prophets. At the sides are full-length figures of saints under three-lobed arches, disposed in rows; there are three rows at either side. One of the shoulders is adorned with the scenes of the Entry into Jerusalem and the Pentecost; the other, with the Raising of Lazarus, and the Young Christ between Constantine and Helen. The sides of the *sakkos* are embroidered with framed inscriptions in Arabic containing texts from the Koran.

The Kremlin Armoury. Inv. No. 12 003. Length 142 cm. Width 150 cm.
Transferred from the Patriarchal Vestry in the Moscow Kremlin. The *sakkos* is supposed to have been sent to Moscow from Constantinople in the mid-14th century, in connection with the canonization of the Metropolitan Peter.

The sleeves, and the ornamentation in pearls at the hem of the *sakkos*, are of later date.

For related objects, see No. 300, and also the so-called Dalmatic of Charlemagne (Talbot Rice, *The Art*, pl. 195; Айналов, *Византийская живопись*, табл. V—VII).

LITERATURE: Савва, *Указатель*, с. 18—19; Успенский, *Патриаршая ризница*, с. 206, 209, 241; Писарская, *Памятники*, с. 29—30, табл. LXII—LXVII; Beckwith, *Early Christian and Byzantine Art*, p. 156, fig. 298.

308—309 *SAKKOS* OF THE METROPOLITAN SIMON. Late 15th—early 16th centuries

Satin, embroidery
The *sakkos* is embroidered with crosses having a long traverse at the centre and short ones at the top and bottom; and ornamental heart-shaped devices with two scrolls issuing from the top, also enclosing crosses.

The Kremlin Armoury. Inv. No. 12006. Length 140 cm. Width 157 cm.
Transferred from the Patriarchal Vestry in the Moscow Kremlin.

The neck and sleeves are decorated with silver gilt orphreys of Russian work.

LITERATURE: Савва, *Указатель*, с. 19; Успенский, *Патриаршая ризница*, с. 242; Левинсон-Нечаева, *Одежда и ткани*, с. 331, рис. 12; *Художественные памятники Московского Кремля*, М., 1956, с. 111, рис. 79; Писарская, *Памятники*, с. 29, табл. LXVIII.

310—314 MOUNT OF THE ICON OF OUR LADY OF VLADIMIR. 15th century

Gold

The rectangular mount in *repoussé* work comprises the plate to cover the background, with an open space in the middle shaped to fit the outline of the figures. The contour is accentuated by an ornamental band of thin strips of metal welded edgewise into the surface. The borders are decorated with the Twelve Feasts of the Church in *repoussé* work, which appear on rectangular plaques with a five-lobed top part. In the upper border are the Annunciation, the Nativity, the Presentation in the Temple (with the subject of the scene named in the inscription on the roll) and the Baptism; in the left margin are the Dormition and the Ascension; in the right, the Raising of Lazarus and the Entry into Jerusalem; below are the Crucifixion, the Pentecost, the Transfiguration, and the Descent into Limbo. In the spaces between the plaques are crosses and rosettes within circles, lozenges, etc. set against the background of filigree ornament. In the lower portion of the mount is the monogram of the Metropolitan Photius in an inscription: ΦΩΤΙΟC ΡΟCΙΑC ΑΡΧΙΕΠΙCΚΟ-ΠΟC.

The Kremlin Armoury. Inv. No. 15350. Height 105 cm. Width 70 cm. Comes from the Assumption Cathedral of the Kremlin.

Minor damages and repairs.

Frames of the icons in monasteries of Mount Athos may be compared (Кондаков, *Памятники*, с. 161, 188—190).

NOTE. Until recently the mount was erroneously regarded as a work of Russian masters. This opinion has been most convincingly disproved by M. Postnikova-Loseva who considers the framing a Byzantine production.

LITERATURE: И. Снегирев, *Памятники Московской древности*, М., 1842—1845, с. 13; К. Невоструев, «Монограмма всероссийского митрополита Фотия на окладе Владимирской чудотворной иконы», in: *Сборник на 1866 год, изданный Обществом древнерусского искусства*, М., 1866, с. 177—181; Кондаков, *Памятники*, с. 188—190; А. И. Успенский, *Владимирская икона Богоматери в Московском Успенском соборе*, М., 1902; M. Alpatoff, «Die frühmoskauer Reliefplastik», *Belvedere*, 51/52, 126, S. 236—256; Б. А. Рыбаков, *Ремесло древней Руси*, М., 1948, с. 632, 643—644; В. Н. Лазарев, «Московская живопись, шитье и скульптура первой половины XV века», in: *История русского искусства*, т. 3, М., 1955, с. 206—207; М. М. Постникова-Лосева, Т. Н. Протасьева, «Лицевое евангелье Успенского собора как памятник древнерусского искусства XV века», in: *Древнерусское искусство XV — начала XVI века*, М., 1963, с. 162—172; Писарская, *Памятники*, с. 18—19, табл. XIX—XXV; А. Н. Свирин, *Ювелирное искусство Древней Руси XI—XVII веков*, М., 1972, с. 78—81; Grabar, *Les Revêtements*, N° 41, p. 68—72, fig. 89—97.

315—316 ICON OF THE DESCENT INTO LIMBO (THE ANASTASIS). 15th century

Egg tempera over gesso, wood

The panel is not hollowed. In the centre is Christ standing on the ledge of a rock, facing right; in his left hand is a scroll; with his right one he raises Adam. Behind Adam are Eve, St John the Baptist, and other personages; left of Christ are David, Solomon, etc. Both the groups are shown against the background of overhanging cliffs. Above are half-figures of angels holding the Emblems of Passion. In the space between are traces of an inscription. In the abyss below are the broken gates of hell, two figures, hinges, nails, etc. On the left is seen part of a sarcophagus. The icon is rich in colouring; the drawing is of great beauty and delicacy. The faces are executied in the so-called fused manner, or *plav* (i.e., modelled by gradations of tones imperceptibly merging into each other). In the representation of garments, a linear manner is felt.

The Hermitage. Inv. No. I 184. Height 32.3 cm. Width 27 cm. Thickness 1.4 cm.
Transferred from the Russian Museum, where it came from Likhachov collection.

The panel is warped. Small losses of paint film and gesso, especially in the corners. The paint layer in the background is abraded and crackled. Numerous minor cracks, mainly in the lower part.

There is a similar icon, the work of Theophanes of Crete (mid-16th century), in the Stauronicetas Monastery on Mount Athos (M. Chatzidakis, «Recherches sur le peintre Théophane le Crétois», *DOP*, 23/24, 1969—1970, p. 326, fig. 76). For a close parallel to our piece in point of iconography—though differing from it stylistically—see: Банк, *Выставка византийских материалов*, с. 346, табл. к с. 348.

LITERATURE: Лихачев, *Материалы*, рис. № 108; Ph. Schweinfurth, *Geschichte der russischen Malerei im Mittelalter*, Den Haag, 1930, S. 419; Lasareff, *Byzantine Ikons*, p. 256; Лазарев, *История*, 1, с. 229, 366; 2, табл. 324; Банк, *Искусство Византии*, фронтиспис, с. 16; Delvoye, *L'Art byzantin*, p. 363, fig. 202; Lazarev, *Storia*, p. 376, 418, tav. 532; M. Chatzidakis, «Recherches sur le peintre Théophane le Crétois», *DOP*, 23/24, 1969—1970, p. 326; Лазарев, *Византийские иконы*, с. 349, вклейка к с. 348.

317—318 ICON OF THE NATIVITY OF ST JOHN THE BAPTIST. 15th century

Egg tempera over gesso, wood

On the left is Elizabeth seated on the couch; at the foot of the couch is the infant John in a crib, and a woman spinning. On the right is Zacharias, seated; he writes. In the middle is a table with diverse vessels on it; and three servant girls standing at the table. The scene is set against an architectural background; on the left there is a building with a velum. The icon is remarkable for the depth and richness of colouring. The ground is gold. The inscription in red reads: Η ΓΕΝΗC[IC] ΤΟΥ ΠΡΟΔΡΟΜΟΥ (The Nativity of the Precursor). On the reverse are traces of slatting. The richness of colouring, the presence of genre motifs, and the dry manner of execution typical of the period of decline in Byzantine painting make the icon datable to the 15th century.

The Hermitage. Inv. No. I 456. Height 65 cm. Width 63 cm. Thickness 1.8 cm.
Acquisitions 1930. Transferred from the Russian Museum.

Vertical cracks in the upper part. Losses of paint film and gesso along the right side and the lower edge. A crack down the female figure on the left. The gilding is worn. A piece broken out of the back surface.
The icon of the Nativity of the Virgin in the Munich National Museum may be compared (Felicetti-Liebensfels, S. 97, 127 b).

LITERATURE: Лазарев, *История*, 1, с. 229, 366; 2, табл. 325; Felicetti-Liebensfels, S. 97, Taf. 126 b; Банк, *Искусство Византии*, № 108—110, с. 123, 126, 129; Lazarev, *Storia*, p. 326, 418, tav. 533; В. Лихачева, «К вопросу об иконографии Рождества Иоанна Предтечи (икона „Рождество Иоанна Предтечи" Государственного Эрмитажа и „Рождество Богоматери" Баварского музея в Мюнхене и Синайского монастыря святой Екатерины)», *Известия на Института за Изкуствознание*, XIII, 1969, стр. 191—198; Лазарев, *Византийские иконы*, с. 349.

319 ICON OF ST GREGORIUS PALAMAS. Late 14th — early 15th centuries

Egg tempera over gesso, wood

The panel is hollowed. St Gregorius Palamas, Archbishop of Thessalonica canonized in 1363, is shown half-length, holding a book in his left hand, and blessing with his right. He wears a red episcopal chasuble decorated with crosses inscribed in circles, and an omophorion with crosses. The nimbus is outlined with a dotted contour. Above is the inscription: ΑΡΧΙΕΠΙϹ ΚΟΠΟϹ ΓΡΗΓΟΡΙΟϹ ΘΕϹϹΑΛΟΝΙ ΚΗϹ Ο ΠΑΛΑ ΜΑϹ (Archbishop of Thessalonica Gregorius Palamas). The execution is extremely dry, the manner graphic; the use of hatching in the treatment of the face is characteristic of the period.

The Pushkin Museum of Fine Arts. Inv. No. 2853. Height 37 cm. Width 28 cm.
Acquisitions 1932. Formerly in the History Museum, Moscow, where it came from the Zubalov collection.

The upper margin and most of the left one have been coated with a new layer of gesso. Losses in the paint film and gesso down to the board in the area of one of the arms. A crack down the beard and the book, with losses of paint film.

LITERATURE: Lasareff, *Byzantine Ikons*, p. 256; Лазарев, *История*, 1, с. 229, 366; Lazarev, *Storia*, p. 376, 418; Лазарев, *Византийские иконы*, с. 345, 348, 352; М. В. Алпатов, «Искусство Феофана Грека и учение исихастов», *BB*, 33, 1972, с. 194.

ABBREVIATIONS

AMIRANACHVILI, *LES ÉMAUX*
: Ch. Amiranachvili, *Les Emaux de Géorgie*, Paris, 1962

AMIRANASCHWILI, *KUNSTSCHÄTZE*
: Ch. Amiranaschwili, *Kunstschätze Georgiens*, Prague, 1971

ANGIOLINI MARTINELLI, *LINEA E RITMO*
: Patrizia Angiolini Martinelli, «Linea e ritmo nelle figure umane ed animali sugli argenti dell'Ermitage di Leningrado dei secoli V—VII», *Corsi di cultura sull'arte ravennate e bizantina*, XX, 1973, Ravenna

ANGIOLINI MARTINELLI, *REALTÀ E FANTASIA*
: Patrizia Angiolini Martinelli, «Realtà e fantasia negli sfondi paesistici ed architettonici delle argenterie paleobizantine del museo dell'Ermitage di Leningrado», *Corsi di cultura sull'arte ravennate e bizantina*, XX, 1973, Ravenna

BANCK, *MONUMENTS (IVe—VIIe s.)*
: A. Banck, «Monuments des arts mineurs de Byzance (IVe—VIIe siècles) au Musée de l'Ermitage», *Corsi di cultura sull'arte ravennate e bizantina*, IX, 1962, Ravenna

BANCK, *MONUMENTS (X^e—XIIe s.)*
: A. Banck, «Monuments des arts mineurs de Byzance (X^e—XIIe s.) au Musée de l'Ermitage (argenterie, stéatites, camées)», *Corsi di cultura sull'arte ravennate e bizantina*, IX, 1962, Ravenna

BANK, *L'ARGENTERIE*
: A. Bank, «L'Argenterie byzantine des XIe—XVe siècles. Classification des monuments et méthodes de recherches», *Corsi di cultura sull'arte ravennate e bizantina*, XVII, 1970, Ravenna

BANK, *LES STÉATITES*
: A. Bank, «Les Stéatites. Essai de classification, méthodes de recherches», *Corsi di cultura sull'arte ravennate e bizantina*, XVII, 1970, Ravenna

BANK, *QUELQUES MONUMENTS*
: A. Bank, «Quelques monuments de l'art appliqué byzantin des IXe—XIIe s. provenant des fouilles sur le territoire de l'URSS durant les dernières dizaines d'années», *Actes du XIIe Congrès International des Etudes Byzantines*, III, 1964, Beograd

BANK, *QUELQUES PROBLÈMES*
: A. Bank, «Quelques problèmes des arts mineurs byzantins au XIe siècle», *The Proceedings of the XIIIth International Congress of Byzantine Studies. Oxford, 5—10 September 1966*, London, 1967

BECKWITH, *EARLY CHRISTIAN AND BYZANTINE ART*
: J. Beckwith, *Early Christian and Byzantine Art* (*Pelican History of Art*), Penguin Books, 1970

BECKWITH, *THE ART*
: J. Beckwith, *The Art of Constantinople. An Introduction*, London, 1961

BECKWITH, *TWO EXHIBITIONS*
: J. Beckwith, "Two Exhibitions of Byzantine Art", *The Burlington Magazine*, C, 667, 1958

BELTING, *DAS ILLUMINIERTE BUCH*
: V. Belting, *Das illuminierte Buch in der spätbyzantinischen Gesellschaft*, Heidelberg, 1970

BM
: *The Burlington Magazine*

BOCK, *POTERIES*
: W. de Bock, «Poteries vernissées du Caucase et de la Crimée», *Mémoires de la Société Nationale des Antiquaires de France*, LVI, Paris, 1897

BS
: *Byzantinoslavica*

BUSCHHAUSEN, *EIN BYZANTINISCHES BRONZKREUZ*
: H. Buschhausen, «Ein byzantinisches Bronzekreuz in Kassandra», *Jahrbuch der Österreichischen Byzantinischen Gesellschaft*, XVI, 1967

BUSCHHAUSEN, *FRÜHCHRISTLICHES SILBERRELIQUIAR*
: H. Buschhausen, «Frühchristliches Silberreliquiar aus Isaurien», *Jahrbuch der Österreichischen Byzantinischen Gesellschaft*, XI/XII, 1962—1963

BUSCHHAUSEN, LENZEN, *EIN KONSTANTINISCHES SILBERRELIQUIAR*
: H. Buschhausen, H. Lenzen, «Ein Konstantinisches Silberreliquiar aus Jabalkovo in Bulgarien», *Jahrbuch der Österreichischen Byzantinischen Gesellschaft*, XIV, 1965

BZ
: *Byzantinische Zeitschrift*

CATALOGUE DES PIERRES GRAVÉES
: *Catalogue des pierres gravées du Cabinet de feu son altesse sérénissime monseigneur le duc d'Orléans, premier prince du sang, dont la vente sera indiquée dans les papiers publiés*, Paris, 1786

CHATZIDAKIS
: *M. Χατζηδάκις, Εἰκόνες ἐπιστολίου ἀπὸ τὸ Ἅγιον Ὄρος, Δελτίον τῆς Χριστιανικῆς Ἀρχαιολογικῆς Ἑταιρείας, περ. Δ, τ. Δ*, 1964—1968

COCHE DE LA FERTÉ, *L'ANTIQUITÉ*
: E. Coche de la Ferté, *L'Antiquité chrétienne au Musée du Louvre*, Paris, 1958

COCHE DE LA FERTÉ, *COLLECTION*
: E. Coche de la Ferté, *Bijoux byzantins de Chio, de Crète, de Salonique. Collection H. Stathatos. Les Objets byzantins et post-byzantins*, Limoges, 1957

CRUIKSHANK DODD
: E. Cruikshank Dodd, *Byzantine Silver Stamps*, Washington, 1961

CRUIKSHANK DODD, *BYZANTINE SILVER TREASURES*

E. Cruikshank Dodd, *Byzantine Silver Treasures*, Bern, 1973

DALTON, *BYZANTINE ART*

O. M. Dalton, *Byzantine Art and Archaeology*, Oxford, 1911

DALTON, *CATALOGUE*

O. M. Dalton, *Catalogue of Early Christian Antiquities and Objects from the Christian East... in the British Museum*, London, 1901

DARCEL, BASILEWSKY

A. Darcel, A. Basilewsky, *La Collection Basilewsky. Catalogue raisonné*, Paris, 1874

DEÉR, *DIE HEILIGE KRONE*

J. Deér, *Die Heilige Krone Ungarns*, Wien, 1966

DEKAN, *ANTROPOMORFNÉ MOTIVY*

J. Dekan, «Antropomorfné motivy na liatych bronzových kovaniach predvel' komorovského typu», *Štdijné Zvesti archeologického ústavu slovenskej akadémie vied. Notra*, 1964

DEKAN, *HERKUNFT UND ETHNIZITÄT*

J. Dekan, «Herkunft und Ethnizität der gegossenen Bronzeindustrie des 8. Jahrhunderts», *Slovenska Archaeologia*, XX(2), 1972

DELBRUECK, *DIE CONSULARDIPTYCHEN*

R. Delbrueck, *Die Consulardiptychen und verwandte Denkmäler*, Berlin—Leipzig, 1927—1929

DELVOYE, *L'ART BYZANTIN*

Ch. Delvoye, *L'Art byzantin*, Bellegarde, 1967

DOP

Dumbarton Oaks Papers

EARLY CHRISTIAN AND BYZANTINE ART EXHIBITION

Early Christian and Byzantine Art. Catalogue of the Exhibition Held at the Baltimore Museum of Art, Baltimore, 1947

FELICETTI-LIEBENSFELS

W. Felicetti-Liebensfels, *Geschichte der byzantinischen Ikonenmalerei*, Lausanne, 1956

FROLOW, *LA RELIQUE*

A. Frolow, *La Relique de la Vraie Croix*, Paris, 1961

FROLOW, *LES RELIQUAIRES*

A. Frolow, *Les Reliquaires de la Vraie Croix*, Paris, 1965

GOLDSCHMIDT, WEITZMANN

A. Goldschmidt, K. Weitzmann, *Die byzantinischen Elfenbeinskulpturen des X.—XIII. Jahrhunderts*, Bde. 1—2, Berlin, 1930—1934

GRABAR, *L'ÂGE D'OR*

A. Grabar, *L'Age d'or de Justinien. De la mort de Théodose à l'Islam*, Paris, 1966

GRABAR, *L'ART DE LA FIN DE L'ANTIQUITÉ*

A. Grabar, *L'Art de la fin de l'antiquité et du Moyen Age*, v. 1—3, Paris, 1968

GRABAR, *LES REVÊTEMENTS*

A. Grabar, *Les Revêtements en or et en argent des icones byzantines du Moyen Age*, Venise, 1975

GRABAR, *UN MÉDAILLON*

A. Grabar, «Un Médaillon en or provenant de Mersina», *Dumbarton Oaks Papers*, VI, 1951

IL TESORO DI SAN MARCO

Il Tesoro di San Marco (*1. La Pala d'oro; 2. Il Tesoro e il museo*). *Opera diretta da H. Hahnloser*, Firenze, 1967—1971

JÖB

Jahrbuch der Österreichischen Byzantinistik

JÖBG

Jahrbuch der Österreichischen Byzantinischen Gesellschaft

L'ART BYZANTIN

L'Art byzantin — art européen. Neuvième exposition sous l'égide du Conseil de l'Europe, Athènes, 1964

LASAREFF, *BYZANTINE IKONS*

V. Lasareff, "Byzantine Ikons of the Fourteenth and Fifteenth Centuries", *The Burlington Magazine*, LXXI, 1937

LASAREFF, *TROIS FRAGMENTS*

V. Lasareff, «Trois fragments d'épistyles peintes et le templon byzantin», *Δελτίον της Χριστιανικῆς Ἀρχαιολογικῆς Ἑταιρείας, περ. Δ, τ. Δ, Ἀθῆναι*, 1964—1968

LAZAREV, *STORIA*

V. Lazarev, *Storia della pittura bizantina*, Torino, 1967

LECLERCQ, *MANUEL*

H. Leclercq, *Manuel d'archéologie chrétienne*, v. 2, Paris, 1907

MACULEVIČ, *ARGENTERIE*

L. Maculevič, «Argenterie byzantine en Russie. L'Art byzantin chez les slaves», *Orient et Byzance*, II, 1932, Paris

MASTERPIECES

Masterpieces of Byzantine Art (Catalogue). Edinburgh International Festival: 1958, Edinburgh—London, 1958

MATZULEWITSCH

L. Matzulewitsch, *Byzantinische Antike*, Berlin—Leipzig, 1929

MEGAW, *ZEUXIPPUS WARE*

A. H. S. Megaw, "The Zeuxippus Ware", *The Annual of the British School of Archaeology at Athens*, 63, 1968

MUÑOZ

A. Muñoz, *L'Art byzantin à l'exposition de Grottaferrata*, Roma, 1906

PEIRCE, TYLER

H. Peirce, R. Tyler, *L'Art byzantin*, v. 1—2, Paris, 1932—1934

PROPYLÄEN KUNSTGESCHICHTE

J. Lafontaine-Dosogne, W. F. Volbach, «Byzanz und der christliche Osten», *Propyläen Kunstgeschichte*, Bd. 3, Berlin, 1968

ROSENBERG

M. Rosenberg, *Der Goldschmiede Merkzeichen*, Bd. 4, Berlin—Leipzig, 1928

ROSS, *CATALOGUE*

M. C. Ross, *Catalogue of the Byzantine and Early Mediaeval Antiquities in the Dumbarton Oaks Collection*, v. 1—2, Washington, 1962—1965

RUDT DE COLLENBERG, *LE «THORAKION»*
W. H. Rudt de Collenberg, «Le "Thorakion". Recherches iconographiques», *Mélanges de l'école française de Rome*, 83, 1971

SCHLUMBERGER, *L'ÉPOPÉE*
G. Schlumberger, *L'Epopée byzantine*, t. 1—3, Paris, 1896—1905

SCHLUMBERGER, *SIGILLOGRAPHIE*
G. Schlumberger, *Sigillographie de l'Empire byzantin*, Paris, 1884

SK
Seminarium Kondakovianum

TALBOT RICE, *THE ART*
D. Talbot Rice, *The Art of Byzantium*, London, 1959

TALBOT RICE, *THE BYZANTINE PAINTING*
D. Talbot Rice, *The Byzantine Painting. The Last Phase*, London, 1968

VOLBACH, *ELFENBEINARBEITEN*
W. F. Volbach, *Elfenbeinarbeiten der Spätantike und des frühen Mittelalters* (3. Auflage), Mainz am Rhein, 1976

VOLBACH, *FRÜHCHRISTLICHE KUNST*
W. F. Volbach, *Frühchristliche Kunst. Die Kunst der Spätantike in West- und Ostrom*, München, 1958

VOLBACH, *IL TESORO*
W. F. Volbach, «Il Tesoro di Canoscio», *Atti del secondo convegno di studi Umbri. Gubbio, 24—28 maggio, 1964*, Perugia, 1964

VOLBACH, *LA STAUROTECA*
W. F. Volbach, *La Stauroteca di Monopoli*, Roma, 1969

VOLBACH, *METALLARBEITEN*
W. F. Volbach, *Metallarbeiten des christlichen Kultes in der Spätantike und im frühen Mittelalter*, Mainz, 1921

VOLBACH, *SILBERARBEITEN*
W. F. Volbach, *Silber- und Elfenbeinarbeiten von Ende des IV. bis zum Anfang des VII. Jahrhunderts. Beiträge zur Kunstgeschichte und Archäologie des Frühmittelalters*, Graz—Köln, 1961

WEITZMANN, *CATALOGUE*
K. Weitzmann, *Catalogue of the Byzantine and Early Mediaeval Antiquities in the Dumbarton Oaks Collection*, v. 3 (*Ivories and Steatites*), Washington, 1972

WEITZMANN, *ICONS*
K. Weitzmann, *The Monastery of St Catherine at Mount Sinai. The Icons*, v. 1 *(From the Sixth to the Tenth Century)*, Princeton, New Jersey, 1976

WEITZMANN, *STUDIES*
K. Weitzmann, *Studies in Classical and Byzantine Manuscript Illumination*, Chicago—London, 1971

WEITZMANN, *THE SURVIVAL*
K. Weitzmann, "The Survival of Mythological Representation in Early Christian and Byzantine Art and Their Impact on Christian Art", *Dumbarton Oaks Papers*, XIV, 1960

WESSEL, *BYZANTINE ENAMELS*
K. Wessel, *Byzantine Enamels from the 5th to the 13th century*, Irish University Press, Shannon, 1969

WULFF, ALPATOFF
O. Wulff, M. Alpatoff, *Denkmäler der Ikonenmalerei*, Hellerau bei Dresden, 1925

АЙНАЛОВ, *ВИЗАНТИЙСКАЯ ЖИВОПИСЬ*
Д. В. Айналов, «Византийская живопись XIV столетия» (оттиск из *Записок классического отделения Русского Археологического общества*, IX, 1917)

АЙНАЛОВ, *ЭЛЛИНИСТИЧЕСКИЕ ОСНОВЫ*
Д. В. Айналов, *Эллинистические основы византийского искусства*, Спб., 1900

АЙНАЛОВ, *СИНАЙСКИЕ ИКОНЫ*
Д. В. Айналов, «Синайские иконы восковой живописи», *Византийский временник*, XI, 1902

АМИРАНАШВИЛИ, *ХАХУЛЬСКИЙ ТРИПТИХ*
Ш. Я. Амиранашвили, *Хахульский триптих*, Тбилиси, 1972

АНТОНОВА, МНЕВА, *КАТАЛОГ*
В. И. Антонова, Н. Е. Мнева, *Каталог древнерусской живописи*, т. 1—2, М., 1963

АРТАМОНОВ, *ИСТОРИЯ ХАЗАР*
М. И. Артамонов, *История хазар*, Л., 1962

БАНК, *ВИЗАНТИЙСКИЕ СЕРЕБРЯНЫЕ ИЗДЕЛИЯ*
А. В. Банк, «Византийские серебряные изделия XI—XII веков в собрании Эрмитажа», *Византийский временник*, XIII, XIV, 1958

БАНК, *ВЫСТАВКА ВИЗАНТИЙСКИХ МАТЕРИАЛОВ*
А. В. Банк, «Выставка византийских материалов в Государственном Эрмитаже», *Византийский временник*, XI, 1956

БАНК, *ДВА ПЕРСТНЯ*
А. В. Банк, «Два византийских перстня из собрания Эрмитажа», *Труды Государственного Эрмитажа*, V *(Культура и искусство народов Востока)*, 1961

БАНК, *ИСКУССТВО ВИЗАНТИИ*
А. В. Банк, *Искусство Византии в собрании Государственного Эрмитажа*, Л., 1960

БАНК, *МЕЖДУНАРОДНАЯ ВЫСТАВКА*
А. В. Банк, «Международная выставка византийского искусства в Эдинбурге — Лондоне», *Византийский временник*, XVII, 1960

БАНК, *МОЗАИЧНАЯ ИКОНА*
А. В. Банк, «Мозаичная икона из б. собрания Н. П. Лихачева», in: *Из истории русского и западноевропейского искусства*, М., 1960

БАНК, *НЕСКОЛЬКО ВИЗАНТИЙСКИХ КАМЕЙ*
А. В. Банк, «Несколько византийских камей из собрания Государственного Эрмитажа», *Византийский временник*, XVI, 1959

БАНК, *ОПЫТ КЛАССИФИКАЦИИ*
А. В. Банк, «Опыт классификации византийских серебряных изделий X—XII вв.», *Византийский временник*, XXXII, 1971

БАНК, *ПОКУШАЈ КЛАСИФИКАЦИЈЕ*
А. Банк, «Покушај класификације споменика византијске глиптике», *Музеј примењене уметности* (зборник, 15), Београд, 1971

БАНК, *ЧЕРТЫ ПАЛЕОЛОГОВСКОГО СТИЛЯ*

А. В. Банк, «Черты палеологовского стиля в византийском художественном металле», in: *Византия. Южные славяне и Древняя Русь. Западная Европа*, М., 1973

БЕНЕШЕВИЧ, *НАДПИСИ*

В. Н. Бенешевич, «Надписи и клейма на сосудах. К изучению Перещепинского клада», *Известия Археологической комиссии*, 49, 1913

БОБРИНСКИЙ, *ПЕРЕЩЕПИНСКИЙ КЛАД*

А. А. Бобринский, «Перещепинский клад», *Материалы по археологии России*, 34, 1914

ВВ

Византийский временник

ВДИ

Вестник древней истории

ВЦНИЛКР

Всесоюзная центральная научно-исследовательская лаборатория по консервации и реставрации музейных художественных ценностей

ДАРКЕВИЧ, *СВЕТСКОЕ ИСКУССТВО ВИЗАНТИИ*

В. П. Даркевич, *Светское искусство Византии. Произведения художественного ремесла в Восточной Европе X—XIII вв.*, М., 1975

ДЬЯКОНОВА, *ИСКУССТВО ВОСТОКА*

Н. В. Дьяконова, *Искусство народов зарубежного Востока в Эрмитаже*, Л., 1962

ЖМНП

Журнал Министерства народного просвещения

ИАК

Известия Археологической комиссии

ИКОНЫ НА БАЛКАНАХ

К. Вейцман, М. Хадзидакис, К. Миатев, С. Радойчич, *Иконы на Балканах. Синай, Греция, Болгария, Югославия*, София — Белград, 1967

ИКДП

Институт книги, документа и письма

ИРАИК

Известия Русского Археологического института в Константинополе

КМЗВИ, КАТАЛОГ

Киевский государственный музей западного и восточного искусства. Каталог западноевропейской живописи и скульптуры, М., 1961

КОНДАКОВ, *ВИЗАНТИЙСКИЕ ЭМАЛИ*

Н. П. Кондаков, *Византийские эмали. Собрание Звенигородского. История и памятники*, Спб., 1892

КОНДАКОВ, *ПАМЯТНИКИ*

Н. П. Кондаков, *Памятники христианского искусства на Афоне*, Спб., 1902

КОНДАКОВ, *РУССКИЕ КЛАДЫ*

Н. П. Кондаков, *Русские клады. Исследование древностей великокняжеского периода*, т. 1, Спб., 1896

КОНДАКОВ, *РУССКАЯ ИКОНА*

Н. П. Кондаков, *Русская икона*, т. 1—4, Прага, 1928—1933

КОНДАКОВ, БАКРАДЗЕ

Н. Кондаков, Д. Бакрадзе, *Опись памятников древности в некоторых храмах и монастырях Грузии*, Спб., 1890

КСИИМК

Краткие сообщения Института истории материальной культуры

ЛАЗАРЕВ, *ВИЗАНТИЙСКИЕ ИКОНЫ*

В. Н. Лазарев, «Византийские иконы XIV—XV веков», in: *Византийская живопись*, М., 1971

ЛАЗАРЕВ, *ИСТОРИЯ*

В. Н. Лазарев, *История византийской живописи*, т. 1—2, М., 1947—1948

ЛАЗАРЕВ, *ТРИ ФРАГМЕНТА*

В. Н. Лазарев, «Три фрагмента расписных эпистилиев и византийский темплон», in: *Византийская живопись*, М., 1971

ЛЕВИНСОН-НЕЧАЕВА, *ОДЕЖДА И ТКАНИ*

М. Н. Левинсон-Нечаева, *Одежда и ткани XVI—XVII веков. Государственная Оружейная палата Московского Кремля*, М., 1954

ЛИХАЧЕВ, *ИСТОРИЧЕСКОЕ ЗНАЧЕНИЕ*

Н. П. Лихачев, *Историческое значение итало-греческой иконописи. Изображение богоматери в произведениях итало-греческих иконописцев и их влияние на композиции некоторых прославленных русских икон*, Спб., 1911

ЛИХАЧЕВ, *МАТЕРИАЛЫ*

Н. П. Лихачев, *Материалы для истории русского иконописания*, т. 1—2, Спб., 1906

ЛИХАЧЕВ, *МОЛИВДОВУЛЫ*

Н. П. Лихачев, *Моливдовулы греческого Востока*. Рукопись (подготовлена к печати и помечена 1937 г. Содержит разностороннее исследование печатей, воспроизведенных на таблицах LVIII—LXXXIII)

ЛИХАЧЕВ, *НЕКОТОРЫЕ СТАРЕЙШИЕ ТИПЫ*

Н. П. Лихачев, *Некоторые старейшие типы печати византийских императоров*, М., 1911

МАР

Материалы по археологии России

МАЦУЛЕВИЧ, *ВИЗАНТИЙСКИЙ АНТИК И ПРИКАМЬЕ*

Л. А. Мацулевич, «Византийский антик и Прикамье», *Материалы и исследования по археологии СССР*, 1, 1940

МАЦУЛЕВИЧ, *ВИЗАНТИЙСКИЕ РЕЗНЫЕ КОСТИ*

Л. А. Мацулевич, «Византийские резные кости собрания М. П. Боткина», *Сборник Государственного Эрмитажа*, II, 1923

МАЦУЛЕВИЧ, *СЕРЕБРЯНАЯ ЧАША*

Л. А. Мацулевич, «Серебряная чаша из Керчи», *Памятники Государственного Эрмитажа*, т. 2, Л., 1926

МИА

Материалы и исследования по археологии СССР

ОАК

Отчеты Археологической комиссии

ПАНЧЕНКО, *КАТАЛОГ*

Б. А. Панченко, «Каталог моливдовулов коллекции Русского Археологического института в Константинополе», *Известия Русского Археологического института в Константинополе*, VIII, 1903, IX, 1904, XIII, 1908

ПЕТРОВ, *АЛЬБОМ*

Н. Петров, *Альбом достопримечательностей церковно-археологического музея при Киевской Духовной академии*, вып. 1 (*Коллекция Синайских и Афонских икон преосвященного Порфирия Успенского*), Киев, 1912

ПИСАРСКАЯ, *ПАМЯТНИКИ*

Л. В. Писарская, *Памятники византийского искусства V—XV веков в Государственной Оружейной палате*, Л.—М., 1965

ПОПОВА, *НОВГОРОДСКАЯ МИНИАТЮРА*

О. С. Попова, «Новгородская миниатюра раннего XIV века и ее связь с Палеологовским искусством», in: *Древнерусское искусство. Рукописная книга*, М., 1972

ПУЦКО, *НЕСКОЛЬКО ВИЗАНТИЙСКИХ КАМЕЙ*

В. Пуцко, «Несколько византийских камей из древнерусских городов», *Зборник Радова Византолошког института*, XII, 1970

РАИК

Русский Археологический институт в Константинополе

СА

Советская археология

САВВА, *УКАЗАТЕЛЬ*

Савва, епископ Можайский, *Указатель Московской Патриаршей ризницы*, М., 1863

СГЭ

Сообщения Государственного Эрмитажа

СМИРНОВ, *ВОСТОЧНОЕ СЕРЕБРО*

Я. И. Смирнов, *Восточное серебро. Атлас древней серебряной и золотой посуды восточного происхождения*, Спб., 1909

ТОЛСТОЙ

И. И. Толстой, *Византийские монеты*, вып. 1—9, Спб., 1912—1914

ТОЛСТОЙ, КОНДАКОВ, *РУССКИЕ ДРЕВНОСТИ*

И. И. Толстой, Н. П. Кондаков, *Русские древности*, т. 1—6, Спб., 1889—1899

ТОВЭ

Труды отдела Востока Государственного Эрмитажа

УСПЕНСКИЙ, *ВТОРОЕ ПУТЕШЕСТВИЕ*

Порфирий Успенский, *Второе путешествие на Синай*, Киев, 1850

УСПЕНСКИЙ, *ПАТРИАРШАЯ РИЗНИЦА*

А. Успенский, «Патриаршая ризница в Москве», *Мир искусства*, 1904, 10

ХС

Херсонесский сборник

ЧУБИНАШВИЛИ, 1957

Г. Н. Чубинашвили, *Грузинское чеканное искусство с VIII по XVIII век*, Тбилиси, 1957

ЧУБИНАШВИЛИ, 1959

Г. Н. Чубинашвили, *Грузинское чеканное искусство. Исследование по истории Грузинского средневекового искусства*, Тбилиси, 1959

ШЕЛКОВНИКОВ, *РУССКОЕ СТЕКЛО*

Б. А. Шелковников, «Русское стекло домонгольского времени, расписанное эмалями», *Советская археология*, 1965, 1, с. 206—224

ЭРМИТАЖ, 1965

Ю. Кузнецов, Н. Никулин, Ю. Русаков, *Эрмитаж*, М.—Л., 1965

ЯКОБСОН, *СРЕДНЕВЕКОВЫЙ ХЕРСОНЕС*

А. Л. Якобсон, «Средневековый Херсонес (XII—XIV века)», *Материалы и исследования по археологии СССР*, 17, 1950

BIBLIOGRAPHY

GENERAL PROBLEMS

Д. Айналов, *Эллинистические основы византийского искусства*, Спб., 1900 (D. V. Ainalov, *The Hellenistic Origins of Byzantine Art*, New Brunswick—New Jersey, 1961)

O. M. Dalton, *Byzantine Art and Archaeology*, Oxford, 1911

O. Wulff, *Altchristliche und Byzantinische Kunst*, Bde. 1—2, Berlin—Neubabelsberg, 1914—1918

J. Ebersolt, *Les Arts somptuaires de Byzance*, Paris, 1923

L. Bréhier, *L'Art byzantin*, Paris, 1924

O. M. Dalton, *East Christian Art*, Oxford, 1925

Ch. Diehl, *Manuel d'art byzantin*, t. 1—2, Paris, 1925—1926

W. F. Volbach, G. Salles, G. Duthuit, *Art byzantin*, Paris, 1933

H. Peirce, R. Tyler, *L'Art byzantin*, v. 1—2, Paris, 1932—1934

L. Bréhier, *La Sculpture et les arts mineurs byzantins*, Paris, 1936

E. Coche de la Ferté, *L'Antiquité chrétienne au Musée du Louvre*, Paris, 1958

W. F. Volbach, *Frühchristliche Kunst. Die Kunst der Spätantike in West- und Ostrom*, München, 1958

D. Talbot Rice, *The Art of Byzantium*, London, 1959

В. М. Полевой, «Искусство Византии», in: *Всеобщая история искусств*, т. 2, М., 1960

А. В. Банк, *Искусство Византии в собрании Государственного Эрмитажа*, Л., 1960

А. В. Банк, А. С. Гущин, «Искусство Византии», in: *История искусства зарубежных стран*, т. 2, М., 1963

L. Nickel, *Byzantinische Kunst*, Heidelberg, 1964

H. Stern, *L'Art byzantin*, Paris, 1965

Ch. Delvoye, *L'Art byzantin*, Paris, 1967

J. Lafontaine-Dosogne, W. F. Volbach, «Byzanz und der christliche Osten», *Propyläen Kunstgeschichte*, Bd. 3, Berlin, 1968

A. Grabar, *L'Age d'or de Justinien*, Paris, 1966

A. Grabar, *L'Art byzantin du Moyen Age*, Paris, 1963

J. Beckwith, *Early Christian and Byzantine Art* (*Pelican History of Art*), Penguin Books, 1970

O. Demus, *Byzantine Art and the West*, New York, 1970

J. Klosińska, *Sztuka bizantyjska*, Warszawa, 1975

CATALOGUES

A. Darcel, A. Basilewsky, *La Collection Basilewsky. Catalogue raisonné*, Paris, 1874

Н. П. Кондаков, *Указатель отделения Средних веков и эпохи Возрождения*, Спб., 1891

O. M. Dalton, *Catalogue of Early Christian Antiquities and Objects from the Christian East... in the British Museum*, London, 1901

A. Muñoz, *L'Art byzantin à l'exposition de Grottaferrata*, Roma, 1906

O. Wulff, *Altchristliche und mittelalterliche byzantinische und italienische Bildwerke*, Bde. 1—2, Berlin, 1909—1911

Собрание М. П. Боткина, Спб., 1911

W. F. Volbach, *Mittelalterliche Bildwerke aus Italien und Byzanz. Staatliche Museen zu Berlin. Bildwerke des Kaiser-Friedrich-Museums*, Berlin, 1930

Exposition Internationale d'Art Byzantin. Musée des Arts Décoratifs. Palais du Louvre, Paris, 1931

Early Christian and Byzantine Art. Catalogue of the Exhibition Held at the Baltimore Museum of Art, Baltimore, 1947

Masterpieces of Byzantine Art. Edinburgh International Festival: 1958, Edinburgh—London, 1958

Catalogue of the Byzantine and Early Mediaeval Antiquities in the Dumbarton Oaks Collection, v. 1 (*Metalwork, Ceramics, Glass, Glyptics, Painting*, by M. C. Ross), Washington, 1961; v. 2 (*Jewelry, Enamels and Art of Migration Period*, by M. C. Ross), 1965; v. 3 (*Ivory and Steatites*, by K. Weitzmann), 1972

L'Art byzantin — art européen. Neuvième exposition sous l'égide du Conseil de l'Europe, Athènes, 1964

Л. В. Писарская, *Памятники византийского искусства V—XV веков в Государственной Оружейной палате*, Л.—М., 1965

Il Tesoro di San Marco (1. *La Pala d'oro*; 2. *Il Tesoro e il museo*). *Opera diretta da H. Hahnloser*, Firenze, 1967—1971

I. Barnea, O. Iliescu, C. Nicolescu, *Cultura byzantina in Romania*, Bucureşti, 1971

Venezia e Bisanzio. Venezia, Palazzo Ducale, 8 giugno/30 settembre 1974

ARCHITECTURE

A. van Millingen, *Byzantine Churches in Constantinople*, London, 1912

J. Ebersolt, A. Thier, *Les Eglises de Constantinople*, Paris, 1913

G. Millet, *L'Ecole grecque dans l'architecture byzantine*, Paris, 1916

J. Hamilton, *Byzantine Architecture and Decoration*, London, 1933

J. Ebersolt, *Monuments d'architecture byzantine*, Paris, 1934

Н. Брунов, *Очерки по истории архитектуры*, т. 2, М.—Л., 1935

Н. Мавродинов, *Византийската архитектура*, София, 1955

Всеобщая история архитектуры, т. 1, М., 1958

R. Krautheimer, *Early Christian and Byzantine Architecture* (*The Pelican History of Art*), Penguin Books, 1965

Н. И. Брунов, «Архитектура Византии», in: *Всеобщая история архитектуры в двенадцати томах*, т. 3, Л.—М., 1966

Ю. К. Милонов, «Строительная техника Византии», in: *Всеобщая история архитектуры в двенадцати томах*, т. 3, Л.—М., 1966

PAINTING

Д. Айналов, «Византийская живопись XIV столетия» (оттиск из *Записок классического отделения Русского Археологического общества*, IX, 1917)

O. Wulff, M. Alpatoff, *Denkmäler der Ikonenmalerei*, Hellerau bei Dresden, 1925

А. П. Смирнов, *Памятники византийской живописи. Государственный Русский музей*, Л., 1928

P. Muratoff, *La Peinture byzantine*, Paris, 1928

Н. П. Кондаков, *Русская икона*, т. 1—4, Прага, 1928—1933

Ch. Diehl, *La Peinture byzantine*, Paris, 1933

V. Lasareff, "Byzantine Ikons of the Fourteenth and Fifteenth Centuries", *The Burlington Magazine*, LXXI, 1937

В. Н. Лазарев, *История византийской живописи*, т. 1—2, М., 1947—1948

O. Demus, *Byzantine Mosaic Decoration*, London, 1948

A. Grabar, *La Peinture byzantine*, Genève, 1953

G. et M. Sotiriou, *Icônes du Mont Sinai*, v. 1—2, Athènes, 1956—1958

W. Felicetti-Liebensfels, *Geschichte der byzantinischen Ikonenmalerei*, Lausanne, 1956

К. Вейцман, М. Хадзидакис, К. Миатев, С. Радойчич, *Иконы на Балканах. Синай, Греция, Болгария, Югославия*, София — Белград, 1967 (*Frühe Ikonen*, Wien—München, 1965)

V. Lazarev, *Storia della pittura bizantina*, Torino, 1967

A. Papageorgiou, *Les Icônes de Chypre*, Paris—Genève—Munich, 1968

D. Talbot Rice, *The Byzantine Painting. The Last Phase*, London, 1968

M. Chatzidakis, «Icônes de Saint Georges des Grecs et de la collection de l'Institut», *Bibliothèque de l'Institut hellénique d'études byzantines et post-byzantines de Venise*, 1, Venise, s. d.

K. Weitzmann, *Studies in Classical and Byzantine Manuscript Illumination*, Chicago — London, 1971

В. Н. Лазарев, *Византийская живопись*, М., 1971

K. Weitzmann, *The Monastery of St Catherine at Mount Sinai. The Icons*, v. 1 (*From the Sixth to the Tenth Century*), Princeton, New Jersey, 1976

SCULPTURE, IVORIES

Л. А. Мацулевич, «Византийские резные кости собрания М. П. Боткина», *Сборник Государственного Эрмитажа*, II, 1923

R. Delbrueck, *Die Consulardiptychen und verwandte Denkmäler*, Berlin—Leipzig, 1927—1929

A. Goldschmidt, K. Weitzmann, *Die byzantinischen Elfenbeinskulpturen des X.—XIII. Jahrhunderts*, Bde. 1—2, Berlin, 1930—1934

S. Bettini, *La scultura bizantina*, v. I—II, Firenze, 1944—1946

A. Grabar, *Sculptures byzantines de Constantinople*, Paris, 1963

R. Lange, *Die byzantinische Reliefikone*, Recklinghausen, 1964

A. Bank, «Les Stéatites. Essai de classification, méthodes de recherches», *Corsi di cultura sull'arte ravennate e bizantina*, XVII, 1970, Ravenna

A. Grabar, *Sculptures byzantines du Moyen Age*, v. 2 *(XIe—XIVe siècles)*, Paris, 1976.

W. F. Volbach, *Elfenbeinarbeiten der Spätantike und des frühen Mittelalters* (3. Auflage), Mainz am Rhein, 1976

SILVERWORK, ENAMELS AND JEWELLERY

Н. П. Кондаков, *Византийские эмали. Собрание Звенигородского. История и памятники*, Спб., 1892

M. Rosenberg, *Der Goldschmiede Merkzeichen*, Bd. 4, Berlin—Leipzig, 1928

L. Matzulewitsch, *Byzantinische Antike*, Berlin—Leipzig, 1929

Л. А. Мацулевич, «Византийский антик и Прикамье», *Материалы и исследования по археологии СССР*, 1, 1940

E. Cruikshank Dodd, *Byzantine Silver Stamps*, Washington, 1961

Ch. Amiranachvili, *Les Emaux de Géorgie*, Paris, 1962

G. Matthiae, *Le Porte bronzea bizantine in Italia*, Roma, 1971

K. Wessel, «Die byzantinische Emailkunst vom 5. bis 13. Jh.», *Studien zur Kunst des christlichen Ostens*, Recklinghausen, 1967 (*Byzantine Enamels from the 5th to the 13th Century*, Irish University Press, Shannon, 1969)

Ш. Я. Амиранашвили, *Хахульский триптих*, Тбилиси, 1972

A. Bank, «L'Argenterie byzantine des XIe—XVe siècles. Classification des monuments et méthodes de recherches», *Corsi di cultura sull'arte ravennate e bizantina*, XVII, 1970, Ravenna

A. Grabar, *Les Revêtements en or et en argent des icones byzantines du Moyen Age*, Venise, 1975

В. П. Даркевич, *Светское искусство Византии. Произведения художественного ремесла в Восточной Европе X—XIII вв.*, М., 1975

EMBROIDERY

G. Millet, *Broderies religieuses de style byzantin*, Paris, 1945

G. Millet, *La Dalmatique du Vatican. Les Elus, images et croyances*, Paris, 1947

GLAZED POTTERY

D. Talbot Rice, *Byzantine Glazed Pottery*, Oxford, 1930

Ch. H. Morgan, *The Byzantine Pottery* (Corinth, XI), Harvard University Press, 1942

А. Л. Якобсон, «Средневековый Херсонес (XII—XIV века)», *Материалы и исследования по археологии СССР*, 17, 1950

А. Л. Якобсон, «Раннесредневековый Херсонес», *Материалы и исследования по археологии СССР*, 63, 1959

R. B. K. Stevenson, "The Pottery", in: *The Great Palace of the Byzantine Emperors of Constantinople. First Report*, London, 1947

A. H. S. Megaw, "The Zeuxippus Ware", *The Annual of the British School of Archaeology at Athens*, 63, 1968